Midwestern
Landscape
Architecture

Midwestern Landscape Architecture

Edited by

William H. Tishler

UNIVERSITY OF ILLINOIS PRESS / URBANA, CHICAGO, AND SPRINGFIELD
in cooperation with Library of American Landscape History / Amherst, Massachusetts

First Illinois paperback, 2004

© 2000 by the Board of Trustees of the University of Illinois

All rights reserved

Manufactured in the United States of America

∞ This book is printed on acid-free paper.

The Library of Congress cataloged the cloth edition as follows:

Midwestern landscape architecture / edited by William H. Tishler.

p. cm.

Includes bibliographical references and index.

ISBN 978-0-252-02593-8 (cloth : acid-free paper)

1. Landscape architecture—Middle West—History.

2. Landscape architects—Middle West—History.

3. Landscape architects—Middle West—Biography.

I. Tishler, William H.

SB470.54.M54M55   2000

712'.0977—dc21   99-050980

1 2 3 4 5 C P 6 5 4 3 2

PAPERBACK ISBN 978-0-252-07214-7

Contents

Preface
Robin Karson   vii

Acknowledgments   ix

Introduction: Shaping America's Heartland
William H. Tishler   1

ONE   Adolph Strauch: Cincinnati and the Legacy of Spring
         Grove Cemetery
         Noël Dorsey Vernon   5

TWO   Horace Cleveland: The Chicago Years
         William H. Tishler   25

THREE   Frederick Law Olmsted: Designing for Democracy
         in the Midwest
         Victoria Post Ranney   41

FOUR   William Le Baron Jenney and Chicago's West Parks:
         From Prairie to Pleasure-Grounds
         Reuben M. Rainey   57

FIVE   Ossian Cole Simonds: Conservation Ethic in the
         Prairie Style
         Julia Sniderman Bachrach   80

SIX   George Edward Kessler: Landscape Architect of the
         American Renaissance
         Kurt Culbertson   99

SEVEN   Jens Jensen: The Landscape Architect as Conservationist
         Robert E. Grese   117

EIGHT   Warren H. Manning and His Minnesota Clients:
Developing a National Practice in a Landscape of
Resources, 1898–1919
Lance M. Neckar   142

NINE   The Olmsted Brothers in the Midwest: Naturalism,
Formalism, and the City Beautiful Movement
William W. Tippens   159

TEN   Wilhelm Miller: Prairie Spirit in Landscape Gardening
Christopher Vernon   174

ELEVEN   Elbert Peets: History as Precedent in Midwestern
Landscape Design
Arnold R. Alanen   193

TWELVE   Genevieve Gillette: From Thrift Gardens to
National Parks
Miriam E. Rutz   215

THIRTEEN   Annette Hoyt Flanders: From Beaux Arts to Modernism
Patricia L. Filzen   231

Contributors   243
Index   245

Preface

FEW OF THE NAMES of the men and women profiled in this collection of essays will be familiar to readers, but millions of Americans have strolled along boulevards, raised children in the suburbs, and buried loved ones in cemeteries designed by them. Every graduate of the University of Michigan has sunned in an Ossian Simonds landscape; every visitor flying into Chicago has had a bird's-eye view of the astounding geometry of William Le Baron Jenney's park system. The origins of these special places, their meaning and significance, constitute far more than curious footnotes in landscape architectural history. They remind us who we were and, in the end, shed light on the land use, management, and conservation challenges we face today.

For five years the Library of American Landscape History has worked on this book with William H. Tishler, a man of great patience and optimism. The essays have been revised several times as new information was discovered in library basements, as historical paradigms gained focus, and as the audience for American landscape history grew and with it the need to produce an engaging book that would speak to broad interests. As the editors of the first offering ever on the subject, we felt a special responsibility to create a book of lasting significance. We are certain that students will find new ideas here, but will be particularly gratified if this volume finds its way into the hands of the profession and the general public—the park commissioners, city planning boards, journalists, and voters who have ultimate responsibility for shaping the land.

The Library of American Landscape History, a not-for-profit corporation founded in 1992, promotes conscientious land stewardship through education. The Library produces clear, engaging books about the cultural and artistic significance of North American landscapes and the people who created them. Intended for general readers as well as specialists, Library books are published in collaboration with university and trade presses. The Library organizes touring exhibitions and educational programs in conjunction with its books for museums, botanic gardens, and other cultural institutions.

Robin Karson
Library of American Landscape History
Amherst, Massachusetts

Acknowledgments

I THANK BILL TISHLER for initiating this publication and for working with such care and patience to see it through to completion. I also thank the volume contributors—their passion and insight inform every page. The text was much improved by suggestions from Arnold Alanen, Leslie Rose Close, Darrell Morrison, Cynthia Zaitzevsky, and Melanie Simo. I am especially indebted to Carol Betsch, who edited the text, and Laura Moss Gottlieb, who created the index. Finally, I thank the staff of the University of Illinois Press, especially Richard Martin and Theresa L. Sears, for seeing the potential of this book and helping us realize it.

Editorial underwriting came from the Graham Foundation for Advanced Studies in the Visual Arts; the Hubbard Educational Trust; Clayton E. and Ann Douglass Wilhite; William Kubley of Landscapes Unlimited, Lincoln, Nebraska; the Illinois Chapter ASLA; the Michigan Chapter ASLA; and the Wisconsin Chapter ASLA.

Royalties from *Midwestern Landscape Architecture* will help fund future programs at The Clearing Institute.

—R.K.

Midwestern
Landscape
Architecture

Shaping America's Heartland

William H. Tishler

DURING THE NINETEENTH CENTURY, America expanded westward along new canals and railroads, through the midwestern prairies and forests, dramatically changing the landscape with cities, farms, and factories. In the wake of the expansion, a handful of visionaries emerged who called for shaping these human environments with beauty and respect for the land. America's first landscape architects were part of this group. Coming from the East Coast and Europe, they brought their fledgling profession to the growing nation's booming heartland. Here, a new generation of practitioners enriched the art and science of landscape architecture with bold innovations inspired by the region's unique sense of place. The landscape legacy of their work has enhanced the quality of life in our nation. This book is about these individuals and the ambitions and ideals they expressed in the midwestern landscape.

Until recently, the history of landscape architecture in America has focused primarily on the profession's development in the more populated and established eastern states. Several reasons account for this emphasis. Two of the most distinguished landscape designers associated with the origins of the profession—Andrew Jackson Downing and Frederick Law Olmsted Sr.—were born in the East and worked mainly on projects in that region. Downing's career was cut short when he died in a tragic accident in 1852, but the indefatigable Olmsted, along with his prolific corps of talented associates, became a major force in shaping the practice of landscape architecture well into the twentieth century.

This eastern nucleus was strengthened when, in 1900, formal education for landscape architects was initiated at Harvard University. For more than half a century the prestigious institution attracted and trained many of the profession's leaders. The growing concentration of landscape architectural offices on the East Coast also influenced the course of the profession. A group of practitioners from New York and Boston (together with a single midwesterner, O. C. Simonds of Chicago) founded the American Society of Landscape Architects in 1899 and dominated its early activities and governing structure. By 1910 the society had launched its official publication, *Landscape Architecture Quarterly,* from editorial offices in New York City. Most of the articles in the early volumes of the journal were contributed by East Coast practitioners who frequently wrote about their own work.

The profession's early development and strength in the East overshadowed the achievements of the small number of unsung landscape architects who ventured into the raw, new cities and vast rural spaces of the nation's heartland. Thus, with only a few exceptions, little is known about their careers and accomplishments: the time is long overdue for illuminating their achievements. As the first book published on this topic, *Midwestern Landscape Architecture* will foster a better understanding of the origins of landscape architecture in the American Midwest and the contributions this profession has made to the interaction of people with their environment in the region.

Several years ago The Clearing (the landscape architect Jens Jensen's home and school in northeastern Wisconsin's Door County), in cooperation with the Department of Landscape Architecture at the University of Wisconsin initiated The Clearing Landscape Institute. Held every two years, these symposiums were established to bring together academicians, professionals, and others interested in the field to experience Jensen's landscape art firsthand while sharing knowledge and ideas about the history and development of landscape architecture in the Midwest. This book evolved from these sessions. Each essay profiles a pioneering landscape architect whose achievements have enriched the lives of countless people in the Midwest and beyond. Included are thirteen practitioners whose careers together span more than a century, arranged in a roughly chronological order according to when their work in the region began. The contributors include professors of landscape architecture as well as landscape historians and practitioners who have a passionate interest in the history of their profession.

The book begins with Noël Dorsey Vernon's essay on Adolph Strauch, the earliest of the emerging group of midwestern landscape designers. Strauch began working in Cincinnati in 1852—nearly a decade before the onset of the Civil War. The German-born designer had come to America trained within the respected European tradition of apprenticeship in landscape gardening, a tradition established long before formal education in landscape architecture developed in America. Strauch devoted his career to working on Spring Grove Cemetery, his crowning achievement. As Strauch's reputation grew, his advice was sought by park and cemetery officials throughout the region, and his parklike burial landscape became a major influence in American cemetery design.

By the end of the nineteenth century, a new and vibrant sense of power had emerged in the Midwest which began to challenge the traditional economic, political, and cultural hegemony of the East. At the same time, with a mighty burst of energy, Chicago's civic renaissance manifested itself in a flowering of the arts. The prairie landscape inspired a new sense of regionalism—the "Prairie style" or "Prairie School"—emerged in both architecture and landscape design. Although it had some affinity for the English Arts and Crafts movement, the Prairie School of architecture drew more directly on the concepts of organic architecture established by Louis Sullivan, who had worked for William Le Baron Jenney. Central to this approach in both architecture and landscape architecture was the quest for an interpretation of midwestern sense of place, or genius loci.

Of the practitioners included in this volume, three—Ossian C. Simonds, Jens Jensen, and Wilhelm Miller—had strong ties to the Prairie style movement in landscape architecture. Historians have associated Simonds with the beginnings of the midwestern movement, which can be traced to his work at Graceland Cemetery in Chicago. There, as early as 1880, he was transplanting from the wilds common Illinois species of oak, maple, ash, thorn apple, witch hazel, and dogwood.

It was the legendary Jens Jensen, however, who became the region's most famous advocate of "natural" parks and gardens. A native of Denmark, Jensen emigrated to America in 1884 and subsequently found employment with Chicago's West Park District. Soon he was making frequent excursions into the countryside beyond the city, where he developed an intimate knowledge of the region's indigenous plants and landscape character. In 1888 he created a popular attraction in Union Park consisting of transplanted wildflowers, which he called the "American Garden." This garden, contrasting sharply with the typical formal, manicured plantings of Chicago's early West Park, was Jensen's first project that utilized native plants in an artistic expression of a natural landscape. As he rose to positions of greater responsibility with the parks system, Jensen protested on numerous occasions against the corrupt actions of self-serving political appointees, and he was fired at least twice. His reputation for integrity and for expertise in naturalistic design grew, however, and Jensen amassed an impressive list of prestigious commissions in private practice. Near the end of World War I, he designed Columbus Park, the last and, in his view, the most successful of his Chicago park projects. His brilliant plan—a masterful expression of the site's indigenous features— included the re-creation of the nearby prairie and a prairie river built on an ancient glacial beach running through the site.

After his wife's death in 1934, Jensen moved to Wisconsin's Door County peninsula to build his lifelong dream at The Clearing. Based on his early experiences in the Danish folk schools, this innovative learning environment emphasized outdoor work and studies of nature integrated with instruction in landscape design and other subjects. From this wooded northern retreat, the independent-spirited Jensen continued his vigorous campaign to conserve wild nature. Fiercely proud of midwestern culture and values, he railed against the use of imported plants and formal styles. Jensen associated these practices with East Coast designers, many of whom were prominent members of the American Society of Landscape Architects. He once wrote, "Many years ago I resigned from that bunch of deadbeats." He considered "those that ruled" the ASLA to be an "eastern klick [sic]."[1]

Women landscape practitioners and conservationists also played important roles in the Midwest. Genevieve Gillette, who was born and grew up on a Michigan farm, became the first woman to graduate from the landscape architecture program at Michigan State Agricultural College (now Michigan State University) in 1920. Midwestern universities generally provided easier access than their East Coast counterparts, many of which were firmly closed to women applicants. Still, it was difficult for women to find jobs, in the Midwest or anywhere else. Gillette found work in the Chicago office of Jens Jensen, where she observed Jensen's wide-ranging conservation activities firsthand. She moved back to Michigan to open her own practice and became a highly effective activist, mustering the political support necessary to create many new state parks.

From Adolph Strauch's early park work at Cincinnati in 1852 to Genevieve Gillette's tireless crusade to save unspoiled Michigan landscapes in the 1960s, the careers of these midwestern landscape architects varied in response to the forces that were shaping their profession: European traditions in landscape gardening, East Coast–born ideas about democratized landscapes, Prairie School philosophy of regional design. The essays in this volume offer insights into the lives and work of these professionals. Each had a unique role in shaping the midwestern landscapes that have become the legacy of all Americans.

Note

1. Jens Jensen, letter to William Evjue, 20 January [1949?], Box 61, Folder 20, Manuscripts Division, State Historical Society, Madison, Wis.

ONE

Adolph Strauch

CINCINNATI AND THE LEGACY OF SPRING GROVE CEMETERY

Noël Dorsey Vernon

ADOLPH STRAUCH (1822–83) was arguably the foremost cemetery designer in the United States in the nineteenth century. His revolutionary "lawn plan" featured a unified landscape treatment of lawns, vegetation, water elements, well-designed outbuildings, and a de-emphasis of monuments. But Strauch was also influential in a wider landscape sphere as well: "Perhaps no man in the United States since A. J. Downing's time," wrote the eminent landscape architect O. C. Simonds, "has done more for the correction and cultivation of public taste in landscape gardening than Adolph Strauch."[1] Simonds himself learned a great deal from Strauch's masterpiece, Cincinnati's Spring Grove Cemetery, before gaining recognition for his own work at Graceland Cemetery, in Chicago. Frederick Law Olmsted, too, admired the designed landscape of Spring Grove Cemetery. Simonds later recalled, "Olmsted used to say that when he needed inspiration he visited Spring Grove."[2] German-born and European-trained, Strauch made substantial contributions to the emerging landscape design tradition of his adopted home, the American Midwest, but in what ways did he influence landscape architectural practice nationwide?[3]

Strauch was born on 30 August 1822 (just four months after Olmsted), in the village of Eckersdorf, then in the Prussian province of Silesia. In the nineteenth century in Europe, training and apprenticeship in landscape gardening were well-established, in marked contrast to the United States, where there were no educational and apprenticeship programs in the field. Strauch began his training at age sixteen when he went to Vienna to learn from the gardeners of Schoenbrunn and Laxenburg. During his six years working under the Hapsburg Imperial gardeners, Strauch became acquainted with Hermann Ludwig Heinrich, Prince von Pückler-Muskau (1785–1871). By that time Pückler-Muskau was highly regarded for his landscape work on his patrimonial estate, Park Muskau, in Silesia.[4] His design was a version of the "picturesque" landscapes of Sir Humphry Repton and John Nash—in a bold departure from the formal geometry of the Schoenbrunn Palace gardens, which rivaled those of Versailles.[5]

Pückler-Muskau was impressed by the young Strauch, and the two formed a lasting acquaintance during Strauch's years in Vienna. The prince's gift of an inscribed copy of his *Hints on Landscape Gardening* became one of Strauch's treasured possessions.[6] In 1845, on his friend's advice, Strauch began an extended European sojourn, carrying letters of reference and making lengthy observations on landscape gardens and gardening procedures in Germany, the Netherlands, and Belgium. During this trip he spent three months with Louis van Houtte at his gardens near Ghent. Strauch also studied in Paris, until leaving France with the onset of the 1848 revolution. Thus, he missed the years after the accession of Louis Napoleon, when Alphand and Haussmann transformed the avenues of Paris and the Bois de Boulogne landscape. He did visit the Père Lachaise cemetery in Paris—one of the only rural landscaped cemeteries in Europe—but later wrote that he considered it inferior to the great rural cemeteries he observed in the United States.[7]

When he left France, the twenty-six-year-old Strauch traveled to London,

Adolph Strauch.
(Reprinted from *Der Deutsche Pionier* 15 [Feb. 1884], 424)

View of Pückler-Muskau's park showing the Pheasantry from the Salon terrace, with the post-bridge over the Neiss River in the background. (Reprinted from Pückler-Muskau, *Hints on Landscape Gardening*, pl. 21)

Prince von Pückler Muskau. (Reprinted from Pückler-Muskau, *Hints on Landscape Gardening*, unnumbered plate)

where he worked at the Royal Botanic Society's gardens in Regent's Park until his departure for America in 1851. Before he left, his vision of landscape gardening must have been broadened by the Great Exhibition, the lavish trade-and-progress fair housed in Joseph Paxton's vast Crystal Palace and set in London's Hyde Park. Being fluent in German, English, French, Polish, and Bohemian, Strauch was asked to serve as a visitors' guide, and in this capacity he met one visitor who would later have a profound influence on his career—Robert A. Bowler, a Cincinnati businessman and "proprietor of the Kentucky Central Railroad."[8] Bowler was also the owner of the Clifton, Ohio, estate Mount Storm and an aficionado of the finest in landscape gardening and horticulture.

Bowler's interest in botanic gardens is best understood in the context of mid-nineteenth-century Cincinnati. For aesthetic as well as economic reasons, Cincinnati's patriarchs had a passion for horticulture. The city was home to a flourishing intellectual and scientific community whose achievements included the historic contributions of Daniel Drake (and other Ohio Valley botanists), Nicholas Longworth's extensive involvement with horticulture, and John Aston Warder's horticultural experiments along with his editorship from 1850 to 1853 of *The Western Horticultural Review*, a periodical that rivaled Andrew Jackson Downing's journal, *The Horticulturist*. The Ernst family owned the premier local nursery, Spring Garden, and several other local landscape gardeners plied their trade and wrote for the *Review*, primarily on plant selection and maintenance. If Strauch came to Cincinnati by a fluke, it was no fluke that he remained there.[9]

Strauch was first lured to this country by the same illustrations of the

Several of Cincinnati's patriarchs who were active in founding Spring Grove Cemetery are included in this Cincinnati Horticultural Society photograph, c. 1850. (Neg. B-88-137; courtesy of the Cincinnati Museum Center Archives, Cincinnati, Ohio)

Southwest which had captured the fancy of so many Europeans.[10] There may also have been political pressures behind Strauch's trip. It is likely that he supported the 1848 uprising in Germany, as he seems to have been one of the many pro-unity and -democracy Germans who could not (or did not wish to) return home after 1850.[11] He planned to earn his way by writing articles on his travels for newspapers in London and "Ausland" in Germany.[12]

In 1851, however, the American Southwest was a dangerous destination. At the time of Strauch's landing in Galveston, Texas, the Comanche Indians were in open conflict with the U.S. military. According to Rattermann, "After a rugged trek on donkey through the Rio Colorado high desert to San Antonio, he learned that further exploration into the mountains would require armed guards."[13] Rather than continue, Strauch passed the winter months among his countrymen in the nearby German American refugee communities of "San Antonio, Neu Braemfels [*sic*], Sisterdale, Boerne, and Fredericksburg."[14] The founders of these communities had taken a moral stance against slavery, a position that Strauch may have shared. (Strauch did in fact appreciate Humboldt's *Cosmos,* which expressed an antislavery perspective).[15] Indeed, these communities had also favorably impressed Frederick Law Olmsted and his brother, John, as the two traveled as journalists through the slave states of the South in 1853 and 1854.[16] Despite the idealism with which they had been founded, and their promise, however, these communities would be tinged with tragedy, and Strauch's own journalistic accounts of life in Texas at midcentury may have helped to correct the prevalent naïveté about conditions there.[17]

By late spring 1852 Strauch was intending to return to Europe, but he changed his plans on hearing of a position for a landscape gardener offered by one of the Cushings of Boston. With the thought of applying for the job, Strauch set out for New England via Niagara Falls. When his steamer arrived in Cincinnati too late for him to meet a train to Buffalo, he was forced to remain overnight. He came across Bowler's card and paid him a visit. Bowler quickly offered Strauch the position as his landscape gardener, and Strauch accepted without hesitation. And so Strauch entered the cultural and horticultural worlds of Cincinnati, whose well-established German American community also would have given him a strong welcome.[18] Something of Strauch's character is revealed in a brief portrait drawn of him by his friend Heinrich Rattermann:

> Strauch was short and of stout physique, with a head which seemed too big
> for his body. He loved to be in the circle of educated people, but he was still
> humble and did not talk about himself, or his accomplishments, as much as
> he loved to show and talk about them with visitors. Only to trusted friends
> did he talk about his battles to reach his goals. Over a period of twenty-five
> years, there was seldom an important personality visiting Cincinnati who did
> not visit with Strauch. These included the Prince of Wales . . . as well as the
> Grand Duke Alexis, the Steubens, the Gerstackers, the Schlaginweits, the
> Rolfs, Bodenstedt, Frau Otto Alvesleben, the Emperor Dom Pedro von Brazil and other notable personalities. . . . Strauch married an American lady
> from a strict Presbyterian family, Miss Mary Chapman. His relationship with
> his wife and children was very sparing. He ate his meals in a rush and went
> off to his business.[19]

Strauch's first "canvas" in the region was Bowler's Mount Storm (now Mount Storm Park), on a west-facing hillside northwest of the city above Millcreek Valley. This work, begun in 1852, was followed by commissions to improve the landscapes of other Clifton properties—the estates of such notables as Henry Probasco, George Schoenberger (whose property, Scarlet Oaks, would later be purchased by John Warder), William Neff, Robert Buchanan, and William Resor.[20] Rattermann notes that Strauch later found other German American gardeners to maintain the properties.[21]

When Strauch arrived in Cincinnati, he had already developed clear theories of park design: he believed that space should be unified through vistas and panoramas without enclosures, hedges, or fences, and he favored lakelets, well-placed statuary framed by suitable trees, lawns and flowers, and "tasteful" outbuildings. The goal was to provide a visually integrated landscape such as Pückler-Muskau had described in his *Hints*.

Many years before Strauch's arrival, Robert Buchanan had gathered together a group of prominent Cincinnati residents to consider the need for a nondenominational rural cemetery in the area. In 1844 a site was chosen: a parcel of 166 acres of sandy soil, beyond Clifton's heights to the northwest, across Millcreek Valley. The valley itself had become something of an eyesore, as industry had spread into Clifton's viewshed. The need to limit the visual blight (and thus maintain Clifton's property values) was an important consideration in the choice of site. The charter of the cemetery corporation was granted by the Ohio legislature on 21 January 1845.[22]

That Spring Grove would be a "landscaped cemetery" carried great Christian significance. In the mid-nineteenth century, death was a constant companion, and grieving was often a way of life. The landscaped cemeteries such as Mount Auburn (1831) in Boston represented a major cultural revolution: they allowed the literal and metaphorical replacement of the grim death's head of the graveyard with an Elysian, picturesque landscape. Sleep replaced death and decay as a means of awaiting the Second Coming. Moreover, the rural cemetery was thought to be a more healthful place to visit than the often crowded urban graveyard: the salutary landscaped, or "garden," cemetery was designed as a physical environment to accommodate death and console the living.[23] As a grove for the honored dead and as the nexus of a community's idealized self-image and history, the landscaped cemetery was, before the advent of the public park, a "heaven-while-waiting" on earth.[24]

From the start, Cincinnati's leading citizens were well aware of and in some ways imitated the achievement of Bostonians at Mount Auburn.[25] At both of these nondenominational cemeteries, the sites were remote, far from the center of town, and landscaped for the comfort of the general public as well as for the consolation of those who grieved. But under Strauch, Spring Grove would follow the lead of Mount Auburn and other early prototypes only in these conceptual ways.

The Spring Grove site was problematic; the southwestern part, a third of the total, was swamp. Nevertheless, by autumn 1845 the cemetery was in use.[26] Within ten years, some of the higher ground had been cleared and landscaped, a hedge of osage orange planted, and an entry drive laid out. One bold feature, an overpass for the Cincinnati, Hamilton, and Dayton railroad built in 1850, provided a strong sense of entry while functioning as a barrier between the cemetery and the less appealing industrial sites beyond.[27] In sum, the site was far from a tabula rasa when Strauch arrived in the winter of 1854–55 to implement his plan of improvement and assume the position of superintendent and landscape gardener.[28]

Why was Strauch's plan for Spring Grove considered revolutionary even within the landscaped cemetery movement?[29] Before Strauch, the question was how to design cemeteries tastefully while meeting the exigencies of enclosure, circulation, and drainage. Earlier landscape theorists, such as John Strang and

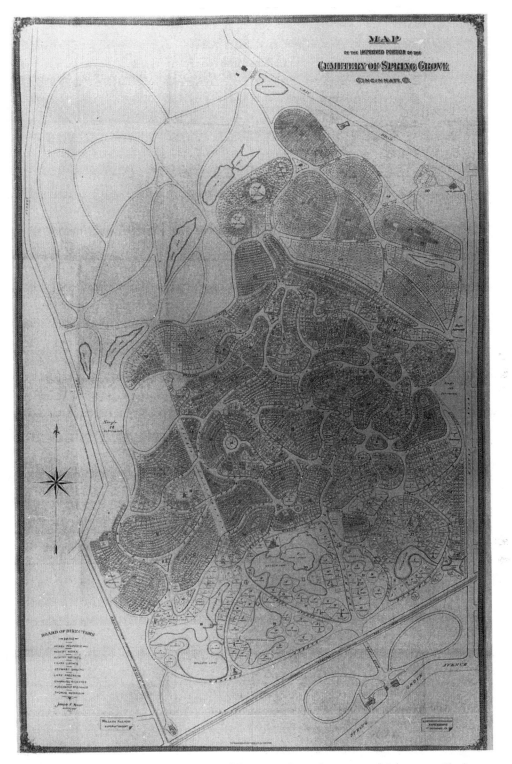

Map of Spring Grove Cemetery. (Courtesy of the Spring Grove Cemetery and Arboretum, Cincinnati, Ohio)

John Claudius Loudon, started with the assumption that graves would be marked with upright stones or other markers and that owners might enclose their plots. While Loudon offered hints for restricting gravestones and monuments to the borders of walks and circulation roads, his own cemetery designs, largely rectilinear, lacked picturesque character.[30] Strauch may have read Loudon's work, but he did not limit himself to Loudon's advice.

Strauch envisioned the cemetery as a unified picturesque landscape with only one monument or sculpture per burial lot. In his plan, headstones could not exceed a height of two feet. Any larger object—a fine work of art, for example—would require special permission from the board.[31] The cemetery designer would determine all site grades and create an overall planting effect. As private enclosures and plantings would be discouraged, the landscape would offer visual unity, a quality lacking in earlier rural landscaped cemeteries.[32] To maintain such a vision Strauch insisted on strict adherence to rules, which sometimes caused major dissension, but in the main his plan was accepted. "Since the adoption of the present style of Improvement," he wrote in 1869, "the financial condition of the association has also very much improved, for not only has the size of the place been extended to more than double its former area, but a large surplus has already been laid aside, for the perpetual care of the grounds after all burial lots shall have been sold." At the lot holders' request, Strauch remodeled areas that had been laid out by his predecessors.[33] He also developed the lower, entry levels of the cemetery along with the lakes (in the former swamp), which so strongly define the site's character.

Pückler-Muskau's design theory appears to have been the strongest guiding force in Strauch's work. For his own landscape, the prince had looked for models in the work of the British landscape gardeners such as Repton (although not uncritically).[34] So the young Strauch was influenced in part, through Pückler-Muskau as well as through his own sojourn in Britain, by English landscape models.

To trace the strong influence of Pückler-Muskau's *Hints* on Strauch's Spring Grove, one may walk the cemetery with a copy of the book in hand, searching out common principles.[35] Pückler-Muskau recommended that a park possess "the character of untrammeled Nature"; only "the well-kept roads and the judiciously scattered buildings" should reveal a human designer. While he did not seek a perfect illusion of wild nature, for visitors should not have to wade through tall grass and thorns, vegetation should be deep, luxuriant: "The first requirement of a landscape is the vigorous growth of all plants," he stated. Pückler-Muskau also believed that like elements (including fields and buildings) should be massed for visual unity. Visual drama and unity-in-complexity were important concerns, and well-composed views—especially those from a building—were critical.

Strauch's Spring Grove design is notable for just such views and visual unity. Its road system also suggests the influence of the *Hints*. The prince warned that roads should not follow the perimeter or surprise visitors by suddenly ending but rather lead visitors "as by an invisible hand, to the most beautiful spots," allowing them to comprehend the picture as a whole. Any roads running parallel should be separated by clear divisions, for example, a hill and a valley. Footpaths and roads should be interconnected to offer a variety of routes.

Many of the lakes at Spring Grove also illustrate the prince's theories. An expanse of water, Pückler-Muskau observed, could be made to seem larger, more like a river, by concealing boundaries with shrubbery, and by creating islands and deep bays. On the banks, however, woods and thickets should give way to the occasional single tree or broad, grassy bank that gives full entry to the sun and thus preserves the water's "transparency and brilliancy."

Spring Grove's "Strauch Island" may have had its origin in Pückler-Muskau's *Hints* (in fortuitous combination with the site's naturally marshy

Winter scene at Spring Grove Cemetery shows the subtle use of expanses of water. (Neg. B-93-193; courtesy of the Cincinnati Museum Center Archives, Cincinnati, Ohio)

topography): "A lonely spot on a well-wooded island, or the distant view of a mass of arching foliage swimming on the crystal surface of the water, is more attractive to many than all the charms available on dry land," the prince noted. But a round or oval island would seem artificial. Strauch Island first appears to be a peninsula; its outlines, like those of the entry lakes, are complex, apparently flowing onward before disappearing.

Imperfections in design should never be accepted, Pückler-Muskau warned, for "nineteen times out of twenty a firm will and patience make the so-called 'impossible' quite easily possible." However diverse in its parts, a plan must reflect a unified idea, and it is the long-term resident designer—willing to rework each mistake until the whole is perfect—not the expert brought in to quickly run up a plan, who produces the finest work. Strauch embodied this approach, seeking a unified plan and working for twenty-eight years at Spring Grove to realize his dream.

Strauch's plan for Spring Grove also reflects a European understanding of Chinese parks, which as Humboldt noted predated the parks of England.[36] In *Cosmos*, first published in 1844, Humboldt referred to a poem by the eighteenth-century emperor Kien-long (Qian Long), who admired nature subtly embellished by art. Here Humboldt recognized a fusing of "the cheerful images of the luxuriant freshness of the meadows, of the forest-crowned hills, and the peaceful dwellings of men, with the somber picture of the tombs of his forefathers."[37] A longer excerpt of this passage from *Cosmos* appears in Strauch's *Spring Grove Cemetery* (1869) and was likely an inspiration for Strauch's design of Spring Grove.[38]

By the 1860s this 412-acre cemetery was said to be the largest in the world and was highly acclaimed. Strauch's success at Spring Grove led to requests for advice and assistance with cemetery design and park projects elsewhere.

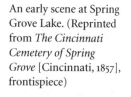
An early scene at Spring Grove Lake. (Reprinted from *The Cincinnati Cemetery of Spring Grove* [Cincinnati, 1857], frontispiece)

Chinese cemetery scene reproduced in Strauch's *Spring Grove Cemetery.* (Neg. B-93-192; courtesy of the Cincinnati Museum Center Archives, Cincinnati, Ohio)

In Cincinnati, he was associated with the park system as a whole and contributed to the early development of Eden Park,[39] and in Detroit he worked for many years at Woodmere, where, with the architect G. W. Lloyd, Strauch furnished plans for the grounds and structures in 1867. An opening address by C. I. Walker, a prominent Detroit lawyer, praised Strauch's ability and gratitude for his generosity: "No one has done so much for the improvement of rural cemeteries, and the correction and cultivation of public taste upon this subject." Citing Spring Grove as the model cemetery in the United States, finer than Mount Auburn (which contained more sumptuous monuments), Walker announced that Woodmere's board of directors had unanimously resolved to follow in general the plan of Spring Grove. He added that "Mr. Strauch very kindly and generously gave us the benefit of his experience, his genius and his taste in the laying out of the grounds, and in valuable suggestions for their improvement."[40] Walker's acknowledgment may have been a response to Strauch's refusal of remuneration for his services: Rattermann observed that, except when serving as superintendent of a city park, Strauch typically did not accept payment: "The spreading of his ideas was, for him, enough compensation."[41]

Various sources credit Strauch with providing advice and designs for cemeteries in other cities as well, including Nashville, Chicago, Buffalo, Cleveland, Indianapolis, and Hartford. It seems likely that he also advised on the design of Cincinnati's new German Catholic Maria Cemetery.[42] In 1864 Strauch assisted in the formation of Oakwoods Cemetery near Chicago.[43] Other cemetery associations including Laurel Hill in Philadelphia also used Strauch's ideas (some solely, some in combination with those of other designers). In 1874 the annual report on Woodlawn Cemetery observed that "to Mr. Adolph Strauch, a Prussian landscape gardener, and the present accomplished superintendent of Spring Grove Cemetery, Cincinnati, is due the credit of having organized the Landscape-Lawn Plan, which bids fair, before many years, to revolutionize all of our principal cemeteries."[44] The majority of citations in this report are from Strauch's *Spring Grove Cemetery,* but advice from Jacob Weidenmann, Loudon, Downing, and H. W. S. Cleveland was also included.

Given his talent and the extent of his influence, why is Strauch so little known today? One answer may be that he worked predominantly in a single region. Possibly another is that that region was the Midwest, when the greatest professional prominence, especially in the early years of the American Society of Landscape Architects, came to designers associated with the large East Coast firms such as Olmsted Brothers. (O. C. Simonds was the only midwestern founder of the ASLA, and the literature was long dominated by East Coast design work.) Moreover, Strauch was not a prolific writer in English, and, although many cemetery boards and associations did cite his *Spring Grove Cemetery* book, his German writings remained largely unexplored.[45] (Apart from Rattermann's writings, the German press appears to have provided little coverage of Strauch's work. Rattermann noted other mentions of Strauch but remarked that Germans seemed reluctant to praise American ideas—especially those of transplanted Germans.)[46]

Strauch's work, however, was not entirely overlooked by the contemporary American press. In an article on Cincinnati published in the *Atlantic Monthly* in August 1867, James Parton gave low ratings to some elements of the cultural life of "Porkopolis" but praised Spring Grove—although he neglected to mention Strauch's role in its creation.[47] But a lengthy article by F. B. Perkins in *The Galaxy* (1871) at last gave Strauch his due. After devoting a page and a half entirely to a description of Strauch's efforts, Perkins added, "The best instance of this complex and difficult work [of cemetery design] is Spring Grove Cemetery; . . . indeed it is the only one in the United States where sufficient time has passed and sufficient space and work have been bestowed to permit an adequate judgment upon the method. The judgment, however, can be but one."[48] Perkins's article is the only substantive critical tribute to Strauch written in English during the nineteenth century.

Spring Grove Cemetery. (Reprinted from Robinson, "Garden Cemeteries," 186)

Acknowledgment of Strauch's contribution was also limited in England and Europe. When William Robinson, editor of the English periodical *The Garden*, wrote an article on American cemeteries, he published two engravings of Spring Grove Cemetery which he had received from Strauch by way of Olmsted Sr.[49] At the end of the article, Robinson briefly credited Strauch as Spring Grove's "superintendent and landscape gardener" at whose suggestion "the present plan of improvement was adopted," but he did not acknowledge Strauch for his illustrations. It was less credit, certainly, than was due him as initiator of the "lawn plan."[50] Robinson further developed his ideas about American contributions to cemetery design in his book *God's Acre*

Beautiful, or The Cemeteries of the Future (1880). In it, he supports cremation and urn burial, both for sanitation and to save space, particularly in
crowded urban environments such as London, where land for lawn plan
cemeteries would be costly and soon become overcrowded. But he was clearly
impressed by the new American lawn plan cemeteries, as his book contains
an engraving of a scene in Spring Grove Cemetery and concludes with praise
for its visual integrity. Robinson reprinted an entire section of the "Act of
Incorporation of the Spring Grove Cemetery at Cincinnati," as though he
considered this cemetery an American institution. (If so, perhaps he can be
forgiven for neglecting to mention Strauch's name.)[51]

In the United States, Olmsted Sr. freely acknowledged the ascendancy of
Strauch's work in landscape design—"Cincinnati possesses in Spring Grove
cemetery the best example in the world, probably, of landscape gardening
applied to a burial place," he wrote in one article—but he also neglected to
mention Strauch by name. Writing to Strauch himself, however, Olmsted
credited him with the origin of the lawn system and added, "I know of no
cemetery in the country in which there are any matured effects of landscape
gardening, properly so called, except at Spring Grove."[52]

O. C. Simonds, too, in an article published posthumously in 1932, revealed
his great respect for Strauch: "During the progress of the work [on Grace-
land] Mr. [Bryan] Lathrop would come out frequently and make suggestions.
One time he said, 'You have not had experience in grading, and Mr. [Wil-
liam Le Baron] Jenney does not know about grading. Let us all go and see
Spring Grove Cemetery at Cincinnati and have a talk with Mr. Strauch. . . .'
We found Spring Grove beautiful with its undulating grades, its charming
landscapes, and its superintendent quite generous with his theories and advice." Earlier, in 1903, Simonds had praised Strauch in an article on cemetery
planning and administration, in which he called Spring Grove "the most
beautiful cemetery in the world."[53]

Strauch suffered a stroke in mid-April of 1883 and died on April 25. He
was buried in a place of prominence on Strauch Island in his own Spring
Grove Cemetery. At his death, Strauch was a respected citizen of Cincinnati,
and a landscape designer held in great esteem by his colleagues.[54] It is a sad
irony that the greatest tribute to his work—Rattermann's four articles in *Der
Deutsche Pionier*—was written in a language that few American landscape
architects or historians could read. Through the beauty of his creation at
Spring Grove, however, and the generosity with which he shared his ideas and
skills, Strauch ultimately had a profound effect on American landscape architecture and on nineteenth-century North American perceptions of death
and experiences of bereavement, grief, and solace.

Notes

I am indebted to John Frederick, biographer and bibliographer of the botanists and horticulturists of Cincinnati, who for nearly ten years encouraged me—in letters, phone calls, and leads—to write about the role played by Strauch and Cincinnati's patriarchs in the history of midwestern landscape architecture. My thanks also to Henry Shapiro and to Blanche Linden and David Sloane for immersing me in Spring Grove during the 1985 Spring Grove symposia; to Sherda Williams, who collected material for me on her trips to Cincinnati; and to Robert Grese, who uncovered and sent me two articles by O. C. Simonds which discussed Strauch's work and the article from *The Garden,* which I had been unable to locate. Don Heinrich Tolzman of the University of Cincinnati has helped me see the probable connection between Strauch's settling in Cincinnati and the presence of a strong German American community there. In addition, I am indebted to the Cincinnati Historical Society, especially to Linda Bailey, and to Jeanette Humphries of Spring Grove Cemetery for their help. Ingrid Russell unlocked a new Strauch source for me with her general translation summary of H. A. Rattermann's work. Finally, I thank William Tishler, who urged me into action by asking me to write this essay.

1. O[ssian] C[ole] S[imonds], "Adolph Strauch," in *The Standard Cyclopedia of Horticulture,* ed. Liberty Hyde Bailey, 2d ed. (New York: Macmillan, 1914).

2. Ibid.

3. In this essay I examine some of the issues central to understanding the career and influence of Adolph Strauch: his status as a midwestern German American in American landscape design; Alexander von Humboldt's far-ranging book *Cosmos,* with its comments on both Chinese and German gardening; the work and writings of Pückler-Muskau (with whom, it is said, Strauch was personally acquainted); the history of the rural landscaped cemetery movement; Cincinnati as an epicenter of nineteenth-century landscape gardening and horticulture; Strauch's relations with friends and colleagues; and the extent of Strauch's reputation and influence in his own time.

For an English-speaking audience, the details of Strauch's life and work have come mainly from his long-time friend Heinrich Armin Rattermann's address before the Cincinnati Literary Club, "Spring Grove Cemetery and Its Creator" (1905), which has been published as *Spring Grove and Its Creator: H. A. Rattermann's Biography of Adolph Strauch* [1905], ed. Don Heinrich Tolzman (Cincinnati: Ohio Book Store, 1988). Rattermann, editor of the German American periodical *Der Deutsche Pionier,* also wrote two texts on Strauch in Old German: "Deutsch-Amerikanische Kunstler: Der Pionier der Landschaftsgartnerei," *Der Deutsche Pionier* 10 (June 1878), 82–93, and the four-part series "Adolph Strauch: Der Begrunder der Landschaftslichen Friedhofe" published in *Der Deutsche Pionier* in 1884. This series was reprinted as *Adolph Strauch, der Begrunder der Landschaftslichen Friedhofe: Eine Biographische Skizze* (Cincinnati, 1884). An earlier, unsigned article on Strauch, found in Robson's *Biographical Cyclopaedia of Ohio in the Nineteenth Century* (1876), may also have been written by Rattermann. Biographical materials on Strauch's patrons and mentors in Cincinnati help to enlarge the picture of his career in that city. Strauch himself left a description of his work in his *Spring Grove Cemetery: Its History and Improvements, with Observations on Ancient and Modern Places of Sepulture* (Cincinnati, 1869).

More recently, histories of cemetery design and of Spring Grove Cemetery in particular have appeared. For secondary sources on Spring Grove, see James A. Green, "A Centennial History of the Cemetery of Spring Grove: A Record of a Century of Devoted and Consecrated Effort" (1944), in the manuscript collection of Spring Grove Cemetery, Cincinnati; George B. Tobey, "Adolph Strauch, Father of the Lawn Plan," *Landscape Planning* 2 (1975), 283–94; and Blanche Linden-Ward and David Sloane, "Spring Grove: The Founding of Cincinnati's Rural Cemetery, 1845–1855," *Queen City Heritage* 43 (Spring

1985), 17–32. These sources, along with the broader cultural overviews gleaned from Humboldt and Pückler-Muskau, help to shed light on Strauch and his work.

I have based my biography of Strauch here on a general translation summary of the four 1884 Ratterman articles on Strauch, written for me by Ingrid Russell in 1990 and which is reinforced by Ratterman's now published "Spring Grove Cemetery and Its Creator"; references to the Russell translation cite the original article number and page.

4. Separated by the division of Germany after World War II, the two halves of Park Muskau have been reunited and are undergoing careful study and preservation.

5. Pückler-Muskau mentioned the work of Repton and Nash several times in his *Hints on Landscape Gardening* (see note 6 below) and often used the words "picturesque" and "romantic" in describing landscapes he liked. In writing the *Hints,* he spoke from personal experience with Park Muskau, as well as from acquaintance with many gardens he had seen. While he believed that design must be site-specific, he noted that, in his own country, "a completed example which could be set beside the best English plans has not come within my experience" (7).

6. Rattermann, "Adolph Strauch," 1:431–32. Hermann, Furst von Pückler-Muskau's *Hints on Landscape Gardening,* trans. Bernhard Sickert, ed. with an introduction by Samuel Parsons (Boston: Houghton Mifflin, 1917), was originally published as *Andeutungen uber Landschaftsgartnerei* (Stuttgart, 1834).

7. Strauch, *Spring Grove Cemetery.* With the exceptions of Père Lachaise, the Glasgow Necropolis, and a few other British sites, Europe did not yet offer examples of what might be termed rural landscaped cemeteries.

8. Rattermann, "Adolph Strauch," 1:432. Information on Robert Bowler is provided in Henry D. Shapiro and Zane Miller, *Clifton: Neighborhood and Community in an Urban Setting: A Brief History* (Cincinnati: Laboratory in American Civilization, 1976), 8.

9. Ulysses P. Hendrick, in his *History of Horticulture in America to 1860* (New York: Oxford University Press, 1950), noted, "The Cincinnati Horticultural Society was one of the best in the country and was long a clearinghouse in the whole Middle West for horticultural information" (311). Liberty Hyde Bailey praised the Cincinnati horticulturists in his *Sketch of the Evolution of Our Native Fruits* (New York, 1898): "[in Cincinnati] there developed, by 1850, a center of horticultural interest which eclipsed, in the character of its men and the variety of its interests, any similar community which has ever arisen in the West"—he specifically cites Strauch's presence (65).

10. Rattermann, "Adolph Strauch," 1:433.

11. At least one writer considered Strauch a political refugee; the "Strauch" entry in the "Biographical Dictionary" in *The Forty-Eighters: Political Refugees of the German Revolution of 1848,* ed. A. E. Zucker (New York: Columbia University Press, 1950), states, "[Strauch's] participation in the Revolution drove him to England where he remained for some time" (346).

12. Rattermann, "Adolph Strauch," 1:433. According to Rattermann, the German publication for which Strauch wrote was *Ausland* ("Spring Grove," 3). *Ausland* was published by Georg Cotta, the (more conservative) son of the liberal German publisher Johann Cotta, who had published works by Heinrich Heine, Karl Gutzkow, and Ludwig Boerne in the 1820s and early 1830s. See Frederick Hertz, *The German Public Mind in the Nineteenth Century: A Social History of German Political Sentiments, Aspirations, and Ideas,* ed. Frank Eyck, trans. Eric Northcott (Totowa, N.J.: Rowman and Littlefield, 1975).

13. Rattermann, "Adolph Strauch," 1:433.

14. Rattermann, *Spring Grove Cemetery,* 3.

15. Rattermann, "Adolph Strauch," 1:439; "Spring Grove Cemetery," 6. In discussing "The Races of Man," Humboldt observes, "While we maintain the unity of the human species, we at the same time repel the depressing assumption of superior and inferior races of men. . . . All are in like degree designed for freedom" (Alexander von Humboldt, *Cosmos: A Sketch of a Physical Description of the Universe,* trans. E. C. Otee [New York,

1851], 1:358). This belief, which Strauch apparently shared, should help to absolve Humboldt (and Strauch) from accusations of "fellow-traveling" in the recent debates about connections between plant geography, German landscape design, and National Socialism.

16. Laura Wood Roper, *FLO, A Biography of Frederick Law Olmsted* (Baltimore: Johns Hopkins University Press, 1973).

17. Rattermann, "Adolph Strauch," 1:433.

18. Rattermann, "Adolph Strauch," 1:434.

19. Rattermann, "Adolph Strauch," 4:66–69.

20. Rattermann, "Adolph Strauch," 1:434.For more details on Mount Storm, and other extensive properties in Clifton, see Sidney D[enise] Maxwell, *The Suburbs of Cincinnati* (1870; reprint, New York: Arno Press, 1974). See also James Barclay, "Report in Memory of Robert Buchanan," *Journal of the Cincinnati Society of Natural History* 3 (July 1880), 74–76; Richard Davies, "Landscape Gardening," *Western Horticultural Review,* April 1851; and Shapiro and Miller, *Clifton.* A visit to these properties gives one a strong sense of Clifton's prominence, but Strauch's sitework there has remained largely undocumented and most cannot be separated (with certainty) from other remnant landscape fragments from the second half of the nineteenth century.

21. Rattermann, "Adolph Strauch," 1:434.

22. See Linden-Ward and Sloane, "Spring Grove," for an account of the founding of the cemetery.

23. For discussions of the rationales for creating rural landscaped, or garden, cemeteries, see Blanche Linden-Ward, *Silent City on a Hill: Landscapes of Memory and Boston's Mount Auburn Cemetery* (Columbus: Ohio State University Press, 1989), and John Stilgoe, "Folklore and Graveyard Design," *Landscape* 22 (Summer 1978), 22–28. These rationales involve the concept of death as sleep, the acceptance of the "modern landscape style," the popularity of the landscape paintings of Gaspar Poussin, Claude Lorraine, and others, the nineteenth-century cult of melancholy, the transcendental triumph of Nature, the fear of "miasma" in cemeteries, and the economics of urban real estate. The nineteenth-century cult of sentiment and grief and the public's acceptance of the long-term pain of bereavement are almost incomprehensible to us today, when death may trigger "situational depression," typically to be overcome in a year or less through a four-step psychological process, the treatment of which is generally covered by insurance.

24. The concept of the cemetery as a "museum without walls" was first brought to my attention by Blanche Linden-Ward and David Sloane during the 1985 exhibition "Nature by Design," at the Taft Museum, along with the series of three symposia sponsored by the University of Cincinnati Center for Neighborhood and Community Studies, the Joint Program in Human Values and the Built Environment of the Ohio Arts Council and the Ohio Humanities Council, the National Endowment for the Humanities, and Spring Grove Cemetery. The photographs for the exhibition, by Alan Ward, first introduced me to the Spring Grove landscape.

25. Strauch writes of Mount Auburn in glowing terms in *Spring Grove Cemetery.* See also Linden-Ward and Sloane, "Spring Grove," for additional information on Mount Auburn's influence.

26. Initial improvements at Spring Grove had been made on a somewhat haphazard basis. John Notman, designer of Laurel Hill Cemetery (1836) near Philadelphia, developed Spring Grove's first master plan, but it was not implemented. Instead, Spring Grove's original plan was designed and executed in part by Howard Daniels, the cemetery's first superintendent, assisted by his successor, Dennis Delaney, and a cemetery committee under Buchanan and including Thomas Earnshaw (Linden-Ward and Sloan, "Spring Grove," 23–25). "Later improvements," Strauch relates, "were made by the order and under the special direction of the monthly [cemetery] committee." Earnshaw and his sons then did a site survey (Strauch, *Spring Grove Cemetery*).

27. Linden-Ward and Sloane, "Spring Grove," 26. Rattermann described the original drive as "gloomy" (*Spring Grove,* 7).

28. See Charles T. Greve, *Centennial History of Cincinnati and Representative Citizens* (Chicago: Biographical Publishing, 1904), 1:1034. Concurring with Strauch (perhaps his only source?), Greve notes that, beginning in 1855, Strauch's system of landscape gardening was carried out largely by Strauch, assisted by (Thomas's son) Henry Earnshaw. Rattermann notes that it was difficult to pry Henry Earnshaw from the job of superintendent so as to let Strauch assume that role in late 1854 (*Spring Grove Cemetery,* 7).

29. Strauch, *Spring Grove Cemetery,* 9, 13. See John Strang, *Necropolis Glasguensis* (Glasgow, 1831), and John Claudius Loudon, *On the Laying Out, Planting, and Managing of Cemeteries and on the Improvement of Churchyards* (London, 1843). Much of Loudon's book was drawn from his series of articles on cemeteries and churchyards in his *Gardener's Magazine* 19 (1843). See Melanie L. Simo, *Loudon and the Landscape: From Country Seat to Metropolis, 1783–1843* (New Haven: Yale University Press, 1988), 285–86.

30. See Simo, *Loudon and the Landscape,* 285–86, and James Stevens Curl, *A Celebration of Death: An Introduction to Some of the Buildings, Monuments, and Settings of Funerary Architecture in the Western European Tradition* (New York: Scribner's, 1980).

31. Strauch, *Spring Grove Cemetery,* 65.

32. The directors of Mount Auburn Cemetery, for instance, had hoped to achieve visual unity in the landscape but made no provision for mandating it. See *The Picturesque Pocket Companion and Visitor's Guide through Mount Auburn* (Boston, 1839). O. C. Simonds observed in 1920: "The wish to have in the cemetery the beauty of trees, shrubs, lawns, and flowers has gradually led to the abolition of fences, coping, and other lot inclosures [*sic*], and a reduction in the number of monuments and the size of headstones" (Simonds, *Landscape Gardening* [New York: Macmillan, 1920], 290). The model for this type of cemetery was Spring Grove.

33. Strauch, *Spring Grove Cemetery,* 29, 28.

34. Samuel Parsons describes Pückler-Muskau as a romantic landscape architect who loved nature, indulged in "wild adventures," and harbored "strange visions and dreams." Parsons also detected a "touch of madness" in Pückler-Muskau's funereal memorials by a lake: "rocks inscribed with names intended to commemorate his ancestors interspersed with and surrounded by weeping willows" (introduction to Pückler-Muskau's *Hints,* xvii, xxii). Indeed, at minimum, Pückler-Muskau seems to have been taken more with the "Picturesque" side of Repton's work than with the (Brownian) "Beautiful" and to have had an intense—even "Wagnerian"—appreciation of the emotional and intellectual experience that could be created through careful use of planting, terrain, and landscape paths and vistas. Despite its limitations and anomalies, Pückler-Muskau was convinced that "England must for a long time remain an unattainable model" for the elevated expression of country life (*Hints,* 4). Strauch was said to "highly admire" the paintings of Claude Lorraine, and he liked the sculpture of Canova and Thorwaldsen; perhaps these also influenced the visually intense yet tranquil quality of the landscape of Spring Grove (Rattermann, "Adolph Strauch," 4:69.

35. The following quotations from *Hints* are from pages 38–39, 80, 93–94, 96, 122–23, and 13–17.

36. For the European fascination with Chinese landscapes (which predates the time of Humboldt), see Osvald Siren, *China and Gardens of Europe of the Eighteenth Century* (1950), reprint, with an introduction by Hugh Honour (Washington, D.C.: Dumbarton Oaks, 1990).

37. Humboldt, *Cosmos,* "Races of Man," 2:103. In a discussion of the gravesites of notable men, Strauch mentioned those of the duke of Saxe-Gotha, Washington Irving, and "the immortal Alexander von Humboldt" (*Spring Grove Cemetery,* 23).

38. Rattermann, "Adolph Strauch," 2:489. The Spring Grove Cemetery we know today was largely Strauch's creation, even though some portions evolved from earlier work and

acreage was added after Strauch's death. Blanche Linden-Ward, *Spring Grove Cemetery: A Self-Guided Walking Tour* (Cincinnati: Center for Neighborhood and Community Studies, 1985), notes that Spring Grove, the largest private, nonprofit cemetery in the United States (a National Historic Landmark) in 1985 contained 733 acres, 35 miles of roads, 14 lakes, and more than 170,000 interments.

39. Green, "Centennial History of the Cemetery of Spring Grove," 17–18; Rattermann, "Deutsch-Amerikanische Kunstler," 91–92.

40. C. I. Walker, "Address," in *Woodmere Cemetery, Its Organization, Act of Incorporation, Rules and Regulations; and Opening Address* (Detroit, 1869), 20. Strauch's participation is detailed on pages 7–8.

41. Rattermann, "Adolph Strauch," 4:62.

42. Robson, *Biographical Cyclopaedia*, 39; ibid.; Simonds, "Adolph Strauch," 1598; and Albert Bernhardt Faust, *The German Element in the United States*, 3d ed. (New York: Arno Press/New York Times, 1969), 2:65, all credit Strauch with influence in other cities. Faust believed that Strauch influenced the development of Woodlawn Cemetery, but this idea is not supported by the text of the *Woodlawn* annual report (see note 44 below). Rattermann notes the Maria Cemetery ("Adolph Strauch," 4:62).

43. Strauch wrote to Olmsted Sr. about it, on 17 March 1875 (Olmsted Letters, Manuscript Division, Library of Congress, Washington, D.C.; hereafter cited as OL).

44. *Woodlawn Cemetery, Annual Report to the Lot Holders for the Year 1874* (New York, 1875), 16.

45. According to Rattermann, Strauch also wrote articles for *The Encyclopaedia Britannica*, "Landscape Gardening" and "Rural Cemeteries" ("Adolph Strauch," 4:69).

46. Rattermann noted that Hermann Jagen mentioned Strauch's work and that a long article on it appeared in *Centralblatt der Bauverwaltung* (Central Paper of the Building Administration), 26 May 1883 (ibid., 65).

47. Less than ten years after Parton's article appeared, Olmsted's article "Parks," in *The American Cyclopaedia* (1875), noted two parks in Cincinnati—Eden Park and Burnett Woods.

48. F. B. Perkins, "Sepulture: Its Ideas and Practices," *Galaxy*, 1871, 844.

49. Robinson had asked Olmsted for material, who in turn contacted Jacob Weidenmann for Strauch's name (Weidenmann to Olmsted, 11 March 1875; OL). Responding to Olmsted's letter, Strauch generously sent a collection of cemetery reports and photographs (including some documenting his own work) to Olmsted, who forwarded the package to Robinson with a letter crediting Strauch.

50. William Robinson [?], "Garden Cemeteries," *The Garden* 10 (August 1876), 188. Contrary to Rattermann, who expressed anger at the "omission" ("Adolph Strauch," 4:63), the article stated that the photographs were of Spring Grove and that they had been sent by Olmsted, but not that Olmsted had designed the cemetery (186).

51. Annoyed by such treatment of his biographical subject, Rattermann also stated that in *God's Acre Beautiful*, Robinson "used Strauch's ideas as his own" ("Adolph Strauch," 4:64). As a veteran journalist, however, Robinson may have stressed information above sources.

52. F. L. Olmsted, "Parks," in *The American Cyclopaedia* (1875), 13:108; F. L. Olmsted to Strauch, 12 March 1875, OL. Rattermann recalled or translated this text in Old German as "I do not know of a cemetery in this land where, through landscape nurseries, there has been developed effective scenery except in Spring Grove Cemetery" ("Adolph Strauch," 4:63).

53. Simonds, "Graceland at Chicago," *American Landscape Architecture* 4 (January 1932), 17. Simonds also noted some flaws in the overall landscape character during Strauch's time, particularly an overabundance of stonework and mounding over graves; see his "The Planning and Administration of a Landscape Cemetery," *Country Life in America* 4 (September 1903), 350.

54. Strauch's naturalization document is dated 2 November 1876. As president of the board of directors of Spring Grove, Cincinnati patriarch Henry Probasco signed an eloquent "Token of Respect" (dated 26 April 1883), which credited Strauch with the design and development of Spring Grove and compared him to Repton and Pückler-Muskau (both documents are held in the Manuscript Division, Cincinnati Historical Society).

TWO

Horace Cleveland

THE CHICAGO YEARS

William H. Tishler

ONE OF THE FIRST landscape architectural practices in the Midwest was that of Horace William Shaler Cleveland (1814–1900), until recently an elusive and almost forgotten figure. Today, new information on Cleveland's work in the West has shed light on his role in helping shape the region.[1] Though initially an Easterner, Cleveland identified with the Midwest, where he became involved with the far-from-glamorous problems of a newly settled area. Wherever the railroad invaded the Great Plains, new towns followed. Development was often crude and graceless. A designer who called for harmonious and efficient use of land for human needs was a proverbial voice crying in the wilderness.[2] Cleveland himself expressed this isolation to Olmsted. In the East, he wrote, "there are enough people to form a class . . . to influence popular opinion with whom one can find sympathy and can talk without fear of misapprehension. Whereas here, it is rare one finds an individual who has the faintest conception of what landscape gardening means."[3]

Cleveland's Chicago years, 1869 to 1886, were the most complex phase of a long and illustrious career. In Chicago Cleveland found the opportunity to develop and test the ideas he had initiated in the East, which would later come to full fruition in Minneapolis, where his ambitious dream of a vast metropolitan open space system was realized.

Horace Cleveland was born in 1814, eight years before Olmsted Sr. He ventured West for the first time as a young man of twenty-one, traveling by railroad as far as it went, to Harrisburg, Pennsylvania, then by canal to Pittsburgh, and by steamboat along the Ohio River. Eventually he reached Illinois. "Dur-

Horace William Shaler Cleveland at the age of sixty-seven, photographed in Chicago by his son Ralph during the summer of 1882. (Courtesy of William H. Tishler)

ing the summer and autumn," he wrote, "I traversed a large portion of the State, on horseback or on foot, . . . exploring wild lands, in the employ of others, with a view to investment."[4] But there was no promise of work in the region, and Cleveland returned east on horseback, arriving in New York late in the year. He was in Illinois again from 1837 to 1839, "engaged in surveying in various parts" of the state. Years later he described the towns in this wild, virtually undeveloped frontier as "mere settlements of log huts" and recalled the vastness of the "adjoining prairie . . . which extended perhaps ten, twenty or thirty miles, an unbroken field of grass" with occasional "sloughs black with [geese]."[5] This sojourn left a lasting impression on the young adventurer, and the destiny he envisioned for the area undoubtedly influenced his decision to move west three decades later.

Back from his second trip, Cleveland purchased a farm on the banks of the Delaware River at Burlington, New Jersey, and there began a career in agriculture, as an innovative scientific farmer. Cleveland also became active in the horticultural societies of New Jersey, Massachusetts, and Pennsylvania, and through the National Pomological Congress, of which he was one of the originators, he associated with Andrew Jackson Downing and corresponded with Frederick Law Olmsted.[6] Cleveland's early experiences bore an uncanny resemblance to Olmsted's: both men traveled by horseback into frontier areas of America, both had a penchant for writing, and each gained valuable skills from a background in agriculture and the study of civil engineering, which served as a springboard for a career in landscape architecture. The two, in fact, became lifelong friends.

In 1854 Cleveland sold Oatlands, his New Jersey farm, and moved to New England. He and Robert Morris Copeland established a landscape architectural practice in Boston, advertising that they would "furnish plans for the laying out and improvement of Cemeteries, Public Squares, Pleasure Grounds, Farms and Gardens."[7] Eventually their successful practice included projects in Massachusetts, Maine, Connecticut, Rhode Island, and Nova Scotia. The new firm also competed for the prestigious commission to design Central Park in New York, but lost to Olmsted and Vaux.[8]

When the Civil War began, Cleveland and Copeland disbanded their practice, and Copeland joined the Union army, serving as a major with the Second Massachusetts regiment of infantry. Cleveland, who was an expert marksman, helped train others and formed rifle clubs. He also experimented with developing better firearm mechanisms, later acting as an agent for the Massachusetts Arms company in the West and Southwest.[9]

In 1868 Cleveland joined Olmsted's staff, recommended by his prominent New England friends George Curtis and Charles Eliot Norton.[10] He worked with the firm for only one season, though, supervising the plantings for Prospect Park in Brooklyn. The next years were unsettled; brief periods of employment in Tarrytown, New York, and Baltimore preceded some time of exploring various business opportunities in the East, including collaboration with his friend Edward Maynard to "open an office as Architects [and] Landscape Gardeners in Washington."[11] When none of these ventures materialized, Cleveland made the bold move to Chicago, in March 1869.[12]

Chicago at midcentury was touted as the new "Empire City of the West."[13] The region was experiencing tremendous growth and development, changing the shape of the landscape. It was an ideal place for Cleveland to settle, with virtually unlimited opportunities for work as the new frontier city invented itself. A concern for creating a healthful urban environment led to the proposal of an extensive park system in the city's south and west sides, and for the creation of a fourteen-mile-long boulevard that would run through the heart of the city.[14] Here was the potential for Cleveland to develop his vision of landscape design, which was rooted in principles of conservation and wise land use. His commitment to realizing this vision was carried out with a missionary zeal.

Taking advantage of contacts he had made in the East, Cleveland quickly secured commissions for his fledgling practice. A one-page announcement heralding the establishment of a new office in the Shepard Building at the corner of Dearborn and Monroe listed thirteen influential references from Chicago and the East. Cleveland stated that he was "prepared to furnish designs for the tasteful arrangement of Villages, Parks, Cemeteries and Private Estates, large and small."[15] The broadside also emphasized his experience designing cemeteries in the East and was likely instrumental in his securing one of his first commissions in Chicago, a design for the expansion of Graceland Cemetery. A prolific writer and engaging speaker, Cleveland seized every opportunity to advocate for orderly land development and proseletize his visionary concepts of planning and design. His ideas quickly began to appear in building and real estate journals, newspaper columns, and a series of informative pamphlets.[16]

Writing to Frederick Law Olmsted, in the first of his many communications from Chicago, Cleveland announced that he had made his "bow to the Chicago public." He also wrote about Chicago's lack of topographic diversity, noting that the city was built on "perfectly flat country extending as far as the eye can reach in every direction." Yet, even in the new towns of the heartland, Cleveland observed, "almost every city has physical and moral character . . . of its own which should indicate the style and character of its adornment."[17]

In the same letter, Cleveland also described the proposed boulevard that would connect the city's new parklands. One plan prepared by a local landscape gardener was being displayed widely. The idea, Cleveland observed, was for a "drive simply made to wobble from one side to the other throughout the whole 14 miles, with rows of trees on each side. Enough," he continued drily, "to give a man the blues to think of driving through." He had himself developed a decidedly more ambitious concept for the boulevard—as "a school for the instruction of people." The first section of it would

> be used as a nursery, in which the whole system of arboriculture could be displayed and yet, managed to make the grounds ornamental & interesting, then a portion devoted to agricultural experiments of all possible descriptions & the testing of all kinds of agricultural products; then fish ponds in which could be shown the whole process of fish culture; then, collections of all different varieties of building stone, & of all the mineral productions of the West, which could be tastefully arranged in rockwork. . . . Throughout the whole length, the plantations should constitute an arboretum, & . . . the different varieties of trees instead of being confined to specimens, could be planted in forests, and so arranged as to secure tasteful effects while exhibiting their natural habits.

Cleveland's proposal called for native species and plants goupings, both of

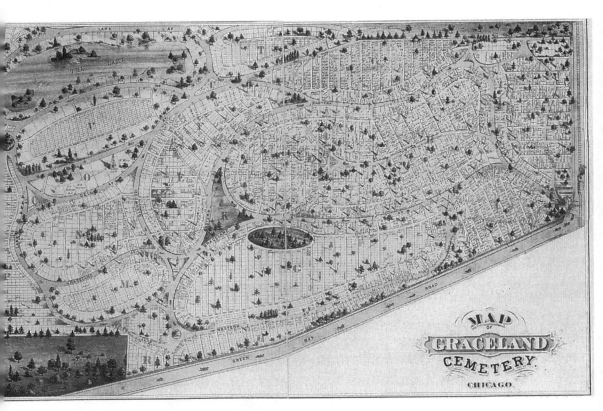

Map of Graceland Cemetery, one of Cleveland's earliest commissions. The initial eighty-acre burial plot, surveyed in 1860 by Samuel S. Greely and Edmund Bixby, was expanded with subsequent purchases. The early sections were designed by Swain Nelson, and in 1870 Cleveland's plan for improvements was laid out. (#0076; courtesy of the Chicago Historical Society, Chicago, Ill.)

The Shephard Block at the corner of Dearborn and Monroe Streets. Cleveland's practice was on the third floor, adjoining the office of Samuel S. Greeley, the city and county surveyor. The structure was destroyed in 1871 by the Great Chicago Fire. (Reprinted from E. J. Goodspeed, *History of the Great Fires in Chicago and the West* [New York, 1871], 177)

which reflected precepts of the Prairie School of landscape architecture later expounded by Wilhelm Miller and practiced by O. C. Simonds and Jens Jensen.

In a matter of weeks, Cleveland was putting forward his planning ideas in the pamphlet titled *The Public Grounds of Chicago: How to Give Them Character and Expression.* He described three major parks in New York, Brooklyn, and Baltimore, which he thought ought *not* be emulated in Chicago. The new site, he noted, was "dead level extending in every direction almost as far as the eye can reach, . . . still unoccupied; for the most part even by a tree or a shrub, a hill or a stone." But before many years passed, he predicted, "the area that has been thus reserved will be enclosed within thickly peopled streets and avenues . . . [so] the problem to be solved is, by what arrangement they can be rendered attractive and interesting as places of recreation and refreshment to the citizens. . . . everything must be created." His solution married the art of landscape gardening with the science of botany: arboretumlike plantations containing "every variety of tree and shrub which will thrive in this climate" would be grouped according to species, consisting of many varieties within each tree type, with a broader palette of shrubs and vines planted among the trees.

Despite Cleveland's promotional campaign, in April 1870 the South Park Commission hired Olmsted and Vaux to furnish plans and specifications for park improvements.[18] Once again, Cleveland had been bypassed for his more established colleague. His friendship with Olmsted was not injured, but it

William Merchant Richardson French, director of the Art Institute of Chicago. A New England native, French first visited Chicago in 1867 while working as an engineer. Two years later he began his association with Cleveland. In 1879 he became secretary of the Chicago Academy of Fine Arts, which later became the Chicago Art Institute. (Portrait by Louis Betts [American, 1873–1961], oil on canvas, c. 1905, 129.5 x 88.9 cm, gift of Mrs. William M. R. French, 1908.46; courtesy of the Art Institute of Chicago, Chicago, Ill.)

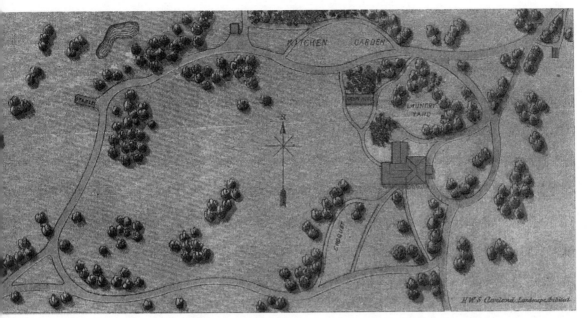

must have been a bitter pill for the older man to swallow. The rejection was, in fact, just the first in a series of staggering disappointments Cleveland would experience while residing in Chicago, even after his propitious start there.

The same year he lost the park commission, Cleveland formed a professional affiliation with Samuel Greely, a surveyor. Together they shared office space in a central city location.[19] Cleveland's wife, Maryann, and son, Ralph, moved to join him, a sign that he was intending to remain permanently. Optimistic about his future, Cleveland wrote to Olmsted in August, "I have got as much work in hand as I can possibly manage, a good deal in this vicinity and more in surrounding States."[20] Cleveland's commissions in the Chicago area included several estates, a ten-acre plan for the grounds of the original University of Chicago campus, and an expansion to the nearby subdivision of Hinsdale. Projects in Indiana, Michigan, and Wisconsin, and a variety of jobs in states to the west, including Iowa and Kansas, were also under way during these years.[21]

In 1870 Cleveland expanded his professional range through an association with William M. R. French, the elder brother of the renowned sculptor Daniel Chester French and a creative civil engineer who later became the first director of the Chicago Art Institute.[22] But then disaster struck. On 7 October 1871, the Great Fire broke out. Both Cleveland, who was out of town working on a project at the time, and Olmsted, who visited Chicago shortly afterward, wrote of the ruinous effects of the massive conflagration that destroyed the city. Greely later described how Ralph Cleveland and John Newman, Cleveland's draftsman, had returned early the night of the seventh

Cleveland's design for the J. Young Scammon estate in Chicago's Hyde Park. Scammon, a University of Chicago trustee, was undoubtedly influential in retaining Cleveland to prepare a plan for the campus before the Great Fire. (Reprinted from Cleveland, *A Few Hints on Landscape Gardening in the West,* following p. 4; courtesy of William H. Tishler)

The Great Chicago Fire advancing near Cleveland's office on Dearborn Street. Only two rolls of plans, the contents of a trunk, and a few momentos escaped destruction. (Reprinted from Frank Luzerne, *Through the Flames and Beyond: Chicago as It Was and as It Is* [New York, 1872], 81; courtesy of William H. Tishler)

to move office papers to another location, "which they thought to be out of the range of the fire," only to have "all the books, papers and instruments . . . burned in the place of deposit" after the direction of the fire's advance changed.[23]

By 1872 Cleveland's thoughts turned to rebuilding the city that was about to rise from the ashes of the Great Fire. The recent disaster demanded immediate planning to prevent a recurrance. Strategically located parks and wide tree-lined boulevards could check the onslaught of such a blaze, Cleveland wrote in a commentary in the *Lakeside Reviewer,* an influential Chicago journal.[24] The article was one of Cleveland's several diatribes against the grid plan, widely used to structure planning in new western communities. Cleveland also wrote of the serious social and economic problems resulting from the exodus of the upper and upper middle classes from the center city. (Since the fire, many of Chicago's most affluent citizens had taken up residence in the suburbs.) It was "desirable," Cleveland emphasized, "for every city to

Letterhead used by Cleveland and French from 1873 to 1878, after they relocated their office in the Portland Block at Dearborn and Washington Streets in downtown Chicago. Their collaboration began early in 1871 and continued, on an occasional basis, until as late as 1881. (Courtesy of the Library of Congress, Washington, D.C.)

secure and retain the home affection and local pride of such men instead of being merely regarded by them as a workshop or a place of business."[25]

The Great Fire had curtailed work on the new parks, especially in the South Park district, where the offices of the commission had been burned out, "with all its plans, accounts, contracts and vouchers."[26] But the following April, Cleveland received an overture regarding the position of park superintendent.[27] By the end of the year his plans for Grove Parkway had been adopted, and his work progressed on other projects for the district. He was doing private consultation work elsewhere, and in 1873 his book *Landscape Architecture as Applied to the Wants of the West,* with an addendum "Forest Planting on the Great Plains," was published. The small volume received positive reviews from Olmsted, among others, who saw the publication as "valuable, timely and altogether of good omen for the West."[28] At this time, too, Cleveland was considering a potential collaboration with William Le Baron Jenney on the design of a conservatory greenhouse for the South Park.[29]

The financial panic of 1873 caused severe problems for the South Park Commission. Property owners who had been demanding exorbitant prices for the land needed for parks rebelled against being paid in installments. No funds were available to extend improvements. The economic setback continued for several years; as French later wrote, it "killed our business."[30]

In fall 1874 Cleveland's South Park Commission salary was stopped for lack of funds. In July a second major conflagration, Chicago's "Little Fire," destroyed large segments of the city center, exacerbating the already distressed situation. Cleveland continued to write and lecture about the need for parks and boulevards to combat these disasters, but his words fell on deaf ears. By May of 1875 he was in desperate financial straits and appealed to Olmsted: "No new business has come to us. . . . I write to ask if you have need of any assistance which I can render. . . . I would gladly work for small remuneration in order to stave off the necessity of encumbering the small property I have been able to lay aside for the not distant day when my working days will be past." In a subsequent letter he related his difficulties with city officials,

Plan of Highland Park. In 1871, Cleveland staked out initial avenues and a path for J. W. Preston, a wealthy Chicago merchant. Subsequently, Cleveland and French platted the suburb's original 1,200 wooded acres, with smaller lots proposed for level areas and five- to ten-acre parcels adjoining the bluffs and steep ravines. (IChi-27588; courtesy of the Chicago Historical Society, Chicago, Ill.)

which caused him deep embarrassment: "I was under the disagreeable necessity . . . of entering a suit at law against the Park Commissioners for payment for my services."[31]

Cleveland was beset by personal problems as well as professional disappointments and hardship. Early in 1874 he had learned the disturbing news of the untimely death of his old Boston partner, Robert Morris Copeland, at the age of forty-four.[32] His wife had become chronically ill with dyspepsia and rheumatism. Then, in the summer of 1880, their son Richard, a brilliant engineer, whom Cleveland deeply loved and admired, died in South America, leaving the troubled couple with the responsibility of their two granddaughters.

Cleveland considered the possibility of moving from the city where so much misfortune had befallen him. His first thought was to return to his native New England; then he toyed with the idea of living in Virginia, but finally settled on Minneapolis. The Clevelands' younger son, Ralph, resided there, and business prospects in the area looked promising. Ironic as it might seem, when he finally left Chicago to take up his new abode in Minneapolis in the spring of 1886, the seventy-two-year-old landscape architect was not moving into retirement but toward his major professional triumph. Had Cleveland lived into the twentieth century, he would have seen the completion of his boldest and most skillfully conceived plan: the vast Twin Cities regional park system. This stellar achievement remains one of the great works of landscape architecture in America.[33]

Sheep grazing on the South Open Green in Washington Park, c. 1890s. In 1872, Cleveland succeeded Olmsted and Vaux as the South Parks landscape architect. He designed the treeless tract's planting plan, and by the end of the following year more than 500 large trees were planted in the park and along Drexel Boulevard. (Courtesy of William H. Tishler)

Drexel Boulevard looking north from 46th Street. A link in Chicago's originally conceived twenty-eight-mile boulevard system, it extends from Washington Park and is an important segment of the continuous greenway encircling the central city. (Courtesy of William H. Tishler)

Awareness of Cleveland's accomplishments has not been widespread. Not only was his a lone voice, it was a modest one as well. "The trial of my life here," he wrote from Chicago in 1870, "is the necessity of flaunting my own merits in the eyes of the world as a means of getting business . . . but I came here with the determination to blow my own trumpet loud enough to be heard and I have been doing it with all my might, but am all the while trampling upon my own feelings."[34] The small size of Cleveland's staff also contributed to his obscurity in history. Although his son Ralph worked with him near the end of his career, the affiliation lasted only a few years.[35] Without descendants or associates to carry it on, the practice essentially dissolved when Cleveland's health began to fail, and the subsequent destruction of his office records further obliterated his impact.

It is critical that as we fill in the picture of the profession's early years, we recover the lives and work of its bold visionaries such as Horace Cleveland. The idea of landscape design founded on a balance between the needs of human development and the resources of the land is as important today as it was in Cleveland's time, and underlies our role as environmental stewards which must be carried into the future.

Notes

1. Cleveland's family background, his early years in the East, and better-known accomplishments were first documented by Theodora Kimball Hubbard, "H. W. S. Cleveland: An American Pioneer in Landscape Architecture and City Planning," *Landscape Architecture* 20, no. 2 (1930), 92–112. Cleveland's most important written work was reprinted with an introduction that contains a penetrating social commentary on his career: Horace W. Cleveland, *Landscape Architecture as Applied to the Wants of the West*, ed. Roy Lubove (1873; Pittsburgh: University of Pittsburgh Press, 1965). Unfortunately, this edition omitted the insightful essay "Forest Planting on the Great Plains," which Cleveland included in the first edition. J. B. Jackson and Norman Newton published influential books that included general references to Cleveland: J. B. Jackson, *American Space* (New York: Norton, 1972); Norman T. Newton, *Design on the Land: The Development of Landscape Architecture* (Cambridge: Harvard University Press, 1971). Eleanor M. McPeck, "Horace W. S. Cleveland in the East, 1854–1878," unpublished paper, Graduate School of Design, Harvard University, 1972, further documents Cleveland's early commissions.

Karl Haglund, "Rural Tastes, Rectangular Ideas, and the Skirmishes of H. W. S. Cleveland," *Landscape Architecture* 66, no. 1 (1976), 67–70, 78, drew from a newly available collection of important Cleveland letters donated to Harvard's Houghton Library. These nineteen letters, written to William Merchant Richardson French, Cleveland's partner from 1870 until 1881, were donated by French's son Prentice, a landscape architect and Harvard Graduate School of Design alumnus.

A far more comprehensive assessment of Cleveland's career is Virginia Luckhardt, "Horace William Shaler Cleveland: An Overview of the Life and Work of an Early American Landscape Architect, 1814–1900" (MALA thesis, University of Wisconsin at Madison, 1983). Nancy J. Volkman, "Landscape Architecture on the Prairie: The Work of H. W. S. Cleveland," *Kansas History* 10, no. 2 (1987), 89–110, offers a meticulous investigation of Cleveland's work in Kansas. The powerful influence that literary ideas and transcendentalism had on Cleveland is explored in Daniel Joseph Nadenicek, "The Literary Landscape of Horace Cleveland" (MALA thesis, University of Minnesota, 1991). Two subsequent articles about Cleveland are Daniel Joseph Nadenicek, "Sleepy Hollow Cemetery: Transcendental Garden and Community Park," *Journal of New England Garden History Society* 3 (Fall 1993), 8–15, and Lance Neckar, "Fast-Tracking Culture and Landscape: Horace William Shaler Cleveland and the Garden in the Midwest," in *Regional Garden Design in the United States*, ed. Marc Treib and Therese O'Malley (Washington, D.C.: Dumbarton Oaks, 1995), 99–123.

2. Jackson suggests this reason in *American Space,* 74–76.

3. H. W. S. Cleveland, letter to F. L. Olmsted, 12 February 1881, Olmsted Letters, Manuscript Division, Library of Congress, Washington, D.C. (hereafter cited as OL).

4. H. W. S. Cleveland, "East and West," *American Builder* (1872), unpaged.

5. H. W. S. Cleveland, letter to William French, 26 September 1871.

6. H. W. S. Cleveland, "Cleveland Genealogy," unpublished (1882), 87, on file in the Library of Congress. As early as 1846, Cleveland served as corresponding secretary for the New Jersey Horticultural Society. See *Horticulturist* 1, no. 2 (1846), 100. The following year he wrote an informative article, "Notes on the Market Gardening of New Jersey," in *Horticulturist* 1, no. 9 (1847), 403–6.

As mentioned in "Domestic Notices," *Horticulturist* 3, no. 5 (1848), 246–48, the National Pomological Congress convened in New York. It was, as the article pointed out, "by far the most important assemblage of horticulturists ever convened in the United States." The article also notes A. J. Downing's appointment to a "business committee" and the election of "H. W. S. Cleveland, of New Jersey," as one of nine vice presidents. At the same meeting both Cleveland and Downing were appointed to a "special fruit committee," which Downing chaired. Both Cleveland and Olmsted also attended the American Pomological Congress in Philadelphia. See *Proceedings of the Second Session of the American Pomological Congress* (Philadelphia, 1852), 29–35, 50–51.

7. A photostat copy of the announcement of Copeland and Cleveland's new practice is on file at the Harvard Graduate School of Design library and is also reproduced in Hubbard, "W. H. S. Cleveland," 95. Many of their projects were cemeteries and estates, but they also collaborated with the architect Arthur Gilman in the layout of Boston's Back Bay. In an attempt to obtain the commission to design Central Park, Copeland wrote to Henry Longfellow, who was a close friend of Cleveland's brother Henry and, like Cleveland, a member of the Five of Clubs literary group. Robert Morris Copeland, letter to Henry Longfellow, 14 June 1856, Longfellow Letters, Houghton Library, Harvard University. Copeland and Cleveland also published a pamphlet, *A Few Words on the Central Park* (Boston, 1856), which set forth their ideas for designing the new park.

8. The "Descriptions of Plans for Improvement of the Central Park," on microfilm at the New York City Public Library, does not refer to a Copeland and Cleveland entry but does state that two plans (entry no. 15, "Rusticus," and entry no. 19, "Sigma") were submitted by "Copeland of Boston" (3–4).

9. Cleveland had an almost legendary reputation as a highly skilled rifleman and wrote several publications on the subject. See, for example, H. W. S. Cleveland, *Hints to Riflemen* (New York, 1864), and "Rifle-Clubs," *Atlantic Monthly* 10 (1862), 303–10. Cleveland refers to his employment with the Massachusetts Arms Company in "Cleveland Genealogy," 89–90.

10. Cleveland, "Cleveland Genealogy," 90; George Curtis, letter to F. L. Olmsted, 30 March 1868, and C. E. Norton, letter to F. L. Olmsted, 10 April 1868, OL.

11. While at Tarrytown, Cleveland spent eighteen months on "an important piece of work in the arrangement of private grounds." In Baltimore he worked for an old family friend, George Dugdale, who operated a maritime shipping business. "Cleveland Genealogy," 90.

12. H. W. S. Cleveland, letter to F. L. Olmsted, 20 January 1869 and 8 April 1869, OL. Cleveland's arrival in Chicago is also noted in *American Builder and Journal of Art* 1 (April 1869), 116: "We were pleased, a few days since, in meeting with Mr. H. W. S. Cleveland, who has been long connected with Messrs. Olmsted & Vaux, of New York; . . . it will certainly result in profit to Chicago, the accession of such a landscape gardener as Mr. Cleveland, one so honorably connected with the above firm."

13. For a discussion of early booster visions of Chicago's future, see William Cronon, *Nature's Metropolis: Chicago and the Great West* (New York: W. W. Norton, 1991), 31–41.

14. An editorial in the *Chicago Tribune,* 24 March 1869, gave a hearty endorsement to the park referendum, which had passed the previous day: "Yesterday was the best day's work our city has ever yet done." Cleveland mentions the boulevard proposal in his letter to Olmsted of 8 April 1869.

15. "H. W. S. Cleveland, Landscape Gardener" (n.p., n.d.), in the William Watts Folwell Papers, Minnesota Historical Society, St. Paul. Cleveland had connections through family ties and previous business contacts with important real estate and railroad entrepreneurs, including Dwight Perkins, who was related to his brother Henry's wife, and the Fletchers of Indiana, whom he had known from his earlier work with Copeland. Cleveland also advertised his services in the Chicago area, for example, in *Land Owner* 1, no. 4 (1869), 88.

16. Cleveland's earliest writings from Chicago include articles for the *Atlantic Monthly,* the *American Builder,* the *Architectural Review and American Builders' Journal,* the *Milwaukee Sentinel,* the *Boston Daily Advertiser,* and the *Chicago Tribune,* and his pamphlet *A Few Hints on Landscape Gardening in the West,* and with W. M. R. French, *The Relationship of Engineering to Landscape Gardening.*

17. Cleveland to Olmsted, 8 April 1869.

18. Victoria Post Ranney, *Olmsted in Chicago* (Chicago: Open Lands Project, 1972), 26.

19. Greely, a native of Massachusetts, had moved to Chicago in the 1830s. The two men

used a letterhead with both their names at the top as early as July 1870. Greely also served as city surveyor for Chicago. H. W. S. Cleveland, letter to William French, 29 July 1870; *Land Owner* advertisement.

20. H. W. S. Cleveland, letter to F. L. Olmsted, 22 August 1870, OL.

21. Many of these projects are noted in Cleveland's *A Few Hints on Landscape Gardening.* Cleveland's correspondence with Olmsted in late 1871 alludes to an interesting plan for a joint business venture that would take advantage of the development opportunities afforded by the growing influx of settlers brought by the railroads to the region. The concept involved planting a series of nurseries along the new rail lines through the Great Plains. "Every nursery thus established," Cleveland wrote, "would form the nucleus of a settlement—the opportunity of providing themselves on the spot with trees, being in itself a strong attraction to settlers," while making available a ready source of timber and fruit trees. Cleveland had been offered the position of superintendent of forest planting on the Nebraska extension of the Burlington & Mississippi River Railroad, which he had turned down, as it would have necessitated giving up his present business and moving from Chicago. He and Olmsted developed their scheme contingent on hiring a skilled nurseryman to establish "a primary nursery, fully appointed with all buildings, teams, tools, etc. necessary for propagation." H. W. S. Cleveland, letter to Olmsted, 19 December 1871, OL. Secondary nurseries would then be located at intervals extending westward along the railroad. Further hints about the venture are found in subsequent letters among Olmsted's papers, but unfortunately the information is unspecific and incomplete. One interesting note is found in a letter of 7 April 1871 to Olmsted from the noted English landscape architect William Robinson, who had secured a talented nurseryman who was about to travel to America for an association with Olmsted—quite possibly the railroad nursery venture. Late in February 1872, after his return from a highly successful speaking tour, Cleveland withdrew from the venture, explaining, "I have engaged so much work that I . . . could no longer entertain any proposition to take charge of the work of forest planting." H. W. S. Cleveland, letter to F. L. Olmsted, 26 February 1872, OL. The intriguing speculative endeavor never became a reality.

22. Cleveland and French began working together as early as July 1870. Cleveland, letter to French, 27 July 1870. Cleveland expressed his serious intent to establish a "business connection" with French in his letter to him of 22 January 1871.

23. Cleveland's handwritten account of the fire, dated 10 November 1871, is on file at the Chicago Historical Society. Other details are provided by Cleveland in a letter published in the *Massachusetts Horticultural Society Proceedings* (May 1883), 248. Olmsted's account of the fire was published in James W. Sheahan and George P. Upton, *The Great Conflagration—Chicago: Its Past, Present, and Future* (Chicago, 1872), 281–86. Samuel S. Greeley, "Memories of the Great Chicago Fire of October 1871," April 1904, 4 pp., manuscript at the Chicago Historical Society.

24. H. W. S. Cleveland, "Parks and Boulevards in Cities," *Lakeside Reviewer,* no. 41 (1872), 412.

25. H. W. S. Cleveland, "Our Streets," *Chicago Daily Tribune,* 23 November 1874, 5.

26. Ranney, *Olmsted in Chicago,* 32.

27. Early in September, on the recommendation of a selection committee consisting of the influential South Park commissioners L. B. Sidway and George W. Gage, Cleveland was appointed the district's landscape architect at an annual salary of $2,400. "Chicago South Park Commissioners Minutes of the Meetings," 17 September 1872, 74, on file at the Chicago Historical Society.

28. Frederick Law Olmsted, review in *Nation* 18 (1874), 64–65. Highly complimentary reviews were also published in *Land Owner,* July 1873, 115; *Gardener's Monthly* 15, no. 7 (1873), 217; and *American Builder* 1 (1873), 191.

29. H. W. S. Cleveland, letter to F. L. Olmsted, 28 July 1873, OL. Like Cleveland, Jenney

was a native of Massachusetts; although the two men occasionally competed for work, they remained friends for many years.

30. *Chicago Tribune,* 4 September 1896.

31. This court action dragged on for more than three years; it finally resulted in a judgment in Cleveland's favor with a settlement of more than $2,200 in back salary. H. W. S. Cleveland, letter to F. L. Olmsted, 26 May 1875 and 28 August 1877, OL; *Chicago Tribune,* 27 December 1878, 3; *Report of the South Park Commissioners to the Board of County Commissioners of Cook County from Dec. 1, 1878 to Dec. 1, 1879* (Chicago, 1880), 20.

32. Copeland's death in Cambridge was announced in the *Boston Daily Advertiser,* 30 March 1874.

33. For a detailed account of Cleveland's work in Minneapolis and St. Paul, see William H. Tishler and Virginia S. Luckhardt, "H. W. S. Cleveland, Pioneer Landscape Architect to the Upper Midwest," *Minnesota History* 49, no. 7 (1985), 281–91.

34. H. W. S. Cleveland, letter to William French, 13 August 1870.

35. Cleveland referred to the new association with Ralph in his letter to Olmsted of 6 July 1891. Perhaps the last reference to the collaboration is found in the letter to Olmsted of 6 June 1893, where Cleveland writes, "I have been quite ill . . . and had to send my son to Omaha in my stead," OL.

THREE

Frederick Law Olmsted

DESIGNING FOR DEMOCRACY
IN THE MIDWEST

Victoria Post Ranney

WHEN FREDERICK LAW OLMSTED SR. first encountered the great prairie region of Illinois, he called it "one of the most tiresome landscapes that I ever met with." The recently appointed architect-in-chief of New York's Central Park, stranded for twelve hours in March of 1863 on a railroad platform in central Illinois, found no scenery or architecture to regale the eye—"only this dreary prairie to the monotonous horizon." Characteristically, Olmsted spent the day observing the local population, in this case, a dirty and forlorn-looking family gathered around two rude log cabins in the midst of a cornfield.[1]

The incident was significant. Olmsted was never to share the reverence for the prairie that Jens Jensen, O. C. Simonds, and other midwestern colleagues felt. But, he *was* inspired by the abundant lakes and rivers of the Midwest, and this inspiration is reflected in his plans for the town of Riverside, Illinois, his three large parks on the south side of Chicago, Belle Isle Park for Detroit, and the World's Columbian Exposition of 1893. All are notable for their creative use of water and native plants along the water's edge.[2]

Olmsted was motivated in his work by a strong belief in democracy. He felt that Americans of diverse backgrounds needed to be brought together on common ground, and all four of his major midwestern designs reflect this abiding interest in fostering community. By providing outdoor spaces where people of all classes could come together in relaxed and friendly circumstances, Olmsted was attempting no less than to civilize America—to make democracy work.

Virtually all American landscape architects of the nineteenth century were influenced by Olmsted. By 1893 and the opening of the Columbian Exposition in Chicago, many significant midwestern landscape architects had

Frederick Law Olmsted, c. 1865. (Courtesy of the National Park Service, Frederick Law Olmsted National Historic Site, Brookline, Mass.)

known or collaborated with him. Some had received their training in his firm; others had read his reports and articles or studied his landscapes firsthand.[3] In 1893 Daniel Burnham, chief of construction for the exposition, offered this accolade to the assembled company of artists and architects:

> Each of you knows the name and genius of him who stands first in the heart and confidence of American artists, the creator of your own parks and many other city parks. He it is who has been our best adviser and our common mentor. In the highest sense he is the planner of the Exposition—Frederick Law Olmsted. No word of his has fallen to the ground among us since he first joined us some thirty months ago. An artist, he paints with lakes and wooded slopes; with lawns and banks and forest-covered hills; with mountain-sides and ocean views. He should stand where I do tonight, not for his deeds of later years alone, but for what his brain has wrought and his pen has taught for half a century.[4]

Olmsted brought to his midwestern work principles of landscape design developed over years of reading and observing. His first landscape experiences came when he traveled with his father, a Connecticut merchant, on trips to the White Mountains, Niagara Falls, and other scenic destinations. While still a boy, Olmsted schooled himself in the romantic principles of English landscape gardening by reading the works of theorists such as Humphry Repton and Uvedale Price. As a young man in 1850, he visited many of the great English country estates on a walking tour.

Olmsted added a democratic purpose to the English landscape tradition. He admired the private parks of the English aristocracy but found a better model for America at Birkenhead Park, designed by Joseph Paxton for the people of Liverpool. On his return to the United States, Olmsted submitted an article describing Birkenhead Park to Andrew Jackson Downing, editor of *The Horticulturist* and the leading American authority on landscape gardening. Downing published the article and soon began campaigning for a large park for New York City. Not one large urban park existed at that time in the United States.

Downing publicized the theory that public parks could civilize American society by elevating the taste and behavior of all citizens. When Downing was killed in a steamboat accident in 1852, his partner, Calvert Vaux, joined with Olmsted to carry on his philosophy and put it into practice. They won the design competition for Central Park in 1858 and lived to see the park's success as a democratic experiment. Convinced of the park's social and aesthetic value, Olmsted and Vaux regarded it as "the big art work of the Republic."[5]

During the 1850s and 1860s, Olmsted developed his own analysis of American society based on his firsthand observations of the American people. As an accomplished journalist and travel writer, he objected to English writers such as Charles Dickens and Anthony Trollope who visited the United States and then wrote popular books that criticized American society. Olmsted agreed that the country lacked civilization, but not because of democracy; the root problem, he believed, was "the pioneer condition" of American life.[6] It was a condition he had observed when traveling through the slave states as a newspaper correspondent in the 1850s and while directing large crews of immigrant workers during the construction of Central Park in New York. On the California frontier, where he had managed a large gold-mining property in the 1860s, Olmsted noted the lack of common bonds among whites, blacks, Mexicans, Chinese, and Indians. In his view American society was uncivilized—pioneer—wherever community ties were weak, where people felt little in common with their neighbors and violence was rife, where residence was transient, and where tendencies toward social disintegration were strong.

To combat these forces Olmsted looked to social planning, and especially to thoughtful landscape architectural design. He believed that by providing people with opportunities to come together in healthful outdoor settings, he could encourage a democratic community and help to civilize America.

❖

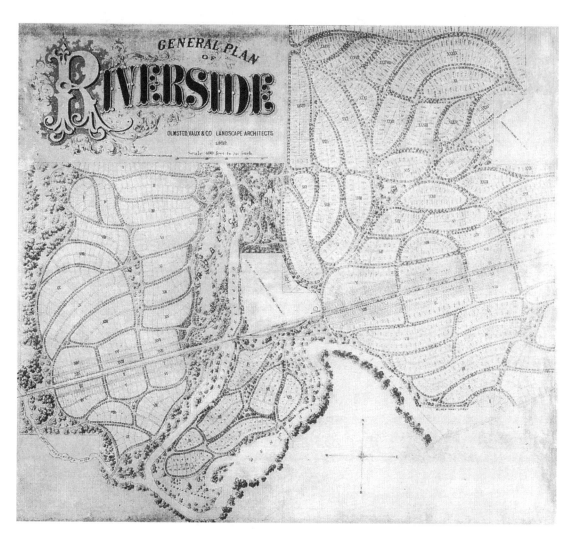

General plan of Riverside by Olmsted, Vaux and Co., 1869. (Courtesy of the National Park Service, Frederick Law Olmsted National Historic Site)

In 1868 Olmsted and Vaux were commissioned to design an entire community, the suburban village of Riverside, near Chicago. As usual, Olmsted began by analyzing the needs of the people. When he looked at the new phenomenon of suburbanization in European and American cities, he saw that although privileged people were moving to the country for pure air and contact with nature, they did not want to relinquish the comforts they enjoyed in the city. In short, they wanted the country with city conveniences and social life. Therefore, Olmsted and Vaux planned their suburb with gas lights, sewers, and all-weather roads. Equally important, they provided settings for recreation and amusement to encourage community through common enjoyment of nature.

Riverside is located nine miles west of Chicago, on 1,600 acres of land the Riverside Improvement Company had purchased where the Chicago, Bur-

Early view of Riverside showing railroad bridge from Blooming Bank Road. (Reprinted from the Riverside Improvement Company, *Riverside in 1871* [Chicago, 1871], 20)

lington and Quincy Railroad crossed a hairpin turn of the Des Plaines River. With its high, wooded riverbanks it was a pleasant site, likely to attract a population of financially successful families. Olmsted and Vaux believed that the essence of a suburb was domesticity and planned a private zone around each house for family living. Outside these clearly demarcated domestic zones were numerous facilities for common recreation. As they explained: "The fact that the families dwelling within a suburb enjoy much in common, and all the more enjoy it because it is in common, the grand fact, in short, that they are Christians, loving one another, and not Pagans, fearing one another, should be everywhere manifest in the completeness, and choiceness, and beauty of the means they possess of coming together, of being together, and especially of recreating and enjoying them[selves] together on common ground, and under common shades."[7]

Common activity was focused along the Des Plaines River. Olmsted and Vaux called for a dam to increase the amount of water for boating in the summer and skating in the winter. They placed a public drive and walk along the riverbanks and suggested vine-covered pavilions from which spectators could watch boat races. The kind of recreation that Olmsted and Vaux valued is clear from their description of a proposed promenade: "The promenade is a social custom of great importance in all the large towns of Europe.

It is an open-air gathering for the purpose of easy, friendly, unceremonious greetings, for the enjoyment of change of scene, of cheerful and exhilarating sights and sounds, and of various good cheer, to which the people of a town, of all classes, harmoniously resort on equal terms, as to a common property."[8]

Olmsted had begun advocating a system of parks and boulevards for Chicago when he first visited the city during the Civil War. As executive head of the U.S. Sanitary Commission, which managed health and other services for the Union soldiers, he met some of Chicago's most public-spirited citizens, including a cultivated lawyer named Ezra McCagg. Once the two men had become friends, Olmsted urged McCagg to take time from his many responsibilities to promote parks for the city. At that time, Chicago had no large park.

Two years later, in Yosemite Valley, Olmsted met William Bross, editor of the *Chicago Tribune* and a former lieutenant governor of Illinois. When Olmsted subsequently sent Bross his report on a park system for San Francisco, Bross invited him to visit Illinois "that we may confer together on a like improvement for Chicago." The newspaperman thought the public could be "brought up to the determination of doing something handsome" through state legislation.[9] He was right. In 1867 Ezra McCagg, following Olmsted's advice, drew up the first of several bills to set aside large tracts of land outside the city for parks. When the first bill lost in a referendum, other friends of Olmsted's joined the campaign. In 1868 John Rauch, a physician and public health reformer, gave a talk to the Chicago Academy of Sciences titled "Public Parks: Their Effects upon the Moral, Physical, and Sanitary Conditions of the Inhabitants of Large Cities: With Special Reference to the City of Chicago." (Before publishing his talk, Rausch sent it to Olmsted for editing.)[10] Real estate developers, including Paul Cornell, founder of the Chicago suburb of Hyde Park, lobbied in Springfield for the parks.

As a result of these efforts, in February 1869 the Illinois legislature passed three bills establishing a connected system of parks and boulevards for Chicago. This system stretched from Lincoln Park in the north to Jackson Park in the south. With Lake Michigan on the east, the parks and boulevards circumscribed the city in a frame of natural beauty, giving form to the urban growth that had sprawled westward across the treeless prairie. The string of parks and boulevards was divided into three sections by the branches of the Chicago River, each to be managed by a separate group: the South Park, the West Park, and the Lincoln Park commissions.

The commissioners then began to buy up the designated sites and hire landscape designers to "improve" them. Rauch attempted to have Olmsted design the entire system, but, probably because jurisdiction for the parks had been divided, he was unsuccessful. The Lincoln Park Commission, with Ezra McCagg its president, authorized Olmsted to prepare a design, but the commission became mired in litigation. In the end the South Park Commission, the largest and wealthiest of the three, hired Olmsted and Vaux.

The 1055-acre South Park, approximately the size of New York's Central Park, consisted of two parks connected by a wide boulevard. The 593-acre tract that was later named Jackson Park, lay along the swampy shore of Lake Michigan six miles south of the city's business district. The 372-acre rectangle that became Washington Park was located a mile inland on the flat prairie. Between them ran a mile-long, ninety-acre boulevard that Olmsted named the Midway Plaisance, because it was literally midway between the two parks.

Olmsted was no more inspired by the prairie landscape around the city than he had been on the railroad platform in central Illinois. He deplored the "low, flat, miry and forlorn character of the greater part of the country immediately about Chicago" and considered the vicinity "not merely uninteresting but, during much of the year, positively dreary."[11] Nonetheless, in the South Park, Olmsted found a creative use for flat terrain. Although he considered flatness to be "the first obvious defect of the site," he pointed out that New York had spent a great deal of money to reduce parts of Central Park to "prairie-like simplicity." Chicago's natural landscape would provide, at low expense, just the psychological relief that city dwellers needed. As he explained: "The element of interest which undoubtedly should be placed first, if possible, in the park of any great city, is that of an antithesis to its bustling, paved, rectangular, walled-in streets; this requirement would best be met by a large, meadowy ground, of an open, free, tranquil character."[12]

The Southopen Ground, a huge meadow at the north end of Washington Park, serves this purpose even today, providing a long, uninterrupted view of nearly a mile. The trees enclosing it give the impression of height that the terrain itself lacks. As Olmsted and Vaux suggested, the field was planted with turf for games, parades, fireworks displays, and other grand public entertainment. Today it is used by numerous athletic teams.

In 1871 Olmsted wrote of Lake Michigan: "There is but one object of scenery near Chicago of special grandeur or sublimity, and that, the Lake, can be made by artificial means no more grand or sublime."[13] Consequently, he and Vaux proposed to extend its influence inland. Lagoons in Jackson Park would connect to a canal down the length of the Midway Plaisance which would open to a pond, or "mere," in Washington Park. People approaching Washington Park by way of the inland boulevards would glimpse the waters of the mere across a mile of open ground.

Olmsted expected that large numbers of Chicagoans would take a steamboat from the city out to Jackson Park at a cost of only a few cents. Such a

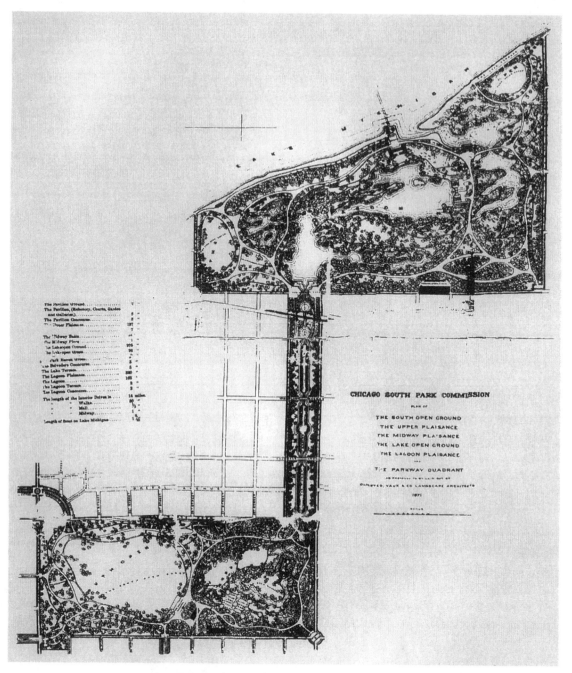

Plan of Chicago's South Park (now Washington and Jackson Parks and the Midway Plaisance) by Olmsted, Vaux and Co. for the Chicago South Park Commission, 1871. (Courtesy of the Chicago Park District Special Collections, Chicago, Ill.)

system was in use at Haga Park in Stockholm, which he considered "one of the most popular and delightful public grounds in the world."[14] Near the pier where the steamboats would land, people could rent small boats and row through the lagoons and along the Midway canal to Washington Park.

Olmsted and Vaux hoped to create distinctive, water-oriented scenery by dredging material from the swamps and elevating the sandbars to provide enough soil for trees to reach their full height. This would make possible wooded lagoons like those of the tropics, where intricate shores were densely overhung with foliage—a prospect they believed would be beneficial to the urban parkgoers. As they reported to the South Park Commissioners:

> If you cannot reproduce the tropical forest in all its mysterious depths of shade and visionary reflection of light, you can secure a combination of the fresh and healthy nature of the North with the restful, dreamy nature of the South, that would in our judgment be admirably fitted to the general purposes of any park, and which certainly could nowhere be more grateful than in the borders of your city, not only on account of the present intensely wide-awake character of its people, but because of the special quality of the scenery about Chicago in which flat and treeless prairie and limitless expanse of lake are such prominent characteristics.[15]

After the Great Chicago Fire of 1871, Washington Park was built essentially to Olmsted and Vaux's design by Olmsted's friend H. W. S. Cleveland. Except for two encroachments—a large school recently constructed at the north end and a garish space-age playground on a peninsula in the tranquil mere—Olmsted's classic pastoral landscape prevails in Washington Park, and generations of Chicagoans have been refreshed by its spacious green meadows and still waters.

Jackson Park as it exists today was built according to Olmsted's third design for the site. The original 1871 plan was not carried out, chiefly because of problems with land titles, and the second, the Columbian Exposition, was only a temporary construction, demolished according to plan in 1894. The present park represents Olmsted, Olmsted and Eliot's 1895 redesign of the site, with certain exceptions. The pond south of the present Museum of Science and Industry was built with natural rather than formal contours, and parts of the lagoons have been filled in and the connections between the lagoons and Lake Michigan blocked off. The park's elegant and well-equipped boathouse has also been torn down. Thus in Jackson Park, Olmsted's vision of a water park on the prairie has been substantially diminished, but it is not lost. Especially around the surviving lagoons, the germ of his concept survives.

The Midway Plaisance served as the site of the Columbian Exposition's amusement section (and from then on, that part of all American fairs was called the "midway"). In 1894 the Olmsted firm redesigned the feature, proposing the straight lines of trees which exist today and a straight canal down the middle, which was never completed. Olmsted's dream of a water connection to Washington Park thus remains unfulfilled, though Daniel Burnham's Plan of Chicago illustrated it in 1909, and it has been proposed a number of times since. Today, the Midway is a series of lawns used for team sports; the sunken portions are flooded for ice skating in winter.

Belle Isle, an island in the Detroit River nearly as large as Central Park, provided Olmsted's second opportunity to create a water-oriented park in the Midwest. When Olmsted visited Detroit in 1882, he found that the average elevation of the island was little more than two feet above the river; there were fine native trees, but the ground below them retained water in an alarming way. He also saw marshy pools covered with bubbles and green scum where dense swarms of mosquitoes bred. Given the danger of malaria and other diseases, he wondered whether the city fathers should invite, or even allow, unwitting people to come near the area. What needed to be done to protect the island from disease, he decided, would also serve a recreational purpose.

Olmsted proposed thinning the trees and underbrush so the river breezes could blow through and cutting little canals, or "rigolettes," through the pools of standing water. These canals would eliminate stagnant water and enable visitors to move by boat through the island's fine native woods. Even children, invalids, and people unaccustomed to boats could feel secure in the shallow interior canals. Boating in sheltered waters had proved a great success in Chicago, and Olmsted predicted that it was "likely to be a more generally popular means of recreation at Belle Isle Park than at any other nearer than the island park of Stockholm." The canals would serve as "highways of pleasure, in which boats would be used instead of carriages."[16] Belle Isle did not need huge expanses of greensward because the river provided a feeling of range and space. The emphasis of the park would be on the woods.

Olmsted's plan for Belle Isle was not fully carried out, and the park has been degraded over the years by the introduction of incompatible facilities. The interior waterways were built on the island, however, and people canoeing them today can sense the pleasure that Olmsted intended.

The World's Columbian Exposition was Olmsted's most fully developed work in the Midwest and the culmination of his efforts to unify and enliven a great public gathering place through the use of water. Called to Chicago in August 1890 to advise on a location for the fair, he selected Jackson Park, of which very little had been constructed. This time he was able to develop the

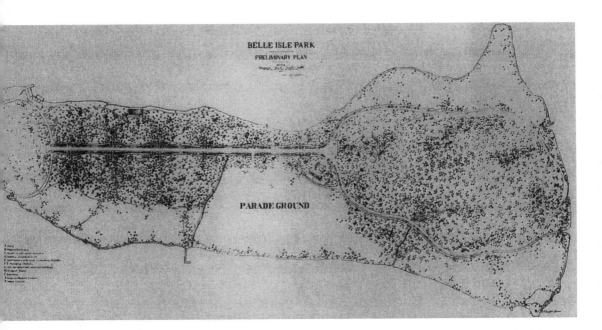

BELLE ISLE PARK
PRELIMINARY PLAN

PARADE GROUND

magnificent Lake Michigan setting to its fullest. The huge white neoclassical
buildings of the fair were grouped around sparkling lagoons and canals. The
cool green shores of the lagoons, planted with masses of willows and rushes,
added softness and delicacy to the scene. The water itself was alive with flocks
of birds and a flotilla of boats. Chicago's fair was the nation's promenade in
the summer of 1893, and Olmsted made sure that the setting gave fairgoers
both a sense of festivity and a feeling of community with people from all over
the world.

The site design was evolved from Olmsted and Vaux's original concept
of lagoons for Jackson Park. Before recommending the site to the exposition
directors in 1890, Olmsted and his young associate Harry Codman consulted
the architects, Daniel Burnham and John Root, who confirmed that Jackson
Park's sandbars, built up with material dredged from the lagoons, could support the huge exposition buildings. As the four men discussed the principal
features of the design, Root quickly sketched them on a piece of brown paper. The entrance was to be a great water plaza surrounded by buildings except at the east end, where the expanse of Lake Michigan could be seen. A
canal would lead north from this Court of Honor to another series of buildings around a lagoon, in the middle of which a wooded island of about fifteen
acres already existed. The island would have a "secluded, natural sylvan aspect" and be left free of conspicuous buildings. The edges of the lagoon would
be planted with aquatic plants. Each large building would have both a water
and a land entrance. Unity of composition would be achieved by connecting bridges and by boats and waterfowl moving throughout the scene.[17] This

View of the Lagoon and Wooded Island at the World's Columbian Exposition. (Courtesy of the Library of Congress, Washington, D.C.)

plan, along with Root's sketch, was approved by the directors and carried out in all its main features.

Olmsted's lagoon landscape was a masterpiece of design using native midwestern plant materials. In less than three growing seasons he clothed "several miles of newly-made, raw, sandy shores with a clean graceful intricate, picturesque green drapery." When he found that commercial nurseries would be unable to supply enough plant material, he promptly deployed collecting parties to Illinois and Wisconsin lakes, rivers, and swamps. There they gathered seventy-five rail carloads of wild herbaceous and aquatic plants—flags, cattails, rushes, irises, and pond lilies—and one hundred thousand bushy willows of different varieties, which they planted along the shores of the lagoons, including the wooded island and several small satellite islands. By using native midwestern plants on such a scale, Olmsted illustrated their potential in designed landscapes to all who visited the fair.[18]

But Olmsted was not concerned with plantings alone. He believed that the boats on the waterways were essential to the scenic effect of the fair, and as such, he considered them part of his province as landscape designer. He proposed a service of boats to run regularly like buses on a city street, stopping at sixteen landings throughout the fair. From the beginning, Olmsted

An electric omnibus boat at the World's Columbian Exposition. A lagoon and the Women's Building are in the background. (Reprinted from C. D. Arnold and H. D. Higinbotham, *Official Views of the World's Columbian Exposition* [Chicago, 1893], n.p.)

insisted that their appearance be light and festive. He objected strongly to the suggestion of cumbersome, roofed steamboats. "The boats," he explained,

> will befit the scene better the less pronounced, the less eminent and obtrusive they are; the further they are from having stately qualities; the lighter, the more nimble, the more bird-like and girlish they are; the less they advertise themselves; the less they disturb all that by, under, over and through which they are passing; the more exquisitely they appear adapted to glide quietly and naturally across the scene; the less fussy they appear; the less the apparent need of effort with which they move through the air and water. To put people on their decks and build a roof over them, especially a high roof, to give boats a breadth that would make them seem to be smashing through, instead of caressing and being caressed by air and water, would be the most mal-adroit thing possible. It would be a great misfortune, a blot and offense upon the whole Exposition, to have such boats in these interior waters. Needless to add that it would be infinitely better to have no boats at all.[19]

Olmsted specified that the boats should be less than thirty feet long, they should ride low in the water, be powered by silent electric motors, and that "nothing should be seen above the gunwale . . . that is decently avoidable unless it is of a floating or fluttering aspect, such as a streamer on a light staff, or a light, low canvas canopy or awning." He made it clear that he should not be expected to provide more detailed specifications, as that was the job of the boat designer: "We do not advise you, be it borne in mind, as boat-builders or as inventors, but as landscape designers."[20] His job was simply to state the problem.

Olmsted's aim was that every detail of the fair should enhance its festive and international character. While he objected to the heavy steamers because they would suggest "a solid, soulless, money-making corporation purpose, rather than a series of light-hearted parties of pleasure,"[21] he proposed other boats that would add an international flavor to the scene: Venetian gondolas, replicas of the ships in which Columbus made his voyage, even a fleet of birchbark canoes to be paddled by Indians in deerskin and moccasins. All kinds of small foreign craft might join the promenade: "Malay proas, catamarans, Arab dhows, Chinese sanpans, Japanese pilot boats, Turkish caiques, Esquimaux kiacks, Alaskan war canoes, the hooded boats of the Swiss Lakes, and so on."[22] When the fair opened in 1893, the omnibus boats had been designed as Olmsted had recommended, and Columbus's ships, gondolas, dhows and other exotic boats plied its waterways.

Shortly after the opening, Olmsted told Burnham that the crowds seemed dull and businesslike, as if they were plodding through the duty of sightseeing. He thought more "vital human gaiety" was needed and proposed the staging of minor incidents that would seem to be part of the crowd: small parties of children or Russians singing, people in full native costume mingling

The shores of the Lagoon at the World's Columbian Exposition, looking east toward the Wooded Island, showing Olmsted's use of native water-edge plants. (Photograph by C. D. Arnold; courtesy of the Avery Architectural and Fine Arts Library, Columbia University, New York, N.Y.)

among the visitors, a trumpeter moving from place to place on the Wooded Island, or Italian dancers with tambourines appearing unexpectedly.[23] Olmsted's suggestions were characteristic: he wanted not only to enliven the mood of the visitors but also to create a vivid experience of community for them—on an international scale.

The Columbian Exposition was Olmsted's crowning work in the Midwest. Water was the dominant feature of the landscape, as it had been at Riverside twenty-five years earlier and would be later in the Chicago and Detroit parks. Yet even though his plan for the exposition featured the abundant water resources of the region and displayed the beauty of native midwestern plants, Olmsted's vision was not so much regional as national or international: his goal was to foster in America a civilization in which people of all types and nationalities might meet on common ground. Although the fair may have seemed artificial or even superficial at a time when millions of Americans were crowded together in urban poverty, it did provide a vision of how life in the cities might be different. Olmsted's careful planning of the fair showed the American public how it might come together, as a people, in a new shared landscape.

Notes

1. J. T. Censer, ed., *Defending the Union: The Civil War and the U.S. Sanitary Commission, 1861–1863*, vol. 4 of *The Papers of Frederick Law Olmsted* (Baltimore: Johns Hopkins University Press, 1986), 548–50.

2. Olmsted also received commissions to design the campus of Washington University in St. Louis and parks for Milwaukee and Kansas City. These jobs, however, like the 1895 redesign of Jackson Park after the demolition of the exposition, were largely carried out by other members of the firm. His reports for Riverside, the Chicago South Park, Belle Isle, and the exposition, on the other hand, reflect deep personal involvement.

3. Olmsted met William Le Baron Jenney, the Paris-trained architect and engineer, at Vicksburg during the Civil War. After the war Jenney wrote Olmsted in New York asking for work, and in 1868 they collaborated at Riverside. Jenney served as engineer for the Riverside Improvement Company and was the architect of both public and private buildings for the town. When Olmsted and Vaux were chosen to design Chicago's South Park, Jenney laid out the West Parks. More than two decades later, Olmsted and Jenney collaborated again at the World's Columbian Exposition, where Jenney was architect of the Horticultural Building.

Olmsted also knew and respected Horace William Shaler Cleveland, the Massachusetts-born landscape architect who had competed against Olmsted and Vaux in the 1858 design competition for Central Park. Cleveland worked one season with Olmsted and Vaux on Prospect Park in Brooklyn and supervised the execution of their design for Chicago's Washington Park.

Other landscape architects who practiced in the Midwest were affiliated with Olmsted or received their training as members of his firm. Jacob Weidenmann, whose work in the region included Mount Hope Cemetery in Chicago, the Iowa State Capitol grounds, and a subdivision in Des Moines, entered into a working agreement with Olmsted in 1874 which lasted for several years. Warren Manning contributed his horticultural expertise to the Olmsted office from 1888 to 1896; he worked on Lake and Washington parks in Milwaukee and was planting supervisor for Jackson Park in Chicago and, after Henry Codman died, for the 1893 Chicago exposition.

Olmsted's two sons, John Charles Olmsted and Frederick Law Olmsted Jr., grew up steeped in their father's work and carried it on during and after his lifetime. (John Charles was actually Olmsted's nephew and stepson, as Olmsted had married his brother's widow and adopted her children, but Olmsted always referred to him as his son.) John Charles joined the firm in 1873, became a partner in 1884, and was the senior partner of Olmsted Brothers for over twenty years. Frederick Law Olmsted Jr., who was eighteen years younger than his stepbrother, joined him as a partner in 1898. In the Midwest the brothers collaborated, as their father had, with Daniel Burnham. During the first two decades of the twentieth century, the Olmsted Brothers firm designed more than a dozen small parks in Chicago; Burnham and Company designed the fieldhouses.

No evidence has yet been uncovered that Jens Jensen or O. C. Simonds, founders of the Prairie School of landscape architecture, had any personal contact with the senior Olmsted. However, they were young men in their thirties when the Columbian Exposition came to Chicago. Jensen was a recent immigrant and supervisor of Union Park on the West side; Simonds had worked for William Le Baron Jenney and might conceivably have met Olmsted through him. At any rate, Jensen and Simonds would have appreciated Olmsted's extensive use of native plant material around the lagoons of the fair.

4. Quoted in Charles Moore, *Daniel H. Burnham: Architect, Planner of Cities,* vol.1 (Boston: Houghton Mifflin, 1921), 74.

5. V. P. Ranney, G. J. Rauluk, and C. F. Hoffman, eds., *The California Frontier, 1863–1865,* vol. 5 of *The Papers of Frederick Law Olmsted* (Baltimore: Johns Hopkins University Press, 1990), 385.

6. Ibid., 594.

7. Olmsted, Vaux and Company, *The Preliminary Report upon the Proposed Suburban Village at Riverside, near Chicago* (New York, 1868), 27–28.

8. Ibid., 12.

9. William Bross, letter to F. L. Olmsted, 28 April 1866, Frederick Law Olmsted Papers, Library of Congress, Washington, D.C.

10. John Rauch, letter to F. L. Olmsted, 12 January 1866, Olmsted Papers.

11. Olmsted and Vaux, *Riverside,* 1, 9.

12. Olmsted, Vaux and Company, *Chicago South Park Commission: Report accompanying Plan for Laying Out the South Park* (Chicago, 1871), 11, 18.

13. Ibid., 12.

14. Ibid., 20.

15. Ibid., 17.

16. [F. L. Olmsted], *The Park for Detroit; Being a Preliminary Consideration of Certain Prime Conditions of Economy for the Belle Isle Scheme* (printed for the author, November 1882), 22, 40–41.

17. F. L. Olmsted, "A Report upon the Landscape Architecture of the Columbian Exposition to the American Institute of Architects," *American Architect and Building News,* 9 September 1893, 152.

18. Ibid., 153.

19. F. L. Olmsted, letter to Daniel H. Burnham, 28 December 1891, Olmsted Papers.

20. Ibid.

21. Ibid.

22. Ibid., 26 January 1891, Olmsted Papers.

23. Ibid, 20 June 1893, Olmsted Papers.

FOUR

William Le Baron Jenney and Chicago's West Parks

FROM PRAIRIES TO PLEASURE-GROUNDS

Reuben M. Rainey

WILLIAM LE BARON JENNEY's legacy of landscape architectural design is clearly visible to the air traveler on the final approach to Chicago's Midway or O'Hare airport. About four miles west of the Loop's orchard of skyscrapers, three polygons of lush greenery emerge from the dull gray urban grid. These three fragments of forest and lawn pivoting around their central lakes are joined by faint green threads, the remnants of once-majestic boulevards. The West Parks, a small but distinguished component of Jenney's work, exemplify one of the finest traditions of nineteenth-century American urbanism, the creation of parks and boulevards as an armature of order and a respite from the burgeoning industrial city.

Jenney's were quintessential nineteenth-century American parks. Combining lofty visions of social reform with the sobering realities of real estate economics, they were landscapes constructed from scratch to enhance the physical and psychic health of all classes of citizens in America's most rapidly expanding city. At the same time, they served as a pragmatic real estate venture to promote the development of the West Side and to nourish Chicago's overall tax base.

Jenney's original 1871 plans for the West Parks also manifest a sophisticated grasp of spatial organization, site engineering, use of water, planting design, circulation systems, and treatment of architectural elements. Only partially realized, they reveal that Jenney was one of the more gifted American park designers of the nineteenth century, worthy of inclusion in the ranks of Frederick Law Olmsted Sr., Calvert Vaux, Horace Cleveland, William Hammond Hall, and Jacob Weidenmann. The West Parks system represented an intelligent synthesis of the leading American park design ideas with those advanced by France's Adolphe Alphand and Britain's William Robinson. These concepts were skillfully adapted to Chicago's challenging prairie landscape—a terrain Jenney viewed as a flat, treeless, poorly drained tabula rasa that offered the designer few clues.

William Le Baron Jenney (1802–1907) was born in Fairhaven, Massachusetts, into a prosperous merchant's family. As a young man he foundered in his early attempts to find a career until he settled on engineering. Disappointed with Harvard's fledgling program, Jenney went to Paris in 1853 to study architecture at the Ecole Centrale des Arts et Manufactures for three years under Louis Charles Mary. Mary's commonsense rationalism stressed the subordination of ornament to structure, the primacy of "fitness," and the functional articulation of building plans and facades generated by the *papier quadrille,* or grid paper, method of J. N. L. Durand, Mary's former teacher. Jenney's curriculum also included site engineering courses in grading and drainage. While a student, he was able to observe firsthand much of the construction of Alphand's Parisian park system, the most brilliant open space concept of its day.

During the Civil War, Jenney's formal education was honed in the field by designing and building earthwork fortifications and bridges under Grant and later Sherman. Jenney also met Olmsted during the war, and he later applied for a job in the Olmsted and Vaux office when they were beginning the design for Brooklyn's Prospect Park. Instead of joining that firm however, Jenney moved to Chicago in 1867.

William Le Baron Jenney. (IChi-19760; courtesy of the Chicago Historical Society, Chicago, Ill.)

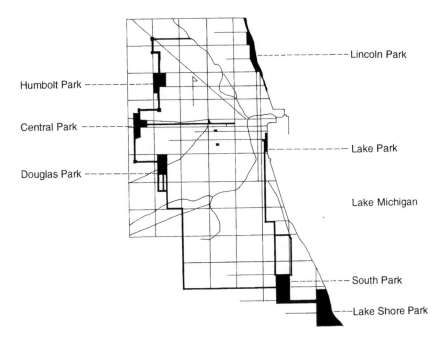

Lincoln Park

Humbolt Park

Central Park

Lake Park

Douglas Park

Lake Michigan

South Park

Lake Shore Park

Plan for the Chicago Park System. (Redrawn by Reuben M. Rainey and John Meder from West Chicago Park reports, 1879–80, on file at the Chicago Historical Society and the Chicago Parks Department, Chicago, Ill.)

Jenney's reputation as an architect and co-founder of the Chicago School is well established; both Louis Sullivan and Daniel Burnham trained in his office. Jenney's talent for structural innovation is supremely evident in high-rises such as the Home Insurance Building (1884) and the second Leiter Building. But his important projects in landscape design are almost forgotten, as is the fact that O. C. Simonds trained under him. His brilliant West Parks system, planned before Chicago's Great Fire of 1871 but built for the most part after it, while often attributed to Frederick Law Olmsted, is Jenney's major achievement in landscape architectural design.[1]

Jenney's West Park System belonged to the same nineteenth-century urban middle-class reform movement that had so fervently supported the construction of the great parks in many eastern cities. The reformers—cosmopolitan in outlook, with strong ties to England and France, intensely preoccupied with national identity and cultural self-definition, increasingly self-assured and assertive, and possessed of an abiding faith in the capacity of the built environment to shape human character for good or ill—envisioned an American urbanism that would address the daunting problems of the rapidly emerging industrial city. Many of them, like Jenney, Olmsted, and Cleveland, had roots in New England Protestant culture. They were intent on dealing decisively with a new kind of American city profoundly shaped by the railroad. It was a city that separated work and residence, created special nodes of commerce and industry, and built enormous "process spaces" such as the Chicago stockyards at the end of trunk lines;[2] a city with a web of arteries that converged on a central commercial and cultural district growing at an unprecedented rate; a city with vast and diverse immigrant populations, polarities of wealth and poverty, and acute problems in public health.

The construction of parks and park systems was seen as one way to address some of the problems of the protean industrial city, and Chicago's reformers demanded parks for the same reasons their counterparts did in New York, Brooklyn, Boston, Richmond, and San Francisco. They believed that parks promoted public health by facilitating beneficial exercise in air purified by leaves that filtered out pollutants. Parks relieved urban stress by providing an experience of landscape which soothed the nerves, supplying a counterpoint to hard urban materials, noise, and restricted views. In addition, parks helped to defuse social tension by bringing together individuals of different economic status and ethnic origin in a shared context of lighthearted recreation or more serious civic ritual, such as military parades or patriotic holidays. Parks also augmented city revenues (not to mention the individual fortunes of real estate developers), by attracting prime development to their perimeters. Finally, parks could house museums and other didactic exhibits that would further the education of the city's citizens, especially its school-children.

Olmsted and Vaux's masterwork, Central Park in New York, and their evolving concept of park systems had established a strong parks tradition, as city after city sought to emulate and surpass the achievements of New York. Alphand's brilliant work in Paris of the 1850s, to which Olmsted and Vaux owed a deep debt, established a powerful precedent on the international scale.[3]

In 1858, when New York's Central Park was just beginning to take shape and Alphand's work was well under way, Dr. John Rauch and other reformers advocated parks for Chicago to purify the air from miasmas in the rapidly growing population (which surged from 100,000 in 1830 to 300,000 in 1867). The common council submitted a bill to the state legislature in 1868, which passed in 1869, to create an elaborate integrated system of parks and boulevards establishing a greenbelt around the city which would provide a coherent structure to Chicago's potentially chaotic expansion. To facilitate construction and administration of this extensive system, the city defined three separate divisions to be headed by teams of appointed commissioners: the North, South, and West Parks districts. The commissioners sought the top design talent of the day, hiring Olmsted and Vaux for the South Park system and Jenney for the West Parks.[4]

The seven West Parks commissioners took an active role in the design process and schooled themselves in the best precedents of their day. They took pains to observe firsthand the work in progress at the new suburban development of Riverside, designed by Olmsted and Vaux, and appropriated funds

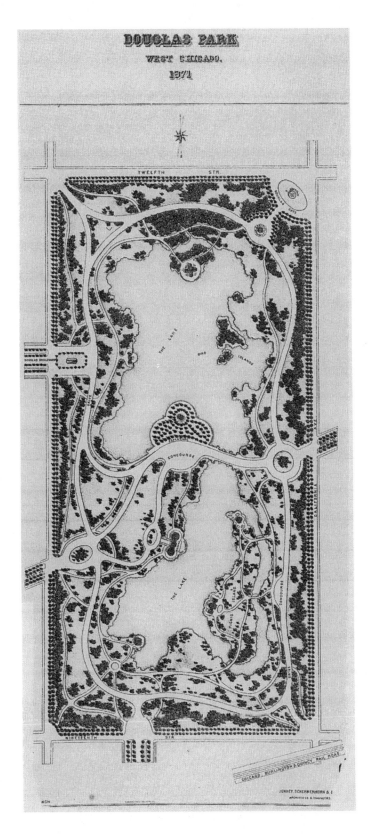

Plan of Douglas Park, 1871. (Courtesy of
the Chicago Park District Special Collections, Chicago, Ill.)

to travel to distant cities to study various efforts—New York's Central Park likely headed the list. No detailed records of Jenney's discussions with the commissioners are available, but one recorded episode suggests that they did not hesitate to critique his designs and, in at least one case, change them.[5]

As Jenney envisioned them, the three West Parks would create a "chain of verdure" and connect the adjacent South and North Park systems.[6] The complex would be oriented around three major open spaces of nearly equal size: Douglas Park at the south end, Humboldt Park in the north, and Central Park between them. (Central Park was renamed Garfield Park in 1887 to honor the assassinated president.) An eight-mile network of boulevards would connect the three, establishing an extensive drive on the perimeter of the then-undeveloped western portion of the city. The boulevards would be extensions of the parks and laid out to conform to the city's expanding grid structure. These elegant thoroughfares typically comprised a commercial highway in the center flanked by pleasure drives, bridle paths, and walks, which were separated from each other by allées of trees or strips of lawn. Where a boulevard changed direction at a right angle on the grid, Jenney proposed a small square to serve the surrounding neighborhood. Intersections would sometimes be marked by fountains, groves, arbors, or elaborate floral displays. In the northern portion of the complex, the formal allées would often be replaced by irregular masses of trees grouped into undulating lines to give a more "picturesque" effect.

Jenney faced multiple challenges in designing the West Parks, including the necessity to provide facilities for such disparate activities as competitive sports, civic rituals, concerts, therapeutic contemplation of landscape scenery, children's play, family picnics, and education in natural history. In response, he designed a clearly defined ensemble of linked spaces that separated potentially conflicting uses. Each of the three parks would have an individual character, yet a similar treatment of water, structures, and planting throughout would unify them into a "harmonious, consistent, and complete" ensemble. His sophisticated planting plans structured those spaces and transfigured the "wild," treeless prairie into a verdant counterpoint of exotic semitropical plants and hardy native vegetation—a variant to the stock-in-trade "pastoral-picturesque" planting schemes of many large nineteenth-century American urban parks. His work reveals some of the richness and variety of this era's park design, which derives some of its principles from those expressed by Olmsted and Vaux's 1858 plan for New York's Central Park.

In fact, Jenney contacted Olmsted for advice and received a "long and highly instructive letter," which has, unfortunately, been lost. However, if we look at Olmsted's surviving letters to Jenney's colleagues, such as William Hammond Hall and Horace Cleveland, and other documents, we can

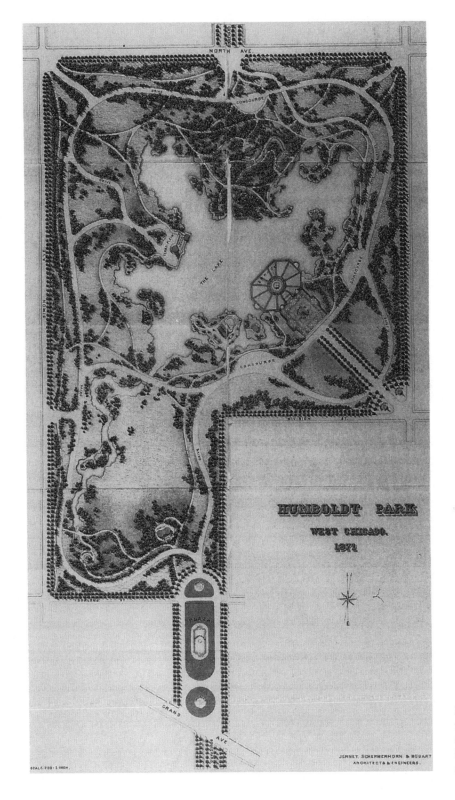

Plan of Humboldt Park, 1871. (Courtesy of the Chicago Park District Special Collections, Chicago, Ill.)

Plan of Central Park,
1871. (Courtesy of the
Chicago Park District
Special Collections, Chi-
cago, Ill.)

View of Grand Boulevard showing allées and median strips. (Reprinted from *Picturesque Chicago*, 3d ed. [Chicago, 1882], n.p.)

surmise that he would have told Jenney to read Adolphe Alphand's great work on the Paris park system, *Les Promenades de Paris* (1867–73), and William Robinson's critique of those parks in *The Parks and Gardens of Paris* (1869).[7] Olmsted would also likely have advised Jenney first to solve the acute drainage problem of the flat site and then design the park around this structural solution. The West Parks were much smaller than their Olmstedian precedents—Douglas and Central, at 171 acres each, and Humboldt, though somewhat larger at 193 acres, were small compared with the 844 acres of New York's Central Park or the 1,055 acres of Chicago's own South Park—and had a rich and complex program envisioned for them. So they required the development of an intermediate-scale design, one that was functionally and typologically somewhere between a small neighborhood park of 5 to 10 acres and a large urban park of 800 to 1,000 acres. As opposed to the sweeping lawns and pastoral scenery of large parks, smaller sites called for what Olmsted and Vaux characterized as a "plaisance" treatment. Such scenery is managed in a "more garden like way." It consists of "lawn, shrubbery underwood and brooding trees" but is treated in an architectonic fashion, like the "kept grounds" or "pleasure-grounds" immediately adjacent to an English country house, where one finds strong symmetry in planting beds and path systems. In contrast to large parks where they can be hidden by the landscape scenery, buildings are featured as focal points and used to enhance vistas. In addition, Olmsted likely reminded Jenney that the parks had to accommo-

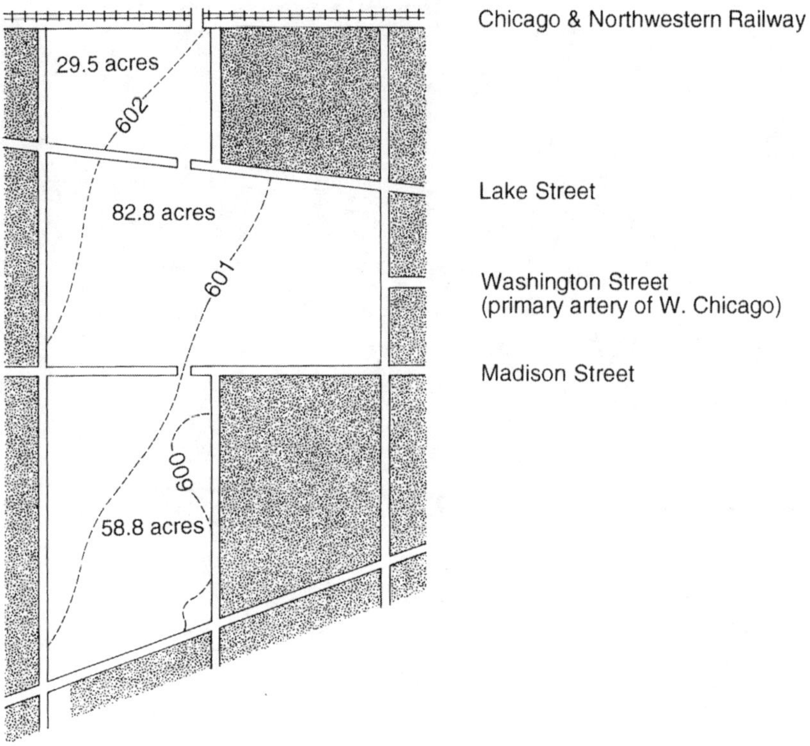

Central Park topography. (Drawn by Reuben M. Rainey and John Meder from information at the Chicago Historical Society, Chicago, Ill.)

Chicago & Northwestern Railway

29.5 acres

602

82.8 acres

601

600

58.8 acres

Lake Street

Washington Street
(primary artery of W. Chicago)

Madison Street

date both "exertive" recreation, involving conscious mental or physical activity (baseball, military parades, chess, and so forth) and "receptive" recreation, which soothes without conscious exertion (picnicking, concerts, solitary walks). Where space had to be provided for potentially conflicting activities side by side, separate precincts should be created, marked by different landscape treatments. Finally, Olmsted would have suggested adding interest to the flat terrain by doubling it in the reflection of large bodies of water.[8]

Jenney set to work with a firm commitment to the Olmstedian concept of an urban park and the specific kinds of recreation it should provide. He expressed his vision in the commission's annual report:

> A park is designed for pleasure and healthful recreation. Within its limits, the man of business can forget the anxieties of the counting house, and rest an overworked brain. The laborer and artisan can forget his toil. The family picnic party can enjoy all the necessary privacy in the grounds allotted to that purpose; can spread their cloth and empty their baskets under the trees amid pleasing surrounding of broad lawns, shady nooks, and glimpses of lakes; with a playhouse nearby for children affording shelter for all in case of a sudden storm.
>
> The invalid and convalescent may seek repose and healthful air under the vine covered arbors; or enjoy the quiet to be found in its groves.

The traffic-road, with its hay-wagons, small carts, lumbering teams, droves of cattle, and the accompanying dust and dirt, is antagonistic to the use and primary object of a park, which is to give relief for a while from all intercourse with the toil and humdrum of life, and afford pleasant and healthful recreation for both mind and body.[9]

Jenney created plans for three individual yet related parks that would offer the visitor a variety of landscape experiences. Douglas Park provides the opportunity to become more absorbed in the lush landscape through a series of lakeside promenades with a changing series of water views. Humboldt is dominated by an elegant esplanade terminating in a terrace thrust forward into the central lake; the architectonic peninsula lends an air of urbanity to the park, which surrounds the terrace almost as an English park frames a stately country house. Central Park is the most diverse in program and facilities, containing athletic fields, a recreational lake, a large conservatory, an arboretum, and zoological gardens.[10]

During the first five years of construction, the West Parks and their boulevards were developed substantially according to Jenney's original 1871 plan; however, budget cuts after the Great Fire, the financial panic of 1873, and mismanagement of funds late in the decade necessitated a scaling back. The principal victims of this fiscal attrition were the elegant buildings and terraces for education and recreation, the memorial to the Great Fire, the elaborate planting plans, and the zoological and botanical gardens. Then, in the early twentieth century, Jens Jensen significantly altered Jenney's vision of the parks. Working primarily in the numerous uncompleted areas of the system, Jensen introduced large numbers of hardy native plants along with abstractions of certain features typical of the regional landscape, such as his "Prairie river" in Humboldt Park. Radically altered concepts of the function of urban parks and inadequate maintenance have more recently obliterated all but faint traces of Jenney's work. As Julia Sniderman Bachrach, Mary O'Shaughnessy, and William Tippens have shown, about all that now remain of Jenney's artistry are the original park boundaries, portions of the original lakes' edges, traces of major road alignments (mostly on the perimeters), and segments of the original grading—rather meager skeletal remnants of the rich and vibrant organism envisioned in 1871 and subsequently approved for construction.

A closer look at the development of Central Park is revealing of Jenney's design process. As is often the case, the landscape architect had no say in the site selection; it was chosen by the commissioners. Although the Central Park site had many strengths, it also posed formidable problems. The 171.1-acre parcel included three rectilinear areas bounded by the north-south grid of

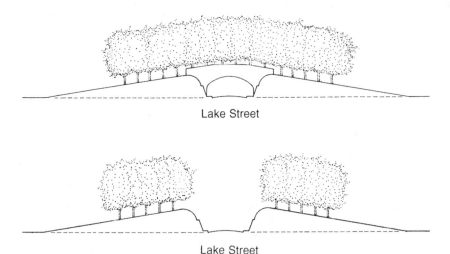

Lake Street

Lake Street

Central Park schematic sections through the principal roadway showing berms and viaduct bridge. (Drawn by Reuben M. Rainey and John Meder from information at the Chicago Historical Society, Chicago, Ill.)

the city's street pattern. The northernmost parcel was 29.5 acres, the central, 82.8, and the southern, 58.8. The park was well integrated with the major streets of West Chicago. Washington Street, the major east-west artery, terminated in the center of the eastern boundary of the park's midsection. Jenney took advantage of the connection by proposing first a statue of Washington and then, in 1872, the Fire Memorial on axis with a view toward the park down Washington Street—in the best Hausmannian fashion. Lake and Madison streets—both major east-west thoroughfares—defined the north and south boundaries of the central section and provided ready access by carriage and foot. The proposed boulevards intersecting the northeast and southwest corners of the site connected it to Humboldt and Douglas parks to the north and south, thus completing the central link in the West Parks' "chain of verdure." Access by public transportation was also good. The Chicago and Northwestern Railway ran along the northern boundary and provided frequent connections with the city's downtown, some 4.5 miles to the east.

The natural features of the site, however, were far less promising. It was poorly drained and almost flat. The change in elevation from the northwest corner to the southeast corner, a distance of 1,000 yards, was only about 2.5 feet. To make matters worse, the site was nearly devoid of attractive vegetation, suggesting the appearance of a landscape victimized by the scorched-earth policy of some marauding army. Also, the relatively small size of the barren parcel made it exceedingly difficult for Jenney to create the long vistas across lush turf bordered by majestic trees which were the quintessential expression of the therapeutic landscape. These interrelated constraints—the pressing need to solve the drainage problem, the necessity of keeping Lake and Madison, the east-west city streets running through the park, open at

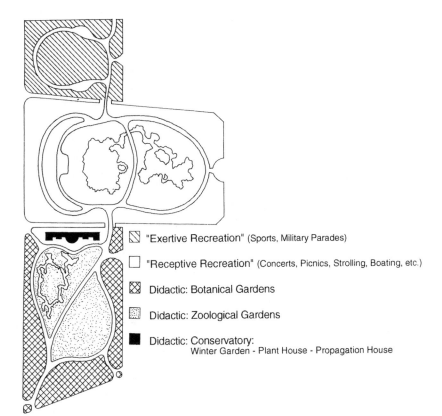

"Exertive Recreation" (Sports, Military Parades)

"Receptive Recreation" (Concerts, Picnics, Strolling, Boating, etc.)

Didactic: Botanical Gardens

Didactic: Zoological Gardens

Didactic: Conservatory:
Winter Garden - Plant House - Propagation House

Central Park zones of activity. (Drawn by Reuben M. Rainey and John Meder from information at the Chicago Historical Society, Chicago, Ill.)

all times, and the restrictions of the small size—were decisive factors in Jenney's design.

The drainage problem was obviously critical, for unless it was solved the flat site would not support vegetation or permit extensive recreational use. In the tradition of his teacher, L. C. Mary, Jenney opted for the most direct, simple, and economic solution: he called for the construction of a large 11.1-acre lake fed by artesian wells in the center of the park, to store surface run-off. He also planned a smaller streamlike body of water in the southern section both to deal with drainage and to provide a water supply for the herds of deer and farm animals in the zoological garden. Creation of the lake profoundly affected the park's design, since it occupied the very center of the middle section.

The mandate to keep the city streets open was also critical. To keep the park a separate precinct apart from the noise and bustle of the city, Jenney had the major roads heavily bermed with the earth excavated for the lake. Thickly planted, the berms created strong visual barriers that made it impossible to see from one section of the park into another; viaducts bridged the three divisions.[11]

Having derived the architectural structure of his park from functional

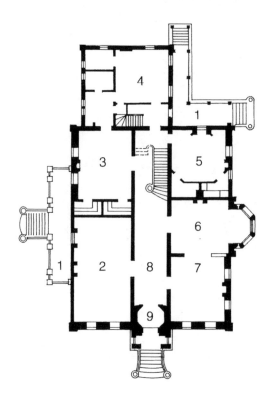

Jenney and Loring's plan
for the John Forsyth
residence, c. 1868. (Re-
drawn by Reuben M.
Rainey and John Meder
from Jenney and Loring,
*Principles and Practice of
Architecture,* ex. C, pl. Z)

1 Piazza   6 Library
2 Parlor   7 Sitting Room
3 Dining Room 8 Hall
4 Kitchen   9 Vestibule
5 Bedroom

necessity, Jenney proceeded to fit the various elements of the program into the three separate sections of his plan. (The plan he generated appears to follow closely the procedure for park design outlined by Alphand in his *Prom-enades de Paris.*)[12]

It is not known precisely who generated Central Park's program, but it most likely reflected the joint efforts of Jenney and the commissioners, with some input from the public and city officials. (One element, the Fire Memorial, was suggested by the Chicago press.) There were no neighborhood residents to appease, since the whole West Parks system was being constructed on land that was mostly undeveloped. One thing is certain: the park as envisioned in the plan of 1871 was a space for all seasons, permitting a vast range of recreational pursuits—had not budget cuts kept the rich program from complete realization.[13]

Jenney provided clearly defined zones to separate potentially conflicting activities. The necessity of breaking the park into three parts to keep the city streets open was thus turned to the park's advantage. The northern part was

THE LAKE IN CENTRAL PARK.

View of the lake in the middle section of Central Park, with the proposed fire memorial in the background. (Reprinted from *Picturesque Chicago*, 3d ed. [Chicago, 1882], n.p.)

used for military parades and active team sports. The western section of the middle part was devoted to concerts, promenades, and other social activities at a music concourse fronting on the lake, while the eastern section was devoted to family picnic areas and special play facilities for children, such as the hoops course. It also contained the Fire Memorial. In the southern part were the large conservatory with its winter garden, a natural history museum, and the zoological and botanical gardens.[14]

Jenney's highly rational zoning of program requirements is reminiscent of mid-nineteenth-century residential plans which allocate rooms for specific domestic functions (dining room, parlor, library, reception hall, etc.). Indeed, his precise zoning of the park recalls the plan of Jenney's Forsythe House (ca. 1868).[15] The Cartesian rationality of this tripartite scheme may reflect Jenney's training under Mary in Paris, which stressed function, symmetry, and correctness of proportion. The clarity of Central Park's tripartite division and the almost bilateral symmetry of the northern and central parts are quite reminiscent of Mary's methods.[16] Indeed, so architectonic is Jenney's park that it appears almost as three adjacent roofless buildings separated by two major streets, with walls of berms and trees rather than masonry. And like the facades of Chicago's streetscapes, each is different in character.

The layout of drives and walks in Central Park is elegant and functional. Like Olmsted and Vaux's design for New York's Central Park, circulation is

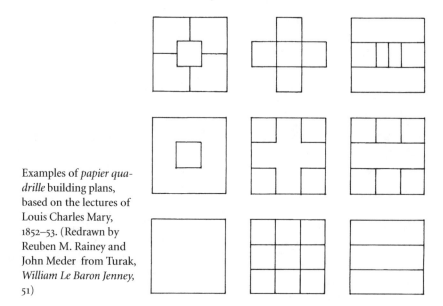

Examples of *papier quadrille* building plans, based on the lectures of Louis Charles Mary, 1852–53. (Redrawn by Reuben M. Rainey and John Meder from Turak, *William Le Baron Jenney,* 51)

organized into three separate but interrelated systems of varying widths: 50-foot carriage drives, 15-foot pedestrian paths, and 20-foot equestrian trails. (However, the flat terrain and limited budget did not allow Jenney to separate these systems by bridges and overpasses.) The three systems are carefully orchestrated to provide the visitor with a wide variety of scenic vistas.[17]

A figure-ground study of the plan reveals the park to be organized into a clear hierarchy of well-defined spaces, appropriately scaled to the activities they were to accommodate. All three sections of the park were surrounded by a wall of trees—some 2.6 miles of American elms that provided shade for promenading. Within this wall, spatial organization varied. The northern section was essentially one large outdoor room of greensward stretching before the concession building, which was centrally sited on its eastern edge like a country house. Nearly bilaterally symmetrical carriage drives and pedestrian walkways encircled the borders of the space. On the eastern perimeter small bosques of trees formed a series of small outdoor rooms. The central section was ordered by a central east-west axis defined by the bandstand, a small island near the eastern shore of the upper lake, and the Fire Memorial column. The ground plane was dominated by the 11.1-acre lake. Numerous bosques in the lawn formed a complex network of linked spaces. A large grove of trees just south of the transverse carriage drive, in the vicinity of the children's hoops course, provided a heavily canopied room for shaded picnics. On the north side of the eastern (or lower) lake, a 1,000-foot corridor of space wove its way in an easterly direction before swinging abruptly toward the northeast corner of the park. Its sinuously curving edge obscured its true dimensions and gave the illusion of a much larger space. The layered

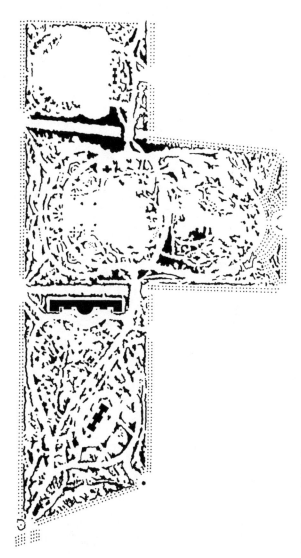

Central Park figure-
ground study. (Drawn
by Reuben M. Rainey
and John Meder from
information at the Chi-
cago Historical Society,
Chicago, Ill.)

spaces created by the bosques broke up the views across the lawn and absorbed large crowds, providing an impression that the park was uncongested.

The southernmost section of the park featured many closely spaced
bosques that broke up the space into a plethora of small linked rooms. Into
these were tucked the botanical garden, the conservatory, the museum, and
various animal paddocks. The diagonal central carriage drive sliced the space
into two almost equal portions. One-half contained the museum, the other,
the animal paddocks and conservatory. The botanical garden wrapped
around the southern and western portions of the site and tied the two halves
together.[18]

The tripartite circulation network and lucid, straightforward spatial
definition were the park's strongest assets. Without this carefully integrated

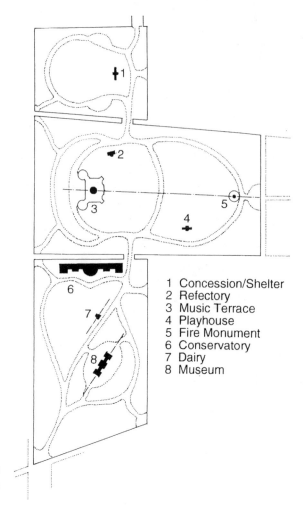

1 Concession/Shelter
2 Refectory
3 Music Terrace
4 Playhouse
5 Fire Monument
6 Conservatory
7 Dairy
8 Museum

Location of principal buildings in Central Park. (Drawn by Reuben M. Rainey and John Meder from information at the Chicago Historical Society, Chicago, Ill.)

system, the conflicting needs of boisterous crowds of baseball spectators, quiet strollers, and picnickers could never have been accommodated at the same time.

Jenney's plantings transformed the site into a lush landscape contrasting with both the spacious "wild" prairie surrounding it and the limited vistas and hard surfaces of the city itself. The use of exotic, large-leafed subtropical understory vegetation, such as *Musa, Artemesia,* and *Dracaena* was reminiscent of the great urban parks of London and Paris. In contrast to the Prairie School landscape architects who followed, Jenney wanted to transform the native landscape into a lush pleasure-ground.[19]

It is unlikely that Jenney was just trying to be au courant with the latest landscape fashions of Britain and Europe. Rather, he probably shared the Olmstedian notion that "tropical effects" in planting provided one of the most powerful contrasts to the city environment, while awakening in the beholder

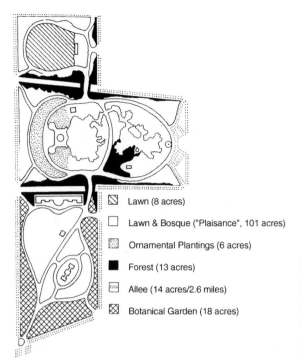

Lawn (8 acres)

Lawn & Bosque ("Plaisance", 101 acres)

Ornamental Plantings (6 acres)

Forest (13 acres)

Allee (14 acres/2.6 miles)

Botanical Garden (18 acres)

Central Park planting
plan diagram. (Drawn
by Reuben M. Rainey
and John Meder from
information at the Chi-
cago Historical Society,
Chicago, Ill.)

"a profound sense of the creator's bountifulness."[20] However, Jenney and
Olmsted differed on how to achieve these tropical effects. Olmsted preferred
to use hardy native and exotic plants, which would not require costly maintenance and wintering indoors, planted close together to mimic the lushness of
tropical scenery or pruned to resemble the habit of tropical plants. Jenney's
preference was for real subtropical species, which would have to have been
wintered in his proposed conservatory and then bedded out in the spring.

Jenney used plants in three basic ways: they structured spaces of the park;
they created prospects and vignettes of varying character; and they provided
instruction in the beauty and order of nature, especially in the botanic garden. His diverse plant palette emphasized seasonal color and variety of form.

Sustaining order in a planting plan of great variety is always a challenge.
Jenney solved the problem by using one dominant vocabulary and playing
the others off against it. About 59 percent of the park is lawn and bosque;
the rest is forest (8 percent), botanical garden (10 percent), perimeter allées
(7 percent), lawn (5 percent), and ornamental planting beds (5 percent), with
the remaining 6 percent a lake. The predominance of lawn and bosque in its
smaller scale "plaisance" treatment suggests an Olmstedian emphasis on the
special therapeutic properties of this type of scenery above all others. Forest
was used to buffer the edges of the park along Lake and Madison streets and
to create the picnic grove in the center section.[21]

Jenney's buildings were prominent in the park's vistas and carefully integrated with the character of the landscape. The upper park's concession building and the music terrace of the middle section established the central axes for their respective spaces. The planned "imposing" Byzantine music pavilion, gilded and ornate, was to be set atop a massive cut stone parapet and complemented by colorful, fan-shaped flower beds set in emerald green turf flanked by clusters of trees. In contrast, the "rustic" shelters, bridges, and children's playground buildings of the east and central sections were "simple and rural" as befits the "pastoral character" of their settings.[22]

In Jenney's envisioned park, on a summer afternoon, Chicagoans could watch a baseball game between neighborhood teams, observe a parade of the city militia, listen to an edifying oration from the bandstand on the music terrace, or dine with friends in the lakeside refectory. They could also contemplate the courage and resiliency of their fellow citizens celebrated by the Fire Memorial, row on the lake, or picnic under the trees with their family. Children of the city could race around the special hoops course or contemplate the wonders of nature in the natural history museum, botanical garden, and 725-foot-long conservatory. Farmers could inspect the herds of fine breeding stock on display in the zoological garden or observe the prancing deer. The harried counting house clerks could take a refreshing solitary walk through tree-lined lawns, while the scions of industry could detour on their way home for a soothing horseback ride through the verdant landscape. In the dead of winter, the inhabitants of the city's congested districts could ride out on the railroad to stroll in the lush oasis of tropical plants housed in the conservatory, or in summer enjoy the cool shade of the groves while the surrounding prairies were scorched brown by the unrelenting summer sun. Free city concerts of carefully selected, soothing music would draw large crowds, who afterward could linger and promenade the park's tree-lined perimeters, or ride in their carriages to other parks in the system.

Nineteenth-century Chicago is an example of a typical American "open city" produced by industrialization in a democratic society. Such a city is pluralistic, "a forum for the freedom of choice." Its primary structuring element is an ever-expanding grid of streets without definite ends or limits, a fitting expression of dynamic opportunity and change. Such a city has no well-defined center but is structured instead around a series of nodes of activity, allowing for a wide range of choices. Its eclectic architecture is yet another expression of an emphasis on freedom of choice within a pluralistic milieu.[23]

Jenney's West Parks clearly manifest many of the characteristics of the "open city." Visitors are allowed movement within, or they can venture onto an eight-mile network of parks and boulevards, affording ever-changing panoramas and choice of routes. Their buildings are eclectic, drawing from the glories of Byzantium (a lighthearted note of fantasy and exoticism) and rustic, rural buildings of a decidedly Alpine flavor, perhaps like those in the Bois de Boulogne. There exists a clear reciprocity between the city and these parks. Their spatial organization and circulation system reflect elements of the urban armature that encloses them.

Efficient differentiation of space allows highly contrasting activities to occur simultaneously with the same smoothness and efficiency as that of the new industrial plants or "process spaces" that were beginning to cluster along the city's rail lines—whether to move cattle through stockyards or to sort out mail orders at Montgomery Ward. In attempting to bring together citizens of all ethnic and economic groups and provide them with a wide range of recreational and educational pursuits structured around a rational system of circulation, the West Parks both mirrored and engendered the democratic values of the open city.

Before he was hired by the West Park Commission, the young Jenney, seeking employment with Olmsted, wrote in 1865: "There is no situation that I can imagine where I should derive more pleasure from the work I might be called upon to perform as one in which Architecture, Gardening and Engineering were associated, and I most earnestly desire and hope that some such position be within my reach."[24] In his masterful vision for the West Parks system, that hope came to fruition. Despite later compromises and cutbacks during construction, the citizens of Chicago were the great beneficiaries of that vision.

Notes

An earlier version of this chapter appeared in *Threshold, Journal of the Chicago School of Architecture* (University of Illinois at Chicago) 5–6 (Fall 1991), 39–59.

1. Jenney's architectural innovations are celebrated in Sigfried Gideon's bible of modernism, *Space, Time, and Architecture* (Cambridge: Harvard University Press, 1974), and have received fresh reassessment by Theodore Turak in *William Le Baron Jenney, A Pioneer of Modern Architecture* (Ann Arbor: UMI Research Press, 1986). Fortunately, Turak's research has begun to restore the fading record of Jenney's accomplishments in landscape architecture, most of which occurred early in his long and productive architectural practice.

2. "Process space" is a term coined by J. B. Jackson. Personal conversation with author, February 1976. See also John Brinckerhoff Jackson, *American Space, the Centennial Years, 1865–1876* (New York: W. W. Norton, 1972), 85–86, where Jackson defines "process space" as one organized as "an orderly system of events leading up to a product."

3. Adolphe Alphand, *Les Promenades de Paris* (Paris, 1867–73); Frederick Law Olmsted, *Public Parks and the Enlargement of Towns* (Cambridge, Mass., 1870); Cynthia Zaitzevsky, *Frederick Law Olmsted and the Boston Park System* (Cambridge: Belknap Press/Harvard University Press, 1982); Daniel Walker Howe, "Victorian Culture in America," in *Victorian America*, ed. Howe (Philadelphia: University of Pennsylvania Press, 1976), 3–28; and

David Schuyler, *The New Urban Landscape: The Redefinition of City Form in Nineteenth-Century America* (Baltimore: Johns Hopkins University Press, 1986).

4. Despite Jenney's never having actually designed a park or boulevard, the West Parks commissioners apparently had sufficient faith in his abilities to hire him. His local residency (no small consideration in Chicago appointments) and his recently co-authored book on architectural theory may also have been factors in their decision. Turak, *Jenney*, chap. 6; Victoria Post Ranney, *Olmsted in Chicago* (Chicago: Donnelley, 1972); Alfred Theodore Andreas, *History of Chicago from the Earliest Period to the Present Time in Three Volumes* (Chicago, 1886), 3:167–89; William Le Baron Jenney and Sanford E. Loring, *Principles and Practices of Architecture* (Chicago, 1869).

5. When Jenney submitted a plan for Douglas Park, the commissioners insisted that he modify the straight diagonal boulevard bisecting it into a more curvilinear drive. Jenney complied, although Ogden Avenue was finally built as a straight diagonal. This drama suggests that the design for the West Parks grew out of a lively dialogue between strong clients and their architect, a situation that often leads to innovative results. "Official Proceedings of the West Parks Commission, 1869–1893," 8 December 1870 (manuscript in Chicago Park District archives); I am indebted to Mary O'Shaughnessy for calling this material to my attention. Jenney left the commission's service in 1877. Thereafter, his former employee O. F. Dubuis supervised the work along the lines of Jenney's original design, which remained the basis of all further work as affirmed by official vote of the West Parks commissioners. There is no evidence that Jenney resigned because of difficulties with the commission, although some evidence suggests that they were not paying him promptly. Probably Jenney simply wanted to devote more time to his burgeoning architectural practice. He maintained a cordial relationship with the commission while serving occasionally as a consultant well into the 1890s and later even designed several park buildings. In fact, it is difficult to separate Dubuis's work from Jenney's, and several of the modifications of the original 1871 plan, necessitated by a shrinking budget, may have been formulated by Jenney in consultation with Dubuis, until the commissioners terminated Dubuis's appointment as chief engineer in 1893.

6. Jenney described his idea for the park system in the *Second Annual Report of the West Chicago Park Commission* (Chicago, 1871). See also *First Annual Report* (1870), *Third Annual Report* (1872), *Fourth Annual Report* (1873), and Turak, *Jenney*, chap. 6. Jenney was not inclined to make elaborate written statements about his design intentions. His description of Central Park in the *Second Annual Report* is a succinct seven pages. Accompanying his statement was a quite elegantly drawn and finely detailed 250-scale plan of the park. In what follows, I have used Jenney's brief statements as a point of departure and supplemented them extensively with my own reading of his plan, taking care to distinguish between the two.

7. While Jenney adopted Alphand's preference for a subtropical planting scheme, he avoided two of what Robinson considered Alphand's "mistakes," carving up the parks with too many roads and ruining the lake edges by bringing pathways too near their shoreline. William Robinson, *The Parks, Promenades, and Gardens of Paris Described and Considered in Relation to the Wants of Our Own Cities* (London, 1869), and Alphand, *Les Promenades.*

8. Olmsted, *Public Parks*; Frederick Law Olmsted, letter to William Hammond Hall, 1874, Olmsted Papers, Library of Congress; Frederick Law Olmsted and Calvert Vaux, "Report Accompanying Plan for Laying Out the South Park," South Park Commission, Chicago, 1871.

9. *Second Annual Report,* 62.

10. *First, Second,* and *Third Annual Report.*

11. *Second Annual Report,* 52–72. Limited funds precluded sinking the roads below grade as in New York's Central Park.

12. Jenney probably consulted chaps. 1–10.

13. A comprehensive history of the West Parks is yet to be written. Valuable preliminary research has been conducted by Julia Sniderman Bachrach. See her manuscripts "Model Preservation Planning Project Survey Analysis, Humboldt Park" (Chicago Park District, 1989) and "The Historic Resources of the Chicago Park District. United States Department of the Interior, National Park Service, National Register of Historic Places Multiple Property Documentation Form" (n.d.; copy in Chicago Park District archives). See also the annual reports of the West Chicago Park Commission, 1870–73. According to Alfred Caldwell, who at one time worked for Jens Jensen, Jensen had deep respect for Jenney's ability as a park designer. Caldwell, personal communication to the author, 24 September 1990.

14. *Second Annual Report*, 52–68.

15. Jenney and Loring, *Principles and Practices of Architecture*, example c, pl. 2.

16. Turak, *Jenney*, chap. 4, esp. p. 50.

17. *Second Annual Report*, 62–68.

18. *Second Annual Report*, 64–68.

19. Early in the next century, Jens Jensen's major additions to the unfinished portions of Jenney's West Parks would transform Jenney's cosmopolitan planting plan into a regional one utilizing native plants and celebrating the prairie's beauty.

20. When Olmsted first saw tropical scenery while crossing the Isthmus of Panama in 1863, he immediately wrote to his chief gardener at Central Park and urged him to attempt to create "tropical character" in portions of the park by the profuse planting of vines and the special pruning of hardy native vegetation. Frederick Law Olmsted, letter to Ignaz Anton Pilat, 26 September 1863, in *The California Frontier, 1863–1865,* ed. V. P. Ranney, G. J. Rauluk, and C. F. Hoffman, vol. 5 of *The Papers of Frederick Law Olmsted,* ed. C. C. McLaughlin and C. E. Beveridge (Baltimore: Johns Hopkins University Press, 1990), 85–92. Olmsted followed a similar strategy in the South Park lagoons.

21. *Fourth* (1873), *Fifth* (1874), and *Sixth* (1875) *Annual Report.*

22. This matching of building style with landscape character was central to the work of Andrew Jackson Downing, whom Jenney greatly admired. *Second Annual Report,* 64–67; Turak, *Jenney,* 91–93.

23. Christian Norberg-Schulz, *New World Architecture* (Princeton: Princeton Architectural Press, 1988), 27–41.

24. Jenney to Frederick Law Olmsted, 15 September 1865, Olmsted Papers, Library of Congress.

FIVE

Ossian Cole Simonds

CONSERVATION ETHIC
IN THE PRAIRIE STYLE

Julia Sniderman Bachrach

A 1914 CIRCULAR PUBLISHED by the University of Illinois urged residents of the state to adopt a new landscape style for their own yards, neighborhood streets, and farms. It praised the work of two Chicago landscape gardeners, Ossian Cole Simonds and Jens Jensen, both of whom were inspired by the "true wonder and beauty" of the region's prairie setting.[1] Simonds and Jensen each held the powerful idea that the beauty of the Midwest's natural environment could be conveyed through designed landscapes, incorporating native plants and natural features. Although Jensen is now the better known of the two designers, Simonds was also pivotal in developing the Prairie style, and, in fact, his contribution actually predated Jensen's—he began gathering native plants for use in Chicago's Graceland Cemetery before Jensen had even emigrated to America from Denmark.

It was at Graceland, as designer and superintendent, that Simonds developed his fundamental landscape ideas, based on the principle of letting nature guide the design. There he laid out paths and drives in response to existing topography so that they encircled naturalistic lakes; burial areas were defined by swaths of native shrubs and trees. Monuments and markers were limited and sited carefully to avoid obscuring poetic views. Simonds used these same design principles to shape hundreds—possibly thousands—of roadways, campuses, golf courses, parks, estates, subdivisions, and other properties, in the Midwest and beyond. Throughout his career, Simonds advocated the use of indigenous plants. His subtly beautiful landscapes appeared to be the work of nature alone, untouched by human hands.

A leader in the profession, Simonds was among the eleven founding members of the American Society of Landscape Architects and the origina-

O. C. Simonds. (Courtesy of the Jens Jensen Collection in the archives at the Morton Arboretum, Lisle, Ill.)

tor of the four-year landscape architecture program at the University of Michigan, one of the first in the country. Underlying all of his work, as a designer and an educator, was a commitment to weaving a conservation ethic into landscape design.

O. C. Simonds was born in Grand Rapids, Michigan, in 1855. During his early childhood, he developed a deep love for nature while exploring the woods and fields of his father's farm. Reminiscing about his boyhood, he noted: "On this farm and throughout the adjacent country there was . . . a most interesting forest. I learned to love the woods with the beautiful flowers of many kinds, the undergrowth of shrubs and young trees, and the ground covering of ferns and flowers . . . I loved the springs and streams, I loved the open spaces that had been cleared for farms—the spaces that allowed us to see the sky, the clouds, the sun rises and sunsets. I loved the rolling country that allowed us to look across valleys to interesting forest sky lines and foliage covered borders."[2]

Simonds began professional training in civil engineering at the University of Michigan in 1874. Two years later, he shifted his concentration to ar-

View of Greenwood Avenue in Graceland Cemetery showing graceful grading of landforms along the road. (Courtesy of Graceland Cemetery, Chicago, Ill.)

chitecture so he could study under William Le Baron Jenney, the architect, engineer, and landscape designer who is now best known as the father of the skyscraper. Unfortunately, budget problems at the university resulted in the elimination of its architecture program; Jenney returned to his Chicago practice and Simonds continued his engineering studies. After graduating in 1878, the young aspiring architect moved to Chicago to work in his former professor's office.

At this time Jenney was commissioned to design an extension to Graceland Cemetery that comprised thirty-five acres of low-lying marsh and celery fields.[3] Jenney's plan included an artificial lake, Willowmere, to solve the site's drainage problems, and Simonds, with his considerable training in engineering, was charged with implementing it. As his first assignment in Jenney's office, Simonds was responsible for excavating the lake, installing drains, and laying out new roads.

The burial site was originally established in 1861 by Thomas Barbour Bryan, a prominent and civic-minded real estate speculator, who came to Chicago from Virginia to make his fortune. Bryan had purchased the eighty-six-acre site so he could inter his son properly.[4] He was familiar with the handful of naturalistic burial grounds which had been designed in other parts of the country and retained the services of William Saunders, the pioneering designer of Philadelphia's Laurel Hill Cemetery. Saunders was to collaborate with Swain Nelson, a local landscape gardener and nurseryman.[5] The cemetery was designed to emulate "a garden, where Grace, Beauty, and Light render the less somber the solemn associations of the tomb."[6]

By 1870 additional property had been acquired and another new plan was needed. Another famous landscape designer, Horace W. S. Cleveland, was hired to collaborate with Nelson on the expansion. Asserting that a crowded landscape with a "sombre and depressing character" would result were lot owners allowed to plant whatever they wanted, Cleveland suggested that the overall composition be considered to produce "the proper mingling of wood and lawn."[7] The full extent of Cleveland's involvement at Graceland Cemetery is not known, yet his ideas clearly shaped the context in which Simonds was first introduced to landscape gardening.

The final parcel at Graceland—the extension that Jenney was retained to design—had been acquired by 1879. Jenney was hired by Bryan's nephew and namesake, Bryan Lathrop, a prominent real estate speculator and philanthropist. The Graceland project proved to be the most influential of Simonds's career, not least because it nurtured his lasting friendship with Lathrop, who became an important colleague and patron.[8] According to Simonds, his work with Lathrop at Graceland provided his real education in landscape gardening.[9]

Lathrop had convinced Simonds that landscape gardening was the "rarest and greatest" as well as the "least understood or appreciated" of the fine arts.[10] Following his mentor's suggestion, Simonds read voraciously A. J. Downing's journal, *The Horticulturalist,* works by Frederick Law Olmsted Sr., and writings of the English landscape school. These studies further deepened Simonds's affinity with nature, which he had begun to develop as a child.

Lathrop also took Simonds to see other important cemeteries and parks. In Cincinnati, Ohio, Simonds met the venerable Adolph Strauch, superintendent of Spring Grove Cemetery. "The charm of Spring Grove," Simonds observed, "was due to its beautiful graded surfaces, its broad open spaces, its simple groups of trees, often with branches sweeping to the ground, its border plantations of shrubbery and its lakes margined with foliage."[11] Simonds received direct instruction from Strauch on ingenious methods to achieve gently curving grades and drives. In addition to explaining his technical methods, the master designer impressed Simonds with the importance of making finishing touches "on the ground," in a manner like "that of the sculptor."[12] Simonds recommended this on-site design process himself in later years, because, he explained, the landscape "must look right when the grade is finished," as Strauch had emphasized, "and the only way to determine that is by using the eye-sight."[13] Simonds's position as superintendent of Graceland aided in this process, giving him detailed field knowledge of the landscape, just as the position at Spring Grove had for Strauch.

Simonds was also influenced by design techniques and tenets of other leading landscape designers. He learned the vocabulary of serene lagoons, winding paths, irregular masses of plantings, and spaces carved from vegetation introduced in Olmsted and Vaux's 1858 Greensward plan for Central Park, New York. (These same techniques were also adapted by Jenney in his 1870 plans for Chicago's West Parks.) Simonds had "drunk deep of the spirit" of Olmsted, and this inspiration went beyond the use of specific design elements.[14] Olmsted Sr. was concerned not only with aesthetic effects but also with psychological responses to his landscapes. Similarly, Simonds believed that cemeteries should be comforting places for the living. Natural landscapes had healing and consoling powers, and he wanted cemeteries to emanate the same "charm which we feel when we go to the woods, . . . the pine forest," and "uncultivated prairies which glow with wild sunflowers, asters and goldenrod."[15]

During Simonds's early years at Graceland, Lathrop afforded him important opportunities for experimentation and the freedom to explore his own ideas. Lathrop's enlightened policies also fostered new and creative design solutions. When the Graceland Cemetery Association began to plan the extension, for example, Lathrop insisted on large lots that would allow for artistic effects and also provide space for naturalistic planting compositions.[16]

His belief that nature was the "greatest teacher" led to the most significant of Simonds's early experiments at Graceland—the use of indigenous plants.[17] In 1880, with Lathrop's encouragement, Simonds began transplanting common Illinois trees and shrubs such as oak, maple, ash, hornbeam, witch hazel, dogwood, and sheepberry to the site. He came to believe that there were "few localities" that lacked the necessary plants "for the most advanced landscape designing" and was often seen "scouring the neighborhood for suitable plants and trees."[18] Simonds's ideas were atypical at a time when enthusiasm for new and exotic flora was widespread, and most people considered native plants invasive weeds. Many visitors to Graceland even assumed that Simonds had used indigenous plants there simply because they were the only things that would grow in the difficult soil.[19]

Although Simonds continued to experiment with materials transplanted from the wild and later began buying native shrubs and trees from nurserymen, he did not entirely exclude exotic materials from his designs. In fact, in one article, he suggested that non-native shrubs and flowering plants— such as forsythia, honeysuckle, lilacs, and roses—"should be used in abundance."[20]

Natural landscapes provided Simonds not only with "tangible raw material" but with "design inspiration" as well.[21] He shunned the practice of dotting the lawn with shrubs in an artificial way, which he believed weakened the artistic effect; at Graceland, trees and shrubs were planted in large groups as they appear in nature. He minimized tree and shrub trimming, suggesting instead that "foliage should meet the lawn," "no attempt should be made to grow grass underneath the branches," and fallen leaves should not be raked.[22] Simonds also believed there should be as few roads in the cemetery as possible. He advocated the removal of fences, borders, and railings as well as the substitution of grass for paved walks.

Moreover, Simonds believed, headstones and monuments had the potential to mar the landscape: "It is in the selection of [them] that we exhibit our weakness, and our lack of appreciation of real beauty. Occasionally there will be a monument which is truly artistic, such as is seen in the work of Augustus Saint-Gaudens, of Daniel French or Lorado Taft. Sometimes even the humblest monuments will have good, unpretentious lines but too often they are meaningless blocks of stone." He asserted that the whole custom of erecting family monuments was "curious."[23] Lathrop's memorial to a family member, a fifty-year-old elm "of exceptional grace and dignity" selected from the woods, seemed to him far more appropriate than one constructed in stone and bronze. In the end, a parklike cemetery with inconspicuous stones was "a fitting monument for all buried within its enclosure."[24]

In an effort to protect the integrity of the landscape design, the Graceland Cemetery Association designated one section for burials without monuments and established a design review process to be administered by Simonds. This process, later called the Court of Appeals, afforded Simonds the opportunity to review all plans for monuments and family plots. In addition to the architectural elements, site plans and planting designs prepared by other landscape architects were subject to Simonds's scrutiny. "Rules for Stonework at Graceland Cemetery" governed the review process and provided a model for smaller cemeteries elsewhere.[25]

Simonds's work at Graceland earned him a national reputation as "dean of cemetery design."[26] Between 1883 and 1888 he worked full time as the superintendent there and saw many of his most important design ideas realized. After 1888 Simonds began to take on independent consulting work. His first job appears to have been done as a favor to his friends William Holabird and Martin Roche, who had been hired to design Fort Sheridan, the military installation north of Chicago. Simonds was commissioned to create a site plan for the 640-acre project. A heavily wooded property fronting Lake Michigan, the site provided Simonds another laboratory for developing his nascent design ideas.

The plan had to include a parade ground for military drills, but rather than making a stiff and formal one, Simonds created a meadow that "extended back from the wooded bluff" with a natural ravine as its border. He laid out a scenic drive along the bottom of another of the site's ravines. Looped and truncated drives through the residential district along the lake afforded natural vistas, and incorporated the simple brick and stone officers' housing as part of a whole composition. An early architectural review noted: "The location and surroundings are so picturesque that their simplicity . . . only adds charm to the effect."[27]

By the late 1890s, Simonds was an active member of several organizations devoted to saving natural areas and acquiring and beautifying urban open spaces. His professional services were increasingly in demand, and his commissions included several prominent parks and estates in Illinois. In 1903 he formed O. C. Simonds and Company, which operated out of a Buena Avenue office located in the cemetery. That same year he was also appointed consulting landscape gardener to Chicago's Lincoln Park.

Originally a cemetery, Lincoln Park had been designed by Swain Nelson, the nurseryman and gardener who had also been involved in the early development of Graceland. Bryan Lathrop and a colleague, Francis T. Simmons, brought their prodigious efforts to bear on Lincoln Park with ambitious plans for improvement and expansion. By the turn of the century, the park covered approximately 275 acres. During Simonds's first year as consultant, he was asked to plan an extension into Lake Michigan which nearly doubled the park's acreage. Soon after this project was under way, he began working on an even larger extension. Lathrop spearheaded the effort to add approximately one thousand acres to the park and extend its boundary to Chicago's northern limits. Simonds's plan included a waterway to allow boats to enter at Belmont Harbor, traverse the inner canal, and reenter the lake at Devon Avenue, the park's northern boundary. Although formally adopted by the board of commissioners in 1912, the plan was never realized.[28]

In addition to his work on the new extensions, Simonds also redesigned some of Lincoln Park's older sections. Despite pressure to accommodate the growing interest in active recreation during this period, he remained true to his intent to "produce the quiet sylvan conditions so much needed and desired by city dwellers."[29] This he achieved by rerouting some of the tightly winding paths and screening the architecture and busy streets within the park. Simonds did, in fact, manage to find ways to integrate facilities for special interest groups without compromising the design. When a rowing club petitioned for a boathouse in 1908, for example, he sited the structure in an embankment camouflaged with native plants.

Simonds warned authorities about the effect that the encroachment of zoo buildings would have but conceded that "if additional buildings in the area would be low and dark in color, and have a setting of trees and shrubbery, the injury to the general scenery to the park would not be great."[30] Even Cafe Brauer, a large park restaurant built by Prairie School architect Dwight H. Perkins, was designed to blend into the setting. The low, curving loggias of the red-brick structure embraced a naturalistic lagoon and was heavily screened with masses of vegetation.

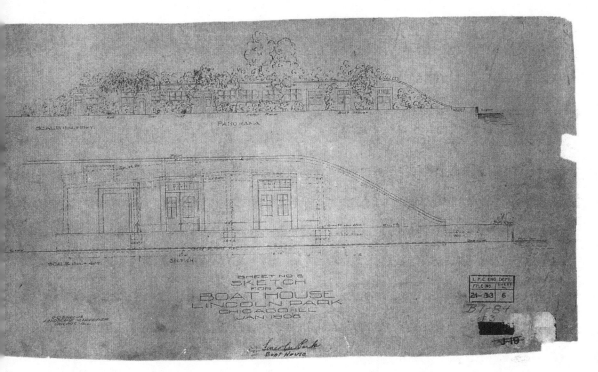

Section and panorama prepared by Simonds for a boathouse in Lincoln Park, 1908. (Courtesy of the Chicago Park District Special Collections, Chicago, Ill.)

Many details regarding Simonds's Lincoln Park projects are not known, but a 1907 newspaper account suggests that he used indigenous plants in naturalistic settings throughout the park. An observer in the *Evening Post* noted that more flowers of "native fragrance" had been planted than ever before; a "visitor who has seen the country or who has walked in an American home garden will not need a botanical text-book to give him the name of the plants that he finds blossoming."[31] This article remarked on the inspiration of Lake Michigan and Simonds's creation of views and vistas of this dramatic natural feature.

Simonds shaped views by carving spaces from existing vegetation and relying on natural topography. His meadows emphasized either broad or long views, two types of spaces particularly suited to a midwestern setting. The broad view, conveyed through large horizontal meadows, "was an attempt to capture some of the openness or feeling of infinity that marked the original" prairie landscape. The long view was created by a narrow corridor leading toward "a hazy ridge or misty piece of the woods," or to a dramatic scene, such as the setting or rising sun.[32] The linear shape of Lincoln Park led Simonds to emphasize long views there.

In much of Simonds's other work, inspiration came from existing features of the unimproved sites. He believed that preserving and restoring natural scenery was especially important in parks, which were, after all, places for "rest, recuperation and undisturbed contemplation of the beauties of

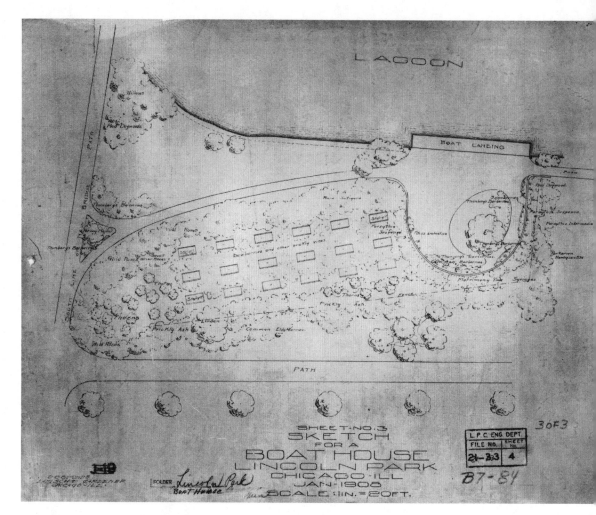

Planting plan by Simonds for a boat landing area in Lincoln Park, 1908. (Courtesy of the Chicago Park District Special Collections, Chicago, Ill.)

nature."[33] This sensitivity toward the value of natural features is particularly evident in his park designs for Quincy, Illinois, where he worked for many years.

After the retirement of H. W. S. Cleveland, Simonds became the consultant for the Boulevard and Park Association of Quincy, where from 1895 until 1912 or later he designed at least eight parks and oversaw landscape management for the system.[34] In the Quincy projects Simonds found sites with extraordinary natural attributes and was given a wide latitude for artistic expression. Creative support came from Edward J. Parker, president of the association, who had also served as an early president of the American Park and Outdoor Art Association.

Parker and Simonds appreciated the dramatic topography of the bluffs, ravines, and Mississippi River shoreline of Quincy's park sites, but not all community members shared their enthusiasm. In 1894, when the association

Quincy, Illinois, railroad yards and the Mississippi River as seen from Riverview Park. An early (1893) design for Riverview Park was drawn by H. W. S. Cleveland and his son Ralph. Simonds designed an addition to the park in 1895. (Courtesy of William H. Tishler)

sought to purchase a river bluff parcel of land that included ancient Indian mounds, there was resistance from city council members who considered the site inappropriate for a park. While acknowledging the location's magnificent views, they suggested that the "ground was barren with deep gullies which would require expensive bridges; the soil was poor, no grass nor trees would grow there."[35] Simonds, however, encouraged the acquisition; the land was, he affirmed, "the best natural site I have seen for a long time. It would make an ideal scenic park of the city. Three thousand dollars? Why, Chicago would give half a million dollars or any other sum of money for a glorious possibility like that. The Indian Mounds, or Sacred Heights, are superior to those anywhere else in your entire system. A genuine Indian Mound in a metropolitan park would have a greater attraction than all the zoological gardens, or all the artificial lakes, or all the monuments that could be crossed into it." To his delight, the land was finally purchased and his 1897 plan implemented. In later years, he remarked that he wished it were possible to transport Indian Mounds Park around the nation "as a sample of what can be done in the development of an unpromising piece of land, at a minimum expense— with native flora and other inexpensive planting."[36]

The Quincy park projects offered the sort of design opportunities Simonds preferred: expansive landscapes where natural attributes could be preserved and existing vegetation could be retained and enhanced with masses of indigenous plants. Dramatic topography could be subtly contrasted

South Park, one of the Quincy, Illinois, parks designed by Simonds. (Courtesy of William H. Tishler)

with gentle grades and drives. Large horizontal meadows could convey broad views—corridor spaces along ravines and creeks could offer long views. Because Quincy's parks emphasized passive rather than active recreation, few structures were required.

But even when landscape projects required buildings (residential estates or subdivisions, for example) Simonds treated them as though they were parks. Further, he believed that the landscape gardener's role in designing "home grounds" should include teaching the client "an appreciation of the beauty of nature."[37] At the Hibbard estate in Winnetka, Illinois, Simonds carved spaces from the existing vegetation to create outdoor rooms. Several different "outdoor salons or sylvan living-rooms" melted one into another, "leading from the house to the country through flowering glades, and returning to the house by woodland trails."[38]

Large estates gave Simonds an opportunity to preserve natural scenery on a grander scale even than urban parks. A premier example is the Governor Lowden estate, also known as Sinissippi Farm, in Oregon, Illinois. The 4,600-acre site, located on a bend of the Rock River, was considered "one of the most dramatic spots on the great plains," according to the well-known writer Wilhelm Miller, who described the estate in *Country Life in America*. It included an "honest self-supporting prairie farm, plus what the English call a 'park,' i.e., an ornamental part which . . . is quiet and enduring—not showy and temporary." Here, Simonds took care not only to preserve natural features but to utilize them to achieve the greatest impact with views and vistas. By connecting the house to the river, woods, and ridges, through an "organic system of drives," he created a series of changing views, which offered enticing glimpses of the river through fringes of the woods rather than allowing it to be seen from all angles. (One of Simonds's tenets was that "a glimpse is usually better than the whole thing.")[39] The Lowden estate farm was surrounded by broad horizontal meadows. Unlike utilitarian structures on farms of the East Coast, which were "scattered about in a showy way," the Lowden farm buildings were sited "to nestle among the woods and gentle hills."[40]

Simonds's ability to group buildings in such a way as to enhance the existing landscape became something of a trademark and can be seen clearly in his plans for four adjacent family estates in Winnetka, Illinois. Simonds was jointly retained by the families of the four estates to design the parcels as one landscape, which would allow each owner to "multiply their grounds by four." The houses had been built on a ridge overlooking a "steep bank,

Simonds's diagram of four residences on a Lake Michigan ridge. (Reprinted from Miller, "How to Multiply Your Grounds by Four," 35)

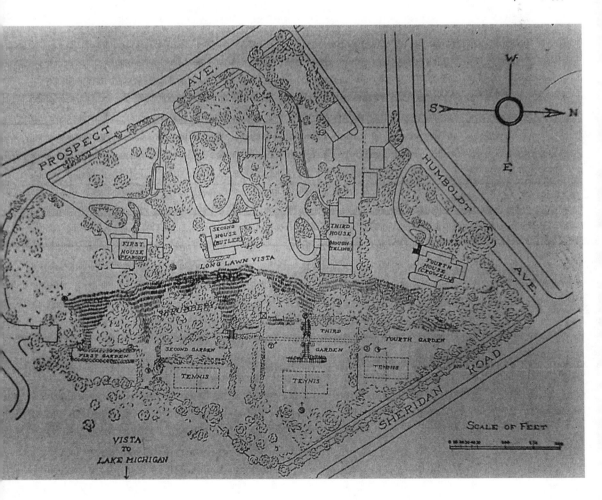

which is clothed with shrubbery, except where openings have been made for vistas of lake and gardens." In Simonds's design each family's garden occupied a roomlike space and was connected to the others by a walk. The plan was considered a model project: "artistic" while "nature-like," having "shut out dust, germs, noise, unsightly objects and curiosity seekers."[41]

Much of Simonds's residential work has not yet been documented, but in 1915 Wilhelm Miller claimed that Chicago's "whole 'North Shore' show[ed] his influence in home grounds."[42] Simonds's client list included such prominent Chicagoans as Cyrus McCormick, Laverne Noyes, Joy Morton, and Charles Dawes, vice president during Calvin Coolidge's administration. Simonds also designed private estates in Wichita, Indianapolis, Ann Arbor, Akron, Locust Valley, Long Island, and Huntsville, Alabama. His impact was felt on a larger scale as well. He created town plans for Kincaid, Illinois, and for a summer community in York Harbor Hills, Maine, where Simonds himself was the developer. Park projects included commissions for Dixon, Springfield, and Kankakee, Illinois; Madison, Wisconsin; Terre Haute, Indiana; Hannibal, Missouri; and Menominee, Michigan. He also created the Nichols Arboretum at the University of Michigan and the Morton Arboretum in Lisle, Illinois. And he designed several campus projects, among them Iowa State and Michigan State universities and the University of Maryland.

Simonds was a prominent member of several influential organizations that were committed to saving and improving landscapes on a national level. He was a member as well of the Association of American Cemetery Superintendents, a forum of administrators of the nation's best-known naturalistic cemeteries which met annually to share ideas and information on management policies, planning, and design. It was a unique exchange that clearly contributed to the momentum of the nascent landscape design movement in late nineteenth-century America. Simonds also served as treasurer of the American Park and Outdoor Art Association and was a member of its Rural Design Committee, which focused on conserving country roads and streams. The association inspired the formation of the American Society of Landscape Architects in 1899, of which Simonds was a founding member and president, in 1913.

The Progressive era dawned at the turn of the century as awareness of the dire effects of industrialization prompted movement for reform. Simonds was involved in many city and regional groups organized to improve and beautify Chicago's urban landscape and to preserve surrounding undeveloped rural land. As president of the Chicago Tree Planting Society and board member of the Illinois Out-door Improvement Association, he initiated programs to inspire greater appreciation of natural beauty.

One of Simonds's most significant volunteer efforts in Chicago was with the Special Park Commission, established in 1899 by Mayor Carter Harrison.

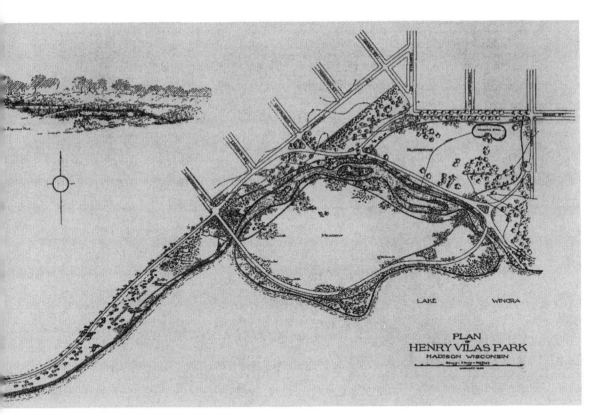

Simonds's plan for
Henry Vilas Park on
Lake Wingra in Madi-
son, Wisconsin. This was
one of several parks in
that city planned by
Simonds. (Reprinted
from *Report of the
Officers of the Madison
Park and Pleasure Drive
Association, 1905* [Madi-
son, Wis., 1905], 32)

This quasi-governmental agency was formed to make comprehensive assess-
ments of the adequacy of existing city parks and playgrounds and to create
additional open spaces. At the time, Chicago's pleasure grounds were located
on its outskirts and no new parks had been established for thirty years, despite the city's burgeoning population. Jane Addams and other settlement
house workers had launched a campaign to create playgrounds, but these
reformers were successful in developing only a small number of such spaces.
Serving on the small parks subcommittee, Simonds was responsible for in-
specting potential sites for new playgrounds on the north side.[43] Simonds's
recommendations were included in a major report in 1904. Written by the
architect Dwight Perkins, the report put forward an expansion program that
comprised not only new inner-city parks and playgrounds but an outer zone
of thousands of acres of conservation lands, now the Cook County Forest
Preserves. Jens Jensen, who had been appointed to the Special Park Commission after Simonds, contributed a sophisticated study of the native flora of
this region which reflected his deep knowledge of indigenous plant communities and was important to the evolution of the Prairie style of landscape
architecture.[44]

It is curious that Jensen's legacy has received considerable scholarly and
popular attention, but Simonds's pivotal role in the development of the

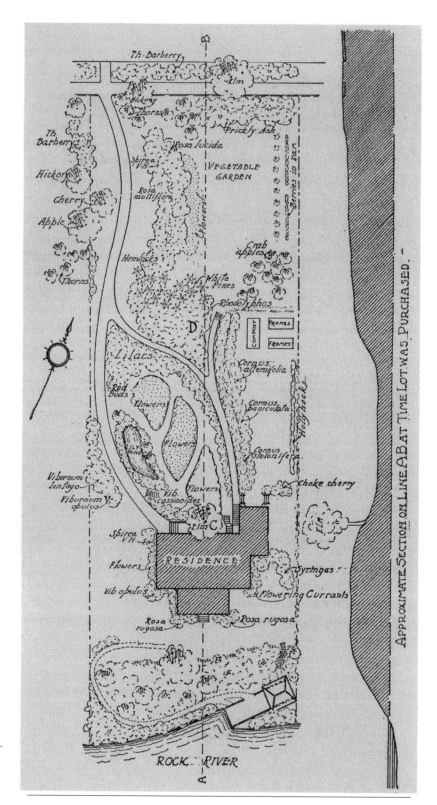

Layout for a medium-size residence and section of site at the "time lot was purchased." (Reprinted from Simonds, *Landscape-Gardening*, 164)

A "naked and defense-less" home compared with a dwelling that is "clothed and protected" with shrubs, vines, and flowers. (Reprinted from Simonds, *Landscape-Gardening,* 54)

Prairie style has largely been overlooked. One reason for Jensen's promi-nence—and Simonds's eclipse—is traceable to the the books written by each of the two men toward the end of their careers. Coupled with scores of other written and photographic documents, *Siftings* provides insight into Jensen's design intent for specific projects. In it, Jensen articulated a spiritual mani-festo for prairie-inspired design and the preservation of natural areas; the text reads almost like a philosophical guide. By contrast, Simonds's book, *Land-scape-Gardening,* strikes a more pedestrian tone in the down-to-earth advice it offers. Simonds does not spell out his design philosophies, and references to his projects tend to be too vague to be useful in documenting his work.

Given the particularly ephemeral nature of the style in which both men worked, it is not surprising that their design legacies would be difficult to discern from what little remains of their landscapes.[45]

Yet there is no question of O. C. Simonds's widespread and enduring influence: at one time, examples of his work could be found in every state.[46] And, though the "prairie spirit" fostered a stronger regional movement in the Midwest than has been documented elsewhere, Simonds may well have influenced other regional styles. Ossian Cole Simonds's simple desire to "make our country more beautiful" resulted in projects that place him among the most significant figures in the history of American landscape architecture.[47]

Notes

1. Wilhelm Miller, The "Illinois Way" of Beautifying the Farm, circular 170 (Urbana: University of Illinois Agricultural Experiment Station, 1914); Jens Jensen, "From a Country Window," Country Life in America 26 (May 1914), 48.

2. Quoted in Marshall G. Simonds, "Simonds's Principles of Cemetery Design," Modern Cemetery 4, no. 11 (1936), 155.

3. Ossian Cole Simonds, "Graceland at Chicago," American Landscape Architecture 6 (January 1932), 12.

4. John Eifler and Associates, Graceland Cemetery Historical Report (Chicago: Eifler and Associates, 1992), 4.

5. Nelson was also the original designer of Lincoln Park four years later. See Julia Sniderman, Bart Ryckbosch, and Laura Taylor, "Lincoln Park," in National Register of Historic Places Registration Form (Washington, D.C.: Department of the Interior, National Park Service, 1994). The original landscape plan for Lincoln Park is in the collections of the Chicago Historical Society. Saunders came to Chicago, inspected the site and determined that it was "admirably adapted" to cemetery purposes. Office of Graceland Cemetery, Charter of the Graceland Cemetery with the Rules and Regulations of the Company (Chicago, 1861).

6. Office of Graceland Cemetery, Statement of the Condition, Property, and Franchises of the Graceland Cemetery Co. (Chicago, 1872), quoted in John Vinci, "Graceland: The Nineteenth-Century Garden Cemetery," Chicago History 6 (Summer 1977), 88.

7. Office of Graceland Cemetery, Catalogue of the Graceland Cemetery Lot Owners (Chicago, 1870), 11–12.

8. An understanding between Lathrop and Jenney apparently allowed Simonds and another young architect in the office, William Holabird, to establish their own firm in 1880, taking the Graceland commission with them. After Simonds was appointed superintendent of Graceland Cemetery, he had less time to devote to the struggling architectural partnership with Holabird. To make ends meet, Holabird had accepted a position as chief clerk in the office of his father, Samuel B. Holabird, quartermaster of the U.S. Army. These added commitments, and the fact that both men had more experience in engineering than architecture, led to the addition of a third partner, who had also come from Jenney's office, Martin Roche. By 1883 Simonds's attention was fully absorbed by his Graceland work. With Lathrop's encouragement he resigned from the firm of Holabird, Simonds and Roche to devote his career exclusively to landscape gardening. (The firm continued as Holabird and Roche and, later, as Holabird and Root, which is still in business today.) See Robert Bruegmann, Holabird and Roche/Holabird and Root: An Illustrated Catalogue of Works,

1880–1940 (New York: Garland, 1991), and Edward A. Renwick, "Recollections" (unpublished manuscript, 1932; Chicago Park District Special Collections).

9. Simonds, "Graceland at Chicago,"12.

10. Ossian Cole Simonds, *Landscape-Gardening* (New York: Macmillan, 1920), dedication.

11. Ossian Cole Simonds, "The Planning and Administration of a Landscape Cemetery," *Country Life in America* 4 (September 1903), 350.

12. Ossian Cole Simonds, "The Grading of Cemeteries," *Park and Cemetery* 18 (November 1908), 447.

13. Ibid.

14. Wilhelm Miller, *The Prairie Spirit in Landscape Gardening,* University of Illinois Agricultural Experiment Station Circular, no. 184 (Urbana, 1915), 2.

15. Ossian Cole Simonds, "Nature in the Cemetery," *Park and Cemetery* 35 (October 1925), 208.

16. Ossian Cole Simonds, "Notes on Graceland," *American Landscape Architecture* 2 (May 1930), 9. "The members of the board shook their heads," Simonds reported, "but finally consented."

17. Ossian Cole Simonds, "How to Develop Beauty and Seclusion in Cemetery Design," *Park and Cemetery* 41 (July 1931), 144.

18. "Marginal Planting," *Park and Cemetery* 9 (October 1899), 174.

19. A review of Graceland reveals the attitude toward landscape typical of the time, noting that it would "compare favorably with any rural cemetery in the country; even if common hardy plants for the north have been freely used in the planting." Edgar Sanders, "Trees and Shrubs That Do Well at Graceland Cemetery, Chicago," *Modern Cemetery* 2, no. 10 (1892), 112.

20. Ossian Cole Simonds, "The Use of Shrubs in Cemeteries," *Park and Cemetery* 10 (October 1900), 177.

21. Frances Copley Seavey, "Fall at Graceland, Chicago" *Modern Cemetery* 4, no. 11 (1895), 124.

22. Simonds, "Use of Shrubs," 177.

23. Ossian Cole Simonds, "Art in the Modern Cemetery," *Park and Cemetery* 22 (September 1912), 166.

24. Ossian Cole Simonds,"Moving Large Trees," *Modern Cemetery* 1, no. 4 (1891), 52; Simonds, "Nature in the Cemetery," 209.

25. Simonds, "Notes on Graceland," 9; Simonds, "Simonds's Principles of Cemetery Design," 155; Ossian Cole Simonds, "Rules for Stonework at Graceland Cemetery," *Modern Cemetery* 1, no. 7 (1891), xx.

Plans filed in the Graceland Cemetery Archives illuminate this process. For instance, on a blueprint for the mausoleum of Mrs. R. T. Crane Jr., Simonds wrote: "approved if lot is made wider." Office of John Russell Pope, "Mausoleum for Mrs. R. T. Crane Jr.," blueprint of plan and elevations, n.d.

26. Robert E. Grese, "Ossian Cole Simonds," in *American Landscape Architecture: Designers and Places,* ed. W. H. Tishler (Washington, D.C.: Preservation Press, 1989), 74.

27. Jenkins, "Holabird and Roche," 29.

28. By the 1890s the Lincoln Park administration had become plagued with political corruption. In 1902 Bryan Lathrop and Francis T. Simmons, both progressive businessmen, were appointed to the Board of Commissioners as part of a reform campaign. One of their first efforts was to recruit Simonds. During Lathrop and Simmons's tenure on the board, Simonds succeeded in implementing a major landfill addition as well as several planting designs for the park. When political turmoil resulted in the resignations of Lathrop and Simmons in 1913, Simonds's position was eliminated. Four years later Simmons was reappointed to the board and elected as its president, and Simonds was

rehired as consulting landscape gardener. He continued to serve in this capacity until 1921, when Simmons died and the position was eliminated once again.

29. Ossian Cole Simonds, "Landscape Gardening and Forestry," in *Annual Report of the Commissioners of Lincoln Park for the Year 1908* (Chicago: Lincoln Park Commission, 1909), 27.

30. Ossian Cole Simonds, "The Problem of the Zoo," report presented to the board, in *Official Proceedings of the Board of Commissioners of Lincoln Park,* 8 March 1911, 16–18.

31. Edward B. Clark, "Formality Ousted in Improvements in Northern Park," *Chicago Evening Post,* 6 April 1907, 1–2.

32. Robert E. Grese, "The Prairie Gardens of O. C. Simonds and Jens Jensen," paper presented at Dumbarton Oaks Symposium on Regional Garden Design, Washington, D.C., 17–18 May 1991 (Dumbarton Oaks Research Library and Collections), 13; Miller, *Prairie Spirit,* 18.

33. Ossian Cole Simonds, "Landscape Design in Public Parks," *Park and Cemetery* 19 (June 1909), 52.

34. A plan for the Quincy Boulevard and Park Association developed by Simonds and his then partner, J. Roy West, in 1931, the year of Simonds's death, indicates that his involvement with Quincy's parks continued through his lifetime. The plan is currently on file with the Quincy Park District in Quincy.

35. Elizabeth Parker, *History of the Park System of Quincy, Illinois, 1888 to 1917* (Quincy: Boulevard and Park Association, 1917), 43.

36. Ibid., 46, 48.

37. Simonds, *Landscape-Gardening,* 151.

38. Wilhelm Miller, "A Series of Outdoor Salons," *Country Life in America* 25 (April 1914), 39.

39. Quoted in Miller, *Illinois Way,* 5.

40. Wilhelm Miller, "A New Kind of Western Home," *Country Life in America* 23 (April 1913), 39–41.

41. Wilhelm Miller, "How to Multiply Your Grounds by Four," *Country Life in America* 22 (August 1912), 34–36.

42. Miller, *Prairie Spirit* 2.

43. "Seek New Small Parks: Commissioners Start Inspection of Possible Sights," *Chicago Tribune,* 3 November 1901.

44. Dwight Heald Perkins, *Report of the Special Park Commission to the City Council of Chicago on the Subject of a Metropolitan Park System* (Chicago: Special Park Commission, 1905).

45. Jens Jensen, *Siftings* (1939; Baltimore: Johns Hopkins University Press, 1990.

One reason for Simonds's current obscurity could be his own modesty: humble in his lectures and writing, he took little credit for what could have been considered prominent commissions. In addition, materials related to his designs are limited and scattered; according to Mara Geldbloom, Simonds's papers at the Buena Avenue office and the Nichols Arboretum were "needlessly destroyed." "Ossian Simonds: Prairie Spirit in Landscape Gardening," *Prairie School Review* 12, no. 2 (1975), 7–8. I did have access to the Graceland Cemetery Archives and found some relevant materials there.

46. Grese, "Prairie Gardens," 2.

47. Simonds, *Landscape-Gardening,* 1.

SIX

George Edward Kessler

LANDSCAPE ARCHITECT OF THE AMERICAN RENAISSANCE

Kurt Culbertson

OVER THE COURSE of his forty-one-year career George Edward Kessler (1862–1923) completed more than two hundred projects in places as farflung as Shanghai, New York, and Mexico City. Kessler began his work as a landscape architect when the new vocation had but a handful of practitioners, Frederick Law Olmsted among them. But while the designs of Olmsted and his early colleagues were having a strong impact in many parts of the country, landscape architecture was virtually unknown in the cities of the Mississippi River valley. Kessler would come to play an important role in the development of city form and urban open spaces in this vast, rapidly changing region.

Kessler's life and work embodies the spirit of the American Renaissance. His image of the City Beautiful combined European influences with the American landscape in a unique blend of Old and New World qualities. Kessler's projects did not always effectively address underlying social needs, yet many proved both influential and enduring. His legacy of magnificent parks, boulevards, and gardens still delights millions of city residents throughout the Midwest. The cityscapes of Dallas, Houston, Kansas City, St. Louis, Denver, Cincinnati, Indianapolis, and a score of other locations bear witness to Kessler's talent.

George Kessler was born on 16 July 1862 in the small village of Bad Frankenhausen in Germany. Three years later, when social and economic unrest erupted during Bismarck's rise to power, Kessler, his mother Clotilde, his merchant father Edward Carl, and his sister Antoine emigrated to the United

George E. Kessler.
(Courtesy of the Kansas
City, Missouri, Parks and
Recreation Archives)

States, living first in Hoboken, New Jersey, then in St. Louis and Hannibal, Missouri, and Wisconsin, before settling in Dallas, Texas, a young town of about 5,000 inhabitants.[1] When George's father died in 1878, his mother returned to Germany with her two children.

Kessler entered a private school for landscape gardening at the Belvedere in Weimar, the thousand-year-old city of Goethe, Schiller, and Liszt, and the center of German literary heritage. The change from Dallas must have been startling. Under hofgartner Julius Hartwig and garteninspector Julius Sckell, he learned botany, forestry, and design. At Belvedere's Neue Garten and the gardens of the adjacent San Souci Palace, Kessler could study firsthand the work of Peter Josef Lenné, the most famous of all German landscape architects. He also studied briefly at the Gaertner Lehr Anstalt, the school of garden design founded by Lenné.[2]

Kessler's mentor, Julius Sckell, had built a strong reputation by introducing the English style, then sweeping the continent, into new designs for the region's palace gardens. Unlike Capability Brown, however, who tended to eliminate all traces of formality in his designs, Sckell sometimes retained naturalistic elements, which he integrated with formal ones, in this way achieving a pleasant balance.

As part of his landscape education, Kessler also toured central and western Europe and southern England, where the grand boulevards of Haussmann's Paris and the great English parks such as Birkenhead were likely attractions. The young artist was profoundly moved by the work of Pückler-Muskau, the German prince, who between 1828 and 1845 had created a beautiful park in the English style on his ancestral grounds at Muskau.[3] This vast estate comprised not only the Pückler-Muskau ancestral forest but several ancient villages that the prince retained as integral elements of the area's history and sense of place. Pückler-Muskau well understood the powerful effect of the outward reach of space and laid out drives to provide sequential glimpses of the chief points of interest—riveting sight lines and great pastoral spaces.[4] The flowing road system tied the entire scheme together, while the park's valley controlled the skyline and provided a sense of cohesion and inward focus. These same design devices would later appear in Kessler's landscapes.

The years immediately following the Centennial of 1876 found the United States intensely preoccupied with national identity. The frontier was closed, and the country had emerged as a world power. Proud of their accomplishments, Americans sought an outlet for nationalist feelings. Many identified with the European Renaissance and believed that its spirit had been captured again in the United States. In the words of one historian, "The civilization envisioned for America was a public life, one of the street, the park, the square or the mall, of large monuments, memorials, and public buildings in the eternal style, adorned with murals and sculptures personifying heroes and symbolizing virtue and enterprise."[5] Who was better prepared to respond to the needs of this time, particularly in the American heartland, than someone fresh from the Continent and schooled in classical European design?

Early in 1882 Kessler sailed to New York, where he spent several months working at LeMoult's, a florist and nursery in the Bowery.[6] While in the city, Kessler wrote to Olmsted, enclosing samples of his work and asking for employment. Olmsted's unencouraging response provides insight into his own sense of the profession and its objectives.

> Your study and practice so far as indicated has been too much limited to small pleasure ground work in which consistent broad effects of natural landscapes are out of the question. The only illustration of what I regard as the higher field of landscape gardening is that which you refer of the work of Puckler Muskau, which I wish much that I had seen. I don't wish to sound disrespectful of pleasure ground and home garden work such as is nearly always called for near a house and which always give much gainful employment to gardeners but only to urge you to be ambitious to be master in higher fields, as to which you can learn or likely to be open to you. Take any of these therefore as means of living and make yourself as perfect as possible in all that you can learn in nature, but by reading and reflection and such excursions as you can afford for enjoyment of natural scenery educate yourself about nature. For the purpose a day's walk along the rolling of any stream or any of the

foothills of any mountain range would be much more to you than a year in the park. I do not mean to advise you to neglect study of improved scenery. There are various places in the Hudson, Hyde Park, laid out by Dr. Hosack, for example, in which magnificent nature gains by foregrounds of art. You will find most referred to in Downing's Landscape Gardening. But bear always in mind that landscape gardening has natural scenery and to conceive art as its highest aim, and that while we are more qualified for work of this higher kind, there are thousands in competition for the lower kind.[7]

Although Olmsted did not offer Kessler a job, he did write a letter of recognition for the young landscape architect which led to a position with the railroad in Merriam, Johnson County, Kansas.[8] Kessler's first work as the railway's station grounds superintendent was to develop a pleasure park, designed to entice Kansas City, Missouri, residents to take a train ride for a day in the countryside across the Missouri River. The position also gave Kessler the opportunity to design railroad stations for the emerging small towns of the Great Plains—Springfield, Nichols Junction, Monett, Thayer, and Hannibal in Missouri, and Pleasanton and Alma in Kansas. Kessler often incorporated floral schemes that spelled out the community's name with accompanying stars and ornamental motifs, a feature that boosted enthusiasm for other civic improvements in the developing regions.

Kessler's work at Merriam was immensely popular and brought additional commissions. The 1887 design of Hyde Park, a Kansas City subdivision, attracted the attention of Jarvis and Conklin, a management firm in that city which was developing Roland Park, a residential subdivision outside of Baltimore. By May 1891 Kessler had been selected topographical and landscape engineer for the project. His plan for the first phase of Roland Park emphasized natural features with gently curving roads that followed existing contours. The firm of Olmsted Brothers was hired to complete later phases of the development, but it was Kessler's original plan that established the character of the project.

Two subsequent designs for residential subdivisions (both undertaken for Jarvis and Conklin), Euclid Heights in Cleveland and a project in Ogden, Utah, further enhanced Kessler's reputation.[9] Together with numerous residences in Kansas City, this work set the stage for his most important project for his adopted hometown. In October 1893 Kessler presented a sweeping plan to the Kansas City park board. It was, in many respects, as bold a vision of the City Beautiful as the World's Columbian Exposition held that year in Chicago. Kessler's plan preserved stream corridors and river bluffs and joined its parks with a continuous open space system of boulevards and parkways.

The notion of a system of parks linked by boulevards was not without precedent. Olmsted and Vaux, in their 1871 design for the South Parks in Chicago, had linked Jackson and Washington Parks with a landscaped mid-

way. Horace Cleveland's farsighted plan for Minneapolis in 1883 used boulevards to link a variety of parks throughout that city. But Kessler's may have been the first to suggest a hierarchy of parks that served a variety of needs. As he explained it:

> A park system may be divided into three parts: the smaller parks and squares, the larger parks and the boulevards connecting them with each other. The smaller ones, in the thickly populated parts of a city, become the breathing spots and often playgrounds, independent or more or less connecting with each other. These are necessarily merely oases in a desert of houses and make life more tolerable in crowded sections.
>
> For just such small places many cities both here and in Europe spend large sums, even removing valuable buildings to make room for a little spot of green.

The real parks, however, whose mission it is to bring within the city the charms of country scenes and clean fresh air, must occupy larger space in order to contain within themselves the quiet repose of the country and must sustain the impression of freedom from the city cares and annoyances.

These parks arranged in a belt about the outskirts of the city, should, to be of any value, be accessible to all by walk, carriage, or rail.

To make them so, the third part of the system, the boulevards, are placed so that they form convenient passages from the city and to each other.

The parks and boulevards when created would quickly demonstrate their value by the constant flow of visitors to them.[10]

As Pückler had at Muskau, Kessler created a "circuit over a route which offers a great variety of pleasing and beautiful scenes, isolated from all traffic and in a world entirely distinct from the active business life of the city." At intervals along the boulevard, he placed "little parks and pleasure grounds,

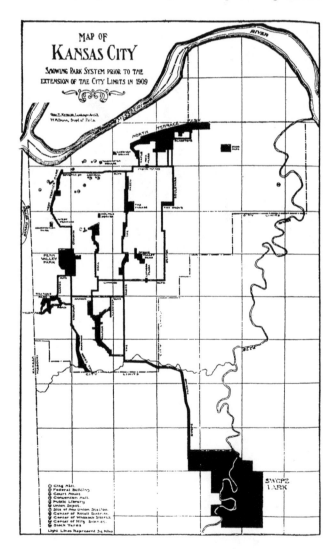

Maps of Kansas City, Missouri, showing the park system prior to extension of the city limits in 1909 (this page) and the park system and extensions to 1915 (opposite page), both prepared by Kessler. (Courtesy of the Kansas City, Missouri, Parks and Recreation Archives)

finally expanding into one of the larger parks."[11] Pückler-Muskau had incorporated ancient villages into his scheme to establish a sense of place and history; in Kansas City, Kessler created his own sense of tradition. A nine-block boulevard known as the Paseo extended through a former slum area and connected a chain of small parks which contained a formal sunken garden, fountains reminiscent of Versailles, a pergola, and flower gardens with a tapestry of patterns. The imagery of Kessler's parks and boulevards was certainly consistent with the eclectic spirit of the American Renaissance. Kessler, perhaps recalling the work of the master Lenné, envisioned the plan so as to provide a contrast to the rigid grid of the city's street system. He designed the network of winding drives to flow easily into the naturalistic landscapes of the North Terrace and Penn Valley parks. "The whole scheme," wrote one historian, "flavored with European touches, bestowed on Kansas City an

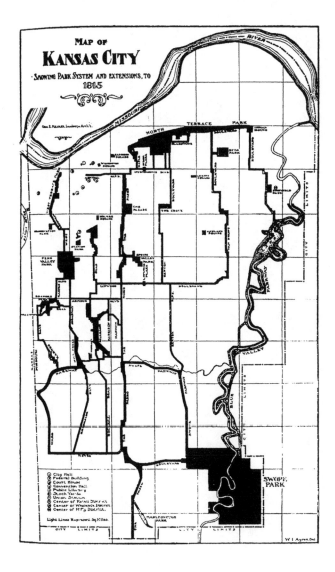

urbanity that was the envy of lesser cities in the unsophisticated midlands of America."[12] The park board described the significance of Kessler's work thirty years after its inception:

> So it fell out that at a time when zoning was unknown, when there was hardly such a thing in the country as a real system of parks and boulevards, when landscape architecture was just becoming recognized as a profession, here in the rough, raw West, in the frontier community at the Kaw's mouth, was worked out a scheme of beauty and utility that was unique in American municipal growth. Visitors from every part of the West caught the vision that had inspired Kessler, and the Kansas City development exercised a profound effect on cities in every direction.[13]

Despite the success of his Kansas City and Roland Park work, Kessler was not invited to join the group of primarily New York and Boston colleagues who established the American Society of Landscape Architects in 1899. Years later, he explained to Samuel Parsons Jr., one of the society's founders, why he still did not wish to become a member:

> Would you please take note of the following quotation from a letter written by one of your members dated 1899. "Such men as . . . yourself have not been invited to join this society because your duties are principally those of superintending park work as an executive and not as a designer. We do not think that the best results in design are likely to follow the combination of these two functions." If that was true in 1899, it is undoubtedly just as true today in that so much of my work is carried on along exactly the same lines as it was then, and had been for at least ten years prior to that time, except that now perhaps a good deal more.[14]

It is ironic that Kessler's peers criticized him for assuming a role far

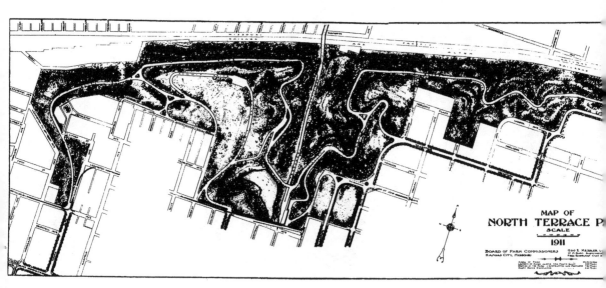

broader than a designer's alone, for while this role alienated him from other members of his profession, it also contributed to his tremendous success. Another reason for Kessler's strained relationship with the circle of landscape architects who followed F. L. Olmsted was the continual misattribution—often by Kansas City residents themselves—of the Kansas City park system to the Boston practitioner. Kessler, a modest but proud man, was deeply hurt by the slight. In 1917 Delbert Haff, his close friend and the attorney for the park board, tried to set the record straight: "I have investigated the matter, and I find that Mr. Olmstead [sic] spent exactly two days in Kansas City, as a guest of Mr. Meyer, and no more, and that was after the plans had been made by Mr. Meyer and Mr. Kessler, and maps had been prepared, park areas selected, routes for boulevards determined and topographic surveys made."[15] Despite Haff's defense, the myth of Olmsted's involvement with the Kansas City park system—as well as with other Kessler designs—lingers still.

The American Renaissance was by nature an art and architecture of capitalism. An enthusiastic proponent of the movement, Kessler spoke eloquently of how his parks and boulevards could provide beauty and relief for the city's crowded masses, but he also emphasized the commercial benefits of such improvements. In this sense, Kessler and many of his American Renaissance colleagues did not rebel against society and the inequalities of wealth but rather joined forces with the elite even while they sought to improve living conditions for the lower class. Kessler moved easily in the business and social circles of the cities where he worked and was a member of prominent business clubs in St. Louis and Cincinnati. His friends and clients included such men as August Busch, the St. Louis brewer, and George Dealey, editor of the Dallas *Morning News.* Many of these men were also of German descent, which further cemented relationships.

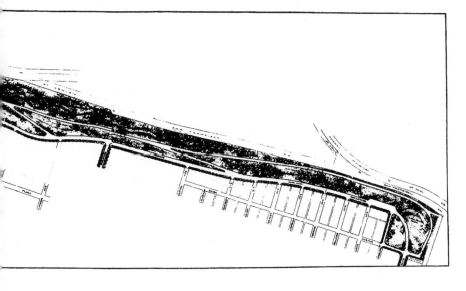

Map of North Terrace Park, 1911, prepared for the Board of Park Commissioners by Kessler. (Courtesy of the Special Collections department, Kansas City Public Library, Kansas City, Mo.)

Kessler's practice continued to grow in scope and breadth. In addition to ongoing residential design in Kansas City, in 1892 he started on plans for a cemetery in Oklahoma City—likely the first work of a professional landscape architect in the Oklahoma Territory. In 1900 Kessler initiated a ten-year association with the park and boulevard system of Memphis which included Riverside, Forrest, Gaspard, Bickford, and Overton Parks. Other projects in Tennessee followed, including the Tri-State Fairgrounds in Memphis, Lancaster Park in Jackson, Vanderbilt University, and the Nashville Zoo (although his plan for the last does not appear to have been executed).

Kessler's success in Kansas City and his ties to the region's businessmen and political leaders led to an invitation to plan the landscape improvements for the 1904 World's Fair, known also as the Louisiana Purchase Exposition. He opened an office in St. Louis to handle the work. One of his employees there was Henry Wright, a native of Lawrence, Kansas, and a graduate of the University of Pennsylvania. (Wright would later earn fame for his work with Clarence Stein at Radburn, New Jersey, and Sunnyside Gardens in New York.) Also joining the staff was Eda Sutermeister, who had studied at the University of Missouri and was one of a handful of women landscape architects practicing in the country at that time. Sutermeister's father owned the stone company that supplied materials for many of Kessler's park improvements. Kessler's sister, Antoine, also worked as a landscape architect on the project, though in a less prominent role than Wright and Sutermeister. When the exposition closed, Kessler also directed the restoration of its setting in Forest Park, creating one of America's great urban parks.

The timing of Kessler's successes in Kansas City and St. Louis could not have been better. Across the country municipal art leagues and civic improvement associations clamored for civic art and beautification. Planning experts were in demand as never before. Kessler traveled widely, and his arrival in a city became front page news and often occasioned a speech before the civic league. City fathers in Cincinnati, Indianapolis, St. Louis, and New York gave him honorary memberships to private clubs and business organizations, further opening access to the power brokers.[16]

Kessler's sphere of influence continued to grow as he extended his practice southward into Texas and northward with projects in Omaha, Hot Springs, South Dakota, and even Syracuse, New York. A park system proposed for Syracuse in 1906 became the focal point of a vicious mayoral campaign, and Kessler's high profile proved a liability—headlines in the *Journal,* which opposed the scheme, proclaimed "Kessler Sneaks Into City Under Cover of Darkness."[17] Although park proponents won the election, momentum and the opportunity to acquire valuable open space had been lost, and the park system was never built.

Kessler's proposal for a park system in Denver, commissioned by Mayor

Undated photograph of Eda A. Sutermeister (back row), who worked in Kessler's St. Louis office and was one of a handful of female landscape architects practicing in the country early in the nineteenth century. (Courtesy of Kurt Culbertson)

Speer in 1907, was one of his most brilliant schemes. Following the principles he had learned from Muskau, Kessler identified the high points of the city from which views to the distant Rockies and eastward to the Great Plains were possible. These vantage points would become parks and be connected by boulevards. Unfortunately, Kessler's plan was only partially realized, but the Cheesman Memorial survives as a striking example of a high point park.

That same year, 1907, Kessler worked in Cincinnati, where he created a park and boulevard plan that had a major impact on the city's future development. Kessler saw that residences along the Ohio River were gradually being absorbed by business, manufacturing, and railway interests. The hills, rising some four hundred feet above the commercial district and providing distant views and overlooks of the city, struck him as a more desirable location for housing. His plan defined this circle of hills as the setting for separate communities that would be linked to a grand central parkway below, created by filling in the Miami and Erie Canal. This corridor would provide "access along fine and easy lines into the very heart of the business portion of the city."[18] Kessler's Cincinnati plan garnered him national attention, and decades later the design was still considered to possess "an integrity and harmony that make it a true work of art, surpassing in scale and complexity anything previously proposed for an American city."[19]

Kessler returned to Dallas, where he had spent his childhood, to begin work on a plan for that city which addressed social as well as aesthetic problems. Published in 1912, the plan reflected an awareness of a need for the "City Practical" as well as the City Beautiful. Kessler had understood that different areas of the city were better suited to some uses than others. "A city should be divided into areas and zones, each devoted to its own particular purpose,"

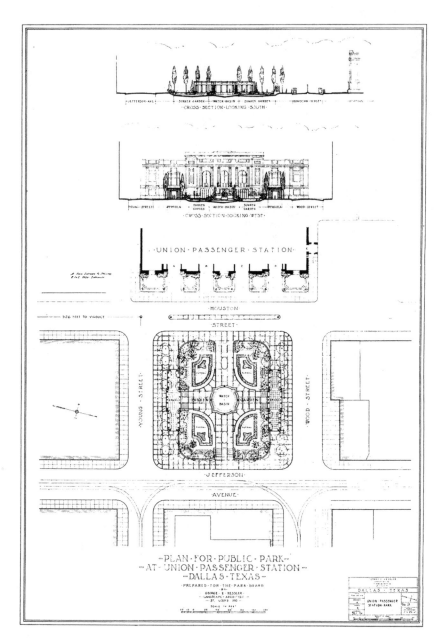

Plan for a public park at Union Passenger Station, Dallas, Texas, 1919, prepared by Kessler. (Courtesy of the City of Dallas, Texas, Park and Recreation Department)

he wrote. "The greatest possible accessibility for all should be provided in ample and direct connecting thoroughfares and all barriers, such as railroad grade crossings, narrow, congested streets and excessively long blocks, should be removed and corrected."[20]

In the Dallas plan, Kessler allocated the lower ground to railroad and industrial purposes, slightly higher land to retail and wholesale outlets near the city center, and the surrounding elevations to residential areas. His scheme included a central freight terminal, a belt railroad around the city, wider streets in the downtown area, levees along the Trinity River to reclaim an area for manufacturing, and a series of playgrounds. This was the kind of practical program which businessmen heartily endorsed. Yet Kessler, while always aware of the commercial elements of a city, was first and foremost a landscape architect. The Turtle Creek Parkway, Lake Cliff Park, and White Rock

Kessler's plan for the north and principal entrance to Hermann Park in Houston, Texas, 1916. The design incorporates a bold geometrical axis with curving forms near the boundaries of the project. (Courtesy of the Houston Metropolitan Research Center, Houston Public Library, Houston, Tex.)

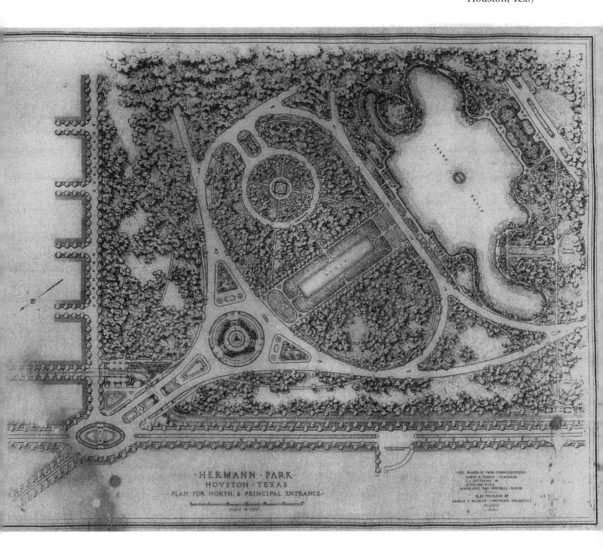

·HERMANN·PARK·
HOUSTON–TEXAS
·PLAN FOR NORTH & PRINCIPAL ENTRANCE·

Parkway, created as a result of his plan, provided natural beauty within the urban environment.

While busy with an array of other projects, Kessler's involvement with Dallas continued throughout the second decade of the twentieth century. This included consultation with city officials regarding the location and grouping of public buildings, advice on railroad-related issues, and the design of parks. Houston also called upon his services, which included the preparation of his majestic plan for Hermann Park.

Between 1911 and 1913, his master plans for St. Joseph, Missouri, and South Bend, Terre Haute, and Fort Wayne, Indiana, established an initial framework for development of those cities. He also designed campus plans for Miami University in Oxford, Ohio, and Shanghai Baptist University and the University of Nanking in China.

Map of the park and boulevard system for Fort Wayne, Indiana, one of the many open-space plans Kessler prepared for American cities. (Courtesy of the Board of Park Commissioners, Fort Wayne, Ind.)

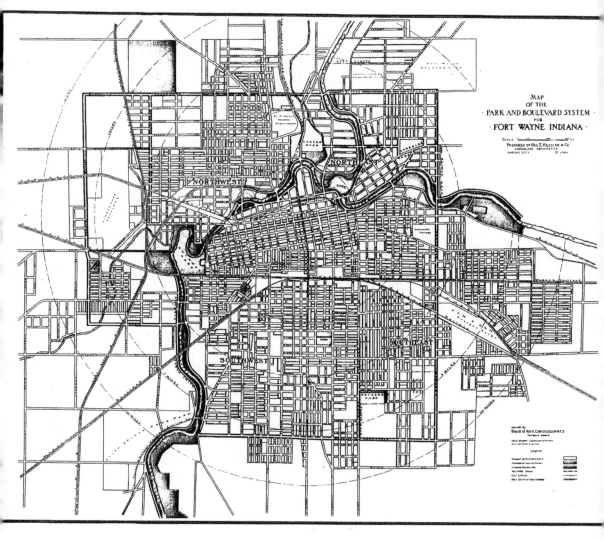

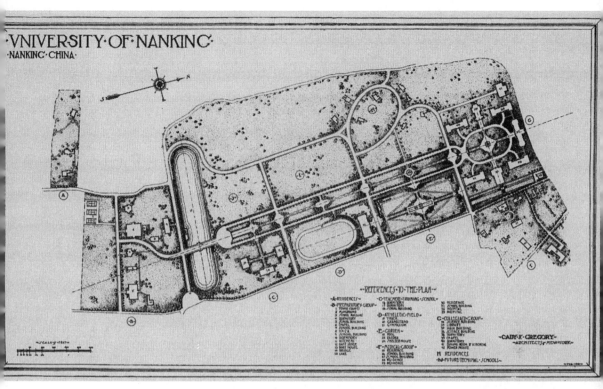

·VNIVERSITY·OF·NANKINC·
·NANKINC·CHINA·

~REFERENCES·TO·THE·PLAN~

·CADY·&·GREGORY·
~ARCHITECTS·of·NEW·YORK~

The outbreak of World War I early in 1917 broadened the scope of city planning and brought Kessler new opportunities. Architects, engineers, and landscape architects were recruited to design and supervise the construction of emergency towns for industrial housing projects in Rock Island and Moline, Illinois. Kessler joined his East Coast colleagues, A. D. Taylor, John Nolen, Warren Manning, Arthur Shurtleff (later Shurcliff), James Pray, and Arthur Comey among them, in these wartime planning efforts.

Kessler maintained a strong commitment to the war effort. He not only held the rank of first sergeant in the National Guard, but he also served in the Camp Planning Division of the War Department, designing cantonments in Lawton, Oklahoma, San Antonio, Texas, Little Rock, Arkansas, and Deming, New Mexico. (He also gave 250,000 francs to the American Hospital in Neuilly.) Kessler worked unstintingly, traveling by rail to Washington, D.C., St. Louis, and many other projects while continuing his involvement with private clients in Cincinnati and other distant cities. The frenetic pace proved impossible to maintain, and in late July, he fell ill and was bedridden for two months; his doctors first diagnosed indigestion, but later termed it a nervous breakdown. Perhaps because he spoke with a German accent all his life, Kessler felt some urgency about proving his patriotism during the war. In any case, he never completely recovered his health. But one benefit of all his work with other landscape architects during this period was an improved relationship

Several of Kessler's projects, including this 1912 master plan for the University of Nanking in China, involved working abroad. (Courtesy of the Special Collections Department, Kansas City Public Library, Kansas City, Mo.)

with the ASLA. In 1919—twenty years after the organization's founding—he applied for membership and was accepted.

After the war, Kessler's professional practice changed. With increased industrial production and agricultural mechanization, the populace moved from the country to the cities. By 1920 the United States had become a predominantly urban nation. Automobile ownership skyrocketed; cars choked central business districts and encouraged sprawling suburban development. As never before, appreciation for city planning grew.

For his postwar project designs, Kessler drew from his wartime experiences. In Wichita Falls, Sherman, and El Paso, Texas, he created not just park and boulevard schemes but comprehensive city plans that reflected a broadening awareness of modern urban needs. In 1919 Kessler became the first city planning consultant to Salt Lake City, Utah, and three years later, he teamed up with the Kansas City landscape architectural firm of Hare and Hare to develop a plan for the new town of Longview, Washington. Master plans for Butler University in Indianapolis and Chapultepec Heights, a residential subdivision in Mexico City, also occupied his time.

In 1923, while on park business in Indianapolis, Kessler again fell ill, and despite surgery his condition worsened. On May 19, George Edward Kessler died at the age of sixty, never having fully recovered from his breakdown during the war. His death was mourned in the many cities where he had worked and prompted friends and colleagues to reflect on his life and career.

A former employee remembered Kessler for his "knack of allowing others . . . to do most of the talking and then crystallizing the whole matter by a timely remark." The same employee described Kessler as a man with high standards who was also utterly fair in his dealings with people: "Mr. Kessler never failed to give proper credit to his assistants. One of his greatest works, of course, was the landscape plan for the World's Fair in St. Louis. He told me at one time that Miss Sutermeister, in his office, was responsible for the color scheme. He could very easily have taken credit for that himself, but did not do so, and many times I have known him to be generous in the same way. As a matter of fact, he was always generous."[21] The editor of the El Paso *Herald* remembered him simply as a "a lovable and companionable genius."[22]

It is remarkable that a man of such professional accomplishments, one so loved and respected throughout a vast region of the country, could be virtually forgotten. Because Kessler wrote very little and was alienated from the leadership of his profession for most of his career, he was to a great extent denied access to communications within his peer group. But Kessler's situation is not unique; few of the many able practitioners who transformed the region's landscape are widely remembered today. Their great parks, city plans, and other public projects, however, continue to enhance of the lives of midwesterners every day.

Notes

1. George Kessler, application for junior membership in the American Society of Land-scape Architects, 26 November 1917. Files of the ASLA Council of Fellows. George Arthur Yarwood, letter to author, 10 December 1984.

2. George Kessler, letter to Frederick Law Olmsted, 22 January 1883. Olmsted Collection. Ac. 16,498, Reel 19, Library of Congress, Washington, D.C. Further instruction in civil engineering at the University of Jena and the Neue Garten with hofgartner Theodore Neitner in Potsdam completed his education. For more on Lenné, see Harri Gunter, *Joseph Peter Lenné* (Berlin: Ost, 1985).

3. Kessler to Olmsted, 22 January 1883. For more on Muskau, see Prince Hermann Ludwig Heinrich von Pückler-Muskau, *Hints on Landscape Gardening,* trans. Bernhardt Sickert, ed. Samuel Parsons (Boston: Houghton Mifflin, 1917).

4. "It is obvious that every interesting feature of the distant landscape should be in-cluded in the park. . . . Distant views . . . lying away beyond the actual grounds, give an appearance of measureless extent." Muskau, *Hints,* 30.

5. Richard Guy Wilson, *The American Renaissance, 1876–1917* (New York: Pantheon/Brooklyn Museum, 1979), 13.

6. Horace Cleveland, *Landscape Architecture as Applied to the Wants of the West* (Chicago, 1873).

7. Frederick Law Olmsted, letter to George Edward Kessler, 5 March 1882, Olmsted Collection.

8. Frederick Law Olmsted, letter to H. H. Hunnewell, President of the Kansas City, Fort Scott and Memphis Railroad Company. Library of Congress, Frederick Law Olmsted Papers, Container No. 20, General Correspondence (1882).

9. William S. Worley. "J. C. Nichols and the Origins of the Planned Residential Com-munity in the United States, 1903–1930" (Ph.D. diss., University of Kansas, 1986), 39.

10. George Kessler, Notes on the Kansas City Park System, May 1892, 1. Kessler Collec-tion, Missouri Historical Society, St. Louis.

11. Ibid.

12. Mel Scott, *American City Planning since 1890* (Berkeley: University of California Press, 1971), 434–35.

13. "Kansas City Board Would Honor Kessler," 25 March 1923. Missouri Historical So-ciety, Vertical File.

14. George Kessler, letter to Samuel Parsons, 1 March 1902. Kessler Collection.

15. Haff continued, "Elsewhere in this report, Mr. Meyer refers in four lines to the fact that he 'consulted the eminent firm of landscape architects, Messrs. F. L. Olmstead & Co.,' but you will find not a single letter, report or recommendation from Olmstead & Co., or F. L. Olmstead, included in this report. You will find, however, attached to the report of 60 pages, with maps and photographs, the report of George E. Kessler of nearly 20 pages of printed matter and 10 large and small maps and drawings, including an exhaustive description of the whole plan adopted by the Board, and the arguments justifying them. If it had been in the slightest degree Olmstead's work, there would have been at least a letter somewhere therein from Mr. Olmstead." Delbert Haff, letter to Henry D. Ashley, 10 May 1917. Kessler Collection.

16. In 1905 Kessler developed the first park and boulevard plan for Indianapolis, thus beginning a lifelong association with that city.

17. Syracuse *Journal,* 1 July 1907, 4.

18. George Kessler, in *The Annual Report of the Park Department of the City of Cincin-nati* (Cincinnati: Park Commission, 1907), 10.

19. August Heckscher, *Open Spaces: The Life of American Cities* (New York: Harper and Row, 1977), 209.

20. George E. Kessler, *A City Plan for Dallas* (Dallas: Park Board, 1912), 8.

21. Lawrence Sheridan, letter to James Pray, 15 May 1923. Files of the ASLA Council of Fellows.

22. Eda A. Sutermeister, letter to J. S. Pray, 19 December 1923. Files of the ASLA Council of Fellows.

SEVEN

Jens Jensen

THE LANDSCAPE ARCHITECT
AS CONSERVATIONIST

Robert E. Grese

JENS JENSEN (1860–1951) was a leading force in promoting a style of design that celebrated the native midwestern landscape. In the mosaic of prairies, wetlands, woodlands, and dunes of his adopted homeland, Jensen saw a diversity and quiet beauty that many other designers overlooked. Throughout his career, he worked to enlighten others of the value of these vanishing resources.

The natural landscape was a source of design inspiration for Jensen, but his work also embraced other important aspects of conservation. He emphasized the value of parks and gardens as wildlife habitat and often integrated other forms of art—sculpture, drama, song, and poetry—with nature and conservation themes into his landscapes. In addition, he used his influence and skills as a charismatic leader to build support for regional conservation movements.

Born in 1860 on the Dybbøl peninsula of the Slesvig region of Denmark, Jensen spent his childhood exploring hedgerows and farm fields and taking excursions with his father into the countryside.[1] He attended the folk school at Vinding, which combined studies of traditional subjects with an intensive emphasis on nature and stressed stewardship of the land and local cultural traditions. Danish culture was a celebration of the seasons, and Nordic folklore provided a rich storehouse of legends and mysteries associated with the land. Soil was viewed as the source of all life, and thus, for Jensen maintaining strong ties to the land was not merely desirable but essential for a healthy society.[2]

Jens Jensen. (Courtesy of
The Clearing, Ellison
Bay, Wis.)

With plans to take over the family farm, Jensen attended Tune Agricul-
tural School near Copenhagen. After graduating, he enlisted briefly in the
German army and returned to Denmark to marry his sweetheart, Anne Marie
Hansen. His parents, however, refused to sanction his marriage to a woman
from a lower social class, so Jensen broke family ties, and in 1884 he and Anne
Marie emigrated to the United States.[3] He worked briefly on farms in Florida
and Iowa before moving to Chicago, where he swept streets in Chicago's West
Parks and worked part-time at a local nursery run by the Swedish landscape
gardener Swain Nelson.[4]

Jensen's career spanned a period of rapid change in the United States.
Chicago in particular was undergoing almost frenzied growth as people re-
built after the Great Fire of 1871 with the aim of making their city both a
national and an international center. From the time Jensen arrived in the
United States until his death, the country moved from primarily an agricul-
ture-based society run on horsepower to one that was thoroughly industri-
alized, centered in large urban areas and dependent on the automobile and
fossil fuels. This transition was already apparent in 1886 as Jensen began his
career with the West Chicago Parks.

An industrious worker, Jensen was gradually given more responsibility, and in 1888 he created his first documented public garden, a planting of native wildflowers in a corner of Union Park, which he named The American Garden to remind the city's people of their rural roots. Jensen saw that city residents were cut off from the surrounding landscape and from nature in general and wanted to reconnect them with the Midwest's natural landscape heritage. To his delight, the garden flourished and became extremely popular. With this small project, Jensen established a conservation theme that would guide his entire career.[5]

Jensen continued his rise through the ranks of park employees, becoming superintendent of Union Park in 1895 and of Humboldt Park in 1896.[6] Four years later, however, he was fired for refusing to accept a "short order" of coal; in a park system rampant with political graft, Jensen was a nonconformist. The ensuing years were lean ones for his growing family, but gradually, with help from influential friends, Jensen established a small landscape design practice working at his kitchen table. As he studied the native landscape, he improvised with various plants and design expressions. Rather than

Jensen photo of ferns taken on one of his many botanizing treks into the landscape surrounding Chicago. (Courtesy of the Jens Jensen Archives, Art and Architecture Library, University of Michigan, Ann Arbor)

attempting to re-create literal translations of nature's scenes, Jensen carefully wove plantings and land forms together into natural gardens symbolic of the larger landscape. Like the painter George Inness, whom he deeply admired, Jensen adeptly manipulated light and shadow, colors, textures, and gently flowing outdoor space to stir the imaginations of the people experiencing his landscapes.[7] Although his early work mixed many traditional garden plants with native species, Jensen's later designs became more restrictive, relying almost entirely on plant associations as found in the wild.[8]

Unlike many landscape architects of the period, who vacillated between a "formal" or a "naturalistic" style, Jensen clearly saw the native landscape as the focus for his design career.[9] But he did not entirely ignore traditional garden forms. Many of his parks and estate grounds, for example, contained rose and vegetable gardens and orchards that incorporated a simple geometric order to facilitate their upkeep.[10] Neither did Jensen completely spurn non-native plants. In areas near a dwelling he often came to use certain imports such as daylilies, hollyhocks, and lilacs, much as pioneers had used these plants for generations.[11] Generally, these special garden spaces and horticultural plantings were set within a framework of native plantings, gently curving walkways or drives, and a free-form arrangement of open spaces and plant massings which dominated the landscape's overall shape. The native landscape and its ever-changing drama became the thread woven through nearly all Jensen's work.

With his colleague O. C. Simonds and the architect Dwight Perkins, Jensen became a member of the Special Park Commission in Chicago. In 1904 this group made sweeping recommendations for creating a regional system of metropolitan playgrounds, parks, and preserves, laying the foundation for a network of neighborhood centers and playground facilities as well as a county forest preserve system for Cook County, Illinois. The following year Jensen was rehired by the new commissioner of the West Parks, this time as superintendent and landscape architect for all of the West Parks, a position he held until 1909, when his title was changed to Consulting Landscape Architect to the West Chicago Park Commissioners.[12] Soon Jensen was given the opportunity to redesign the West Parks, in ways that affected the system's small parks and playgrounds as well as the larger Humboldt, Garfield, and Douglas parks.

Jensen's redesign of Humboldt Park contained a new feature that seemed to embody the ideal prairie landscape. Originally designed by William Le Baron Jenney from 1869 to 1871, the park had been modified later by Oscar F. Dubuis, who built, among other things, a spring-fed lagoon. Jensen adopted Dubuis's lagoon but embellished its banks with native wetland plants to create a "prairie river." This treatment contrasted sharply with Jenney's characteristic large boulders and picturesque rocks that dotted the edges of his

Bur oak on land studied for the Chicago regional park system proposed by Jensen and others. (Reprinted from Perkins, *Report of the Special Park Commission,* 93)

water features. Jensen's river more closely resembled the lagoons created by Frederick Law Olmsted at the Columbian Exposition, where the banks were clothed with a rich mixture of wetland plants. At Humboldt Park and in subsequent "prairie river" designs, Jensen relied almost entirely on the rushes, grasses, and wildflowers found at local streams to evoke a sense of wilderness in the city.

Jensen also experimented with combining formal and naturalistic areas

Wetland garden in
Humboldt Park, c. 1936.
(Courtesy of the Chi-
cago Park District Spe-
cial Collections, Chi-
cago, Ill.)

at Humboldt Park. The rose garden contrasted with the park's prairie river,
open meadow, and woodland plantings and also served as a central gathering space, providing a transition to the city's regular geometry beyond the
park boundaries. Its circular beds contributed a playful quality to the design
which Jensen eventually disavowed, identifying it as a "folly of his youth."[13]

While working on Humboldt Park, Jensen strengthened ties to many of
the "prairie architects." In 1908 he had moved his kitchen table office to
Steinway Hall in downtown Chicago, where several of them practiced, and
he became involved in the City Club, the Chicago Architectural Club, and
the Cliff Dwellers.[14] He was familiar with the evolving prairie movement in
architecture and probably joined in discussions about the developing style.
Jensen's architect friend Hugh M. G. Garden designed Humboldt Park's
graceful refectory, which skillfully combined curving arches with clear horizontal lines. Garden also designed the elegant lanterns for the park's public
spaces. When Jensen designed the park's concrete benches and flower pavilion, he echoed the prairie style's characteristic strong horizontal lines, simple
forms, and honest use of materials.[15]

From 1916 to 1917 Jensen was given considerable freedom to reshape Columbus Park on the western edge of Chicago's city limits. In this important project, he was again able to express his ideal representation of the native Illinois landscape.[16] The site (previously known as Warren Woods, or the Austin Tract) had been used for golf, but unlike the other West Parks it had had little other development before Jensen's involvement. His design preserved and emphasized the site's most notable feature, an ancient beach ridge that formed a broad curve across the northeast quadrant of the property. Jensen created one of his prairie rivers at its base and a walkway along the ridgetop to provide a good vantage point for watching the sunset over the broad landscape to the west. He retained the golf course, which combined with the beach rise resulted in a greater sense of expansiveness than was possible in his other parks. An irregular border of trees and an island planting of trees and shrubs enhanced perspective views over the meadow and made the space seem larger. While the meadow surface was kept in turf for golf, the wooded border and island of trees at the center were underplanted with thousands of native wildflowers.[17]

In Garfield Park, the third of the large West Parks, Jensen's work expressed a different aspect of the midwestern landscape. The Conservatory, as a ref-

Rose garden in Humboldt Park, before 1912. (Courtesy of the Chicago Park District Special Collections, Chicago, Ill.)

erence to the prehistoric landscape of Illinois, featured a junglelike display of primitive Carboniferous-period flora. Whereas most conservatories of the period housed eclectic collections of specimen plants, Jensen's indoor garden was treated as an outdoor space. Limestone ledges, reminiscent of the Chicago area's bedrock, were carefully constructed along the outer edges of the conservatory space to serve as a backdrop for the massed plantings. At the garden's center was a "lawn" of Lycopodium and a quiet pool fed by waterfalls trickling down the limestone ridges. Ferns, cycads, and other primitive plants provided the lush tropical atmosphere characteristic of the region's early geologic period and fossilized in its rich coal deposits.[18]

Jensen eventually curtailed his association with the Chicago parks, although he continued to serve as consulting landscape architect until the early 1920s. In that capacity, he prepared his forward-looking study, *A Greater West Park System,* published in 1920. The book documented Jensen's holistic vision of how conservation attitudes could be nurtured through a network of

Garfield Park Conservatory, 1908. (Courtesy of the Chicago Park District Special Collections, Chicago, Ill.)

parks, playgrounds, school sites, community gardens, large preserves, and linear parkways along streams, canals, and boulevards.[19]

While working on the parks, Jensen continued to build his private practice. He had become extremely knowledgeable about the region's landscape as a result of weekend explorations with his family through the ravines north of the city, the network of forests, wetlands, and prairies of the Des Plaines River, the dunes of northern Indiana, and other wilderness areas.[20] From about 1912 until 1920, Jensen's private client base expanded into Chicago's northern suburbs and throughout the Midwest.[21]

In his residential designs Jensen experimented with the natural landscape at a reduced scale. At the Rubens estate (1903–6) in Glencoe, Illinois, he created a series of outdoor rooms and flowing spaces that linked the garden to long views over Lake Michigan and constructed a small version of the prairie rivers he later created in Humboldt and Columbus parks. Each garden space had its own sense of order; vegetable plots and orchards were laid out in traditional rectilinear form, while the natural gardens derived their rhythm from nature.[22]

Jensen's work for Henry Ford at Fair Lane in Dearborn, Michigan (beginning in 1914) also integrated formal horticultural layout with natural elements. Jensen combined farm fields and orchards with woodlands and meadows to evoke memories of the land as it was when "the American Indians skied down the banks of the River Rouge."[23] A dam built to power Ford's hydroelectric plant was designed to resemble a natural waterfall and cascade. Such falls were not natural to lake plain rivers such as the Rouge, but Jensen carefully extended rock terraces along the river's edge to tie the

The end of the meadow at Fair Lane, the Henry Ford Estate in Dearborn, Michigan, was designed to be in line with the setting sun on the summer solstice. (Courtesy of Robert E. Grese)

dam into the larger landscape, making it appear as though the river were cutting through horizontal beds of limestone.

Clara Ford had requested rose and perennial gardens, which Jensen placed near the house and filled with species long associated with American gardens: lilacs, daylilies, periwinkle, mock orange, and spiraea. The estate's greater landscape was given over to native species grouped as they might be found in the wild. A network of paths linked these features and suggested movement through the various garden spaces. Near the house, paths were built of cut stone wide enough for people to walk two abreast; farther away, however, they were made of rough stepping stones or simply dirt or mowed grass. These narrower paths encouraged people to move single file and at a slower pace, fostering quiet contemplation of the surroundings.

At the center of Jensen's design for Fair Lane was a long meadow oriented toward the setting sun. Busy people, he believed, needed to be reminded of nature's cycles, daily and seasonal. At Fair Lane, viewers could sit out on the terrace or in the music room and watch the summer sunset over this grand space. In the morning, the eastern sun highlighted a group of white birches planted at the far end.[24] Another meadow originally extended across the river from the house to provide a similar sunset view at the winter solstice, although trees have now reclaimed that opening.

At Fair Lane and in his other landscapes, Jensen used plantings that changed with the seasons. Unlike many of his colleagues, who typically used evergreens extensively as spatial frames, Jensen featured deciduous trees and shrubs that turned brilliant colors in the fall or provided a show of spring flowers.[25]

Like Olmsted, Jensen believed that parks and gardens could exert a quieting influence and provide places of rest and comfort for weary city workers. He wanted his landscapes to give emotional and spiritual release and help attune people to the cycles of nature. Of all his parks, Columbus is the preeminent example of this refuge theme. Here people found respite and peace as well as a place to watch the sunset or enjoy the varied colors and forms of plants native to the Chicago region. The habitats developed in Columbus Park were also a haven to many wildlife species, despite the city's rapid growth around it. Jensen was particularly pleased that the re-created wetlands attracted the great blue heron back to the city.[26]

Wildlife habitats were also important in Jensen's residential designs, even in small gardens such as those for Julius Rosenwald and Albert H. Loeb, both in Hyde Park, which Wilhelm Miller featured in his article "Bird Gardens in the City."[27] On these relatively small city lots, Jensen created quiet garden rooms separated from their urban surroundings by native shrubs and small trees that provided a variety of food and nesting habitat for birds. Following the ideas of Baron von Berlepsch of Germany, Jensen installed tall purple martin houses and covered feeding platforms to lure birds.[28] In the Loeb garden, Jensen created a quiet pool bordered by limestone rock ledges, typical of the region, with an artificial spring at its center. Ringing the pool were native prairie grasses and forbs, including blue flag, arrowhead, calamus, and swamp rose mallow.

Jensen also established wildlife habitats in his designs for larger estates. At the Edsel and Eleanor Ford property in Grosse Pointe Shores, Michigan (1926–32), he created a shorebird refuge along the edge of Lake St. Clair. To accommodate Ford's request for a quiet harbor for his boats, Jensen had an area near the shoreline dredged out and used the dredged material to reshape an existing sandbar into a peninsula that jutted into the lake and enclosed the harbor. Its topography was sculpted to include both upland and shallow beach areas, which were then planted as a mosaic of meadow and woodland to create habitat for birds and animal life. Separated by water from the rest of the estate, wildlife on the peninsula would hardly be disturbed.[29]

Many of Jensen's most important design and conservation ideas coalesced in the Lincoln Memorial Garden in Springfield, Illinois, where he created a landscape such as Abraham Lincoln himself might have seen. When Jensen began the project, the site consisted of abandoned farm fields on the newly created Lake Springfield. Because his clients, the Garden Club of America and the Springfield Civic Garden Club, had limited resources, much of the actual planting was done by volunteers. But Jensen turned this limitation into an opportunity to create both long-term landscape change and a sense of stewardship in the many volunteers who participated.[30]

Jensen's planting plan for the island on the grounds of the Edsel and Eleanor Ford house in Grosse Pointe Shores, Michigan. (Courtesy of the Jens Jensen Archives, Art and Architecture Library, University of Michigan, Ann Arbor)

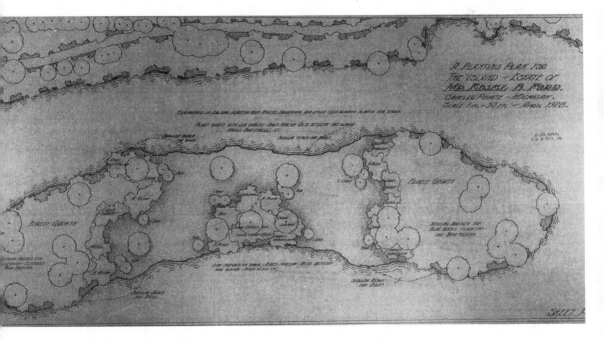

Lincoln Council Ring at Lincoln Memorial Garden, Springfield, Illinois. (Courtesy of Robert E. Grese)

Jensen structured the garden with a series of lanes and fingerlike openings through woodlands of native trees. In this way, he created a play of sunlight and deep shade in the wooded areas. At the clearing edges and along the lanes, he used a wide palette of native Illinois plants, among them his "trademark" edgings—sumac, American plum, flowering dogwood, redbud, prairie crabapple, hawthorn, sheepberry (nannyberry viburnum), and arrowwood viburnum. On the rises above the lake, he created meadows that gave expansive views across Lake Springfield, providing a feel of the vast, open prairie which Lincoln would have experienced. Bordering one of these openings, on the highest hillock above the lake, Jensen planned a grove of white oaks as a timeless, living monument to the former president.

The construction of the Lincoln Memorial Garden became a public celebration. Many of the native plants Jensen recommended were unavailable in nurseries, so volunteers had to rescue them from the wild or plant seeds. For the grove of white oak, children from surrounding states were asked to collect acorns. In a grand ceremony during the spring of 1936, Springfield Girl Scouts and Boy Scouts marched across the site and after a dedication planted their offerings. In subsequent years, garden club volunteers throughout Illinois rescued plants from areas scheduled for development and sent them to be planted in the garden. The result was a landscape made by the loving hands of people from many places over a long period of time.[31]

In addition to providing local citizens with opportunities to become involved in restoring landscapes, Jensen also created places for outdoor celebrations. Many of his designs included "council rings"—low, curving walls of stone where people could sit around a fire for stories, poetry, song, dance, or

Scouts planting oak acorns around the Lincoln Council Ring. (Courtesy of the Lincoln Memorial Garden, Springfield, Ill.)

general discussion. Jensen credited both Nordic and Amerindian traditions for inspiring the feature.[32]

Jensen included council rings in all types of projects, usually placing them at the edge of a woods with views into a large open space such as a meadow or lake. The scale varied from diminutive rings that would accommodate small groups of five to ten people to larger dance rings intended for fifty or more.[33] Although Jensen envisioned the council rings as the social center of his gardens, apparently many of his clients never appreciated or used them as he intended. Edsel Ford, for example, wrote to him that they had not used the ring built at their Jefferson Avenue property in Detroit and he wanted Jensen to drop it from his plans for their Seal Harbor, Maine, estate.[34]

While Jensen was designing Chicago's West Parks, interest grew in staging municipal celebrations to recount local history and create bonds among diverse ethnic groups. Playground festivals and pageants became important events for commemorating the passage of the seasons in the parks.[35] Jensen probably had no direct involvement with the pageant themes, but he supported them as a means of reawakening people to the cycles of nature and related cultural traditions by designing theater spaces or "players' greens" where audiences could sit on a grassy rise and view evening performances.[36] On clear nights, the play was illuminated by the rising moon; at times, flares were set on large rocks at either side of the stage. One of Jensen's largest and most elaborate players' greens was at Columbus Park. Here the audience sat on a grassy field separated from the stage by a narrow branch of the stream that fed the prairie river; small openings in the woods behind the stage served as the performers' dressing rooms.

Although he advocated keeping "the hand of man" to a minimum in his parks and gardens, Jensen did believe that sculpture could augment nature's quieting influence. In 1908 he helped mount an exhibition of public sculpture in Humboldt Park with the Municipal Art League and local sculptors Lorado Taft and Charles Mulligan, both of the Chicago Art Institute. While monumental and portrait sculpture belonged only in city squares, Jensen noted, pictorial or allegorical sculpture had a place "where park and city meet."[37] The Humboldt Park exhibit included allegorical pieces such as Leonard Crunelle's *Boy and Frog* and *Fisher Boy* fountain, along with the pictorial *Panther and Cubs* by Edward Kemeys, which was described as "blending with the lawn so realistically as to make the animals seem almost in their native haunts."[38] Charles Mulligan's *Miner and Child,* in an informal setting of shrubbery and native trees, depicted a weary miner stooping to greet his daughter on returning home from work. Jensen and the other exhibition organizers obviously wanted local people to identify with the artworks and feel that the park was a place they belonged. Another Mulligan

Scene from Shakespeare's *Midsummer Night's Dream* performed in the Player's Green at Columbus Park, 30 July 1940. (Courtesy of the Chicago Park District Special Collections, Chicago, Ill.)

sculpture, *Lincoln, the Rail Splitter,* posed the figure of Abraham Lincoln in a naturalistic setting. The exhibition was so successful that a second one was held the following year in Garfield Park.[39]

Jensen regarded playgrounds as places where children could use their imaginations and also learn about their regional heritage. From 1905 until about 1914, he followed the model of other "reform era" parks that emphasized formal play on gymnastic equipment and strictly defined play courts on small city lots. In 1914, however, at Franklin Park, Jensen initiated a completely different approach to playground design, which emphasized unstructured spaces for unfettered play.[40] At Franklin, and later at Columbus Park, Glenwood Children's Park in Madison, Wisconsin, and South Park, in Allegheny County, Pennsylvania, he created clearings and council rings as settings for impromptu dramatic performances, dances, singing, and other activities.[41] The playground in Columbus Park also included a small pool, birdhouses, and a variety of native trees and shrubs. In addition, there was a large swimming pool designed to resemble a rustic country swimming hole.

Eventually, Jensen extended these ideas to the design of school grounds. The most refined of these plans were for Chicago's Logan and Lloyd School Centers.[42] There he wanted to create places attractive not only to children but also to their parents and grandparents, making the schools true centers for life-long learning. The grounds were to be mosaics of vegetable and flower gardens, naturalistic swimming pools, woodland and prairie plantings, playfields, council rings, and outdoor theater spaces.[43]

In his parks and gardens, Jensen tried to awaken people to the beauty around them that was fast being lost. His landscapes provided ties to a region's natural heritage while they encouraged an appreciation of its cultural history. Jensen hoped that people would learn to respect and love wild lands and places with significant historical associations by interacting with them daily.

Jensen also worked in other ways to advance his conservation ideas. He was a major force in the founding of two organizations devoted to landscape preservation, the Prairie Club, established in 1908, and the Friends of Our Native Landscape, in 1913. Both groups initially focused on the Chicago area and were intended to get people involved with the landscape and encourage their participation in land preservation efforts. The Prairie Club grew out of an idea Jensen had with several friends who made regular weekend field trips to places of botanical or scenic interest in Chicago's outskirts. In 1908, to engage others in these excursions, they instituted a series of Saturday Afternoon Walking Trips as an extension of the activities of Chicago's Playground Association. These sojourns grew in popularity, and a separate organization was formed, which at Jensen's suggestion became known as the Prairie Club.[44] The club organized hiking trips and other outdoor excursions for people otherwise trapped in dense urban areas; recreation was its central purpose. Although the group never drew large numbers from Chicago's tenements, as Jensen and the other organizers had hoped it would, it did attract many middle-class professionals and intellectuals. Through the club's field trips, they became familiar with areas of spectacular natural diversity and scenic beauty in the city's outlying regions that were accessible by rail. Prairie Club members became important lobbyists for legislation to establish the forest preserve network around Chicago and other environmental protection efforts.

Jensen organized the Friends of Our Native Landscape, in contrast, specifically to bring knowledgeable and influential people together to celebrate the native landscape and fight for its preservation.[45] Outings were an important part of its programs also, but the Friends' major objectives were public education and political activism. The group was committed to collecting information about areas of historic and scenic value in Illinois and eagerly promoted legislation for their protection. (Many of Jensen's friends belonged to both groups, which frequently joined forces to engage in major conservation battles.)

Both the Friends and the Prairie Club combined interests in the arts, recreation, and nature study with preservation and stewardship efforts. Both groups' activities merged poetry, song, drama, and dance with general fellowship and a celebration of the outdoors. Perhaps their most dramatic conservation effort was the attempt to establish a national park at the Indiana Dunes, a sacred center for Jensen and many of his colleagues from both organizations. The Prairie Club had a long association with the area. In 1908 the Saturday Afternoon Walking Trips attracted some 338 people for an excursion to the dunes near Gary, Indiana. Five years later, the club built a permanent cabin near Tremont for their activities and dedicated the site with a special masque.[46] For Henry Cowles, the noted plant ecologist and one of Jensen's original walking companions, the dunes were an important botanical crossroads where the relationship of plants and their environment could be studied. (Cowles developed many of his classic theories of succession and ecological change at the dunes.) For others, the dunes were simply a retreat and place for inspiration.

In 1916 Stephen Mather, the newly appointed National Park Service director and a member of the Friends, organized a public hearing for the national park proposal.[47] Jensen (who became known as the "apostle of the dunes") put together testimony by influential members of the Prairie Club and the Friends. Congress turned a deaf ear to their pleas, but the Prairie Club did not give up. A staging of Thomas Wood Stevens's epic dunes pageant, which documented the site's history from 1675 to 1840, was attended by more than sixty thousand people (despite being partly rained out during its first

performance). Although efforts to establish a national park were defeated, the State of Indiana was persuaded to set aside 2,250 acres as the Indiana Dunes State Park in 1926.[48]

In fact, the Friends, with Jensen as president, were far more successful in preserving historic and scenic areas in Illinois as state parks. Each year, the group held a Meeting to the Full Leaf at sundown on the second Saturday in June. Their celebration ultimately included the presentation of Kenneth Sawyer Goodman's masque *The Beauty of the Wild* and a discussion of the site's value and prospects for preservation. Between sixty and one hundred members of the Friends, and often a thousand or more local people, attended these annual celebrations.[49] In 1921 the Friends issued their recommendations for proposed state park areas, highlighting some twenty sites across the state which they targeted for protection. Before this time, historic value was the defining criterion for a potential state park site (except for Starved Rock); the Friends argued that scenic and scientific values should also be considered. Of the twenty sites originally recommended, eight were made state parks, three were protected as segments of state parkways, and several others became part of the Shawnee National Forest in southern Illinois.[50]

Jensen had ambivalent feelings about the automobile. He recognized its negative effect on the urban landscape and urged the development of mass

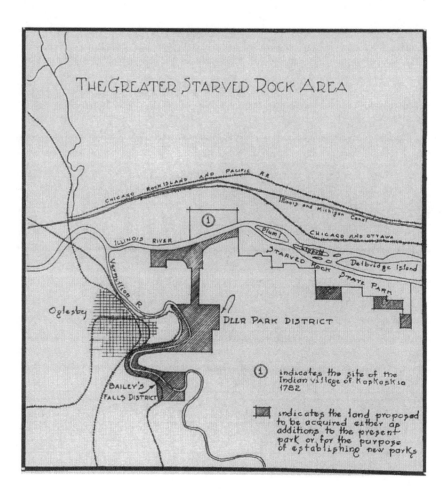

The Greater Starved Rock Area

① indicates the site of the Indian village of Kapkaskia 1782

▨ indicates the land proposed to be acquired either as additions to the present park or for the purpose of establishing new parks

Proposed additions to Starved Rock State Park. (Reprinted from Friends of Our Native Landscape, *Proposed Park Areas,* 56; courtesy of the Jens Jensen Archives, Art and Architecture Library, University of Michigan, Ann Arbor)

transit systems.[51] Yet he believed that Americans' growing love affair with the automobile could also have a positive effect in rural conservation, and he argued for designing and managing attractive roads as a powerful preservation tool. From 1917 to 1925 Jensen worked with the Lincoln Highway Association to develop an "ideal section" of the Lincoln Highway in northern Indiana. The Lincoln Highway Association had been founded in 1913 by several leading automobile manufacturers to promote construction of a coast-to-coast highway. The ideal section was to serve as a prototype for other highway developments.[52]

Jensen planned this stretch of road to highlight the native prairie-savanna-oak woodland character of northern Indiana. He suggested replanting prairie grasses and forbs and preserving bur oak groves and wooded ravines. Along the edge, he carefully wove a pedestrian trail so that hikers could enjoy the scenery too. He also planned a forty-acre campsite and rest area as part of the highway, with attractive picnic areas, a gas station, and a grocery store designed by his architect friend John S. Van Bergen. Characteristically,

View of the countryside around the proposed state park site at the Spoon River in central Illinois. (Reprinted from Friends of Our Native Landscape, *Proposed Park Areas*, 60)

Trail along the "ideal section" of the Lincoln Highway in northern Indiana. (Courtesy of the Lincoln Highway Collection, IS 2, Special Collections Library, University of Michigan, Ann Arbor)

Jensen intended his design to promote a genuine sense of community among the campers and planned council rings for them to gather around common campfires. None of Jensen's campground ideas were implemented, although much of the ideal section was developed according to his design. Sadly, today little remains of his actual work there.

Jensen retired from active practice after his wife's death in 1934, and he moved to the property on Lake Michigan he had bought as a family summer retreat, at Ellison Bay on Wisconsin's Door Peninsula. He continued consulting work, but his major focus until his death in 1951 was the school he founded there and called The Clearing. Modeled loosely after his Danish folk school experiences, The Clearing offered programs directed toward American youth, with an emphasis on learning by doing, thereby building a sense of social responsibility and environmental stewardship. Jensen wanted to clear away what he called "the debris of overstuffed learning" by teaching in the out-of-doors and emphasizing the strong relationship between people and the native landscape.[53]

Schoolhouse and rock garden at The Clearing. (Courtesy of Robert E. Grese)

For a variety of reasons, Jensen's work has long been misunderstood and neglected. Parks and gardens such as Jensen designed, which reflect natural

patterns and processes, are particularly vulnerable to the passage of time and the lack of sensitive management. Often they are regarded as wild areas that should simply be left alone, and as a result, only a handful of his surviving landscapes resemble what he actually designed. Rather than the typical landscape maintenance practices, which unfortunately too often entail mindless clipping and mowing, Jensen's landscapes require both thoughtful care that responds to natural cycles of disturbance and the gradual restoration of biological integrity to what are, essentially, symbolic fragments of nature.

Thus the task of preserving and restoring a Jensen landscape is complicated. His plans were, in a sense, only a starting point for developing design concepts, and he often modified them on site; frequently these modifications were not recorded on drawings. Moreover, Jensen believed that a garden represented a personal relationship between a designer or owner and the landscape, which changed naturally over time. "It matters little," he wrote in *Siftings*, "if the garden disappears with its maker. Its record is not essential to those who follow, because it is for them to solve their own problem, or art will soon decay. Let the garden disappear in the bosom of nature of which it is a part, and although the hand of man is not visible, his spirit remains as long as the plants he planted grow and scatter their seed."[54] Jensen himself would likely suggest that, rather than dwell on the past and what has disappeared, we forge a new landscape art, one that reflects a deeper understanding of nature's processes, centered on ecological principles.

Jens Jensen's designs were exceptional in that they responded to a site's context within broad landscape patterns; they fostered great joy and a sense of wonder regarding the outdoor world. With their council rings, open air theaters, sculpture exhibitions, pageants, poetry readings, and dances, his parks and gardens brought art and the landscape together. From his American Garden in Union Park, to his efforts to save the Indiana Dunes, to the Lincoln Memorial Garden, to his school at The Clearing, Jens Jensen clearly demonstrated that a genuine conservation ethic and a love of the landscape can be raised to the level of art.

Notes

This essay is drawn from research supported in part by grants from the National Endowment for the Arts, Design Arts Program. Materials from several archives containing information relating to Jensen's work were used to prepare it: Chicago Park District Special Collections, Chicago Park District, Chicago (cited as CPD); Jens Jensen Archives, The Morton Arboretum, Lisle, Ill. (cited as MA); Jens Jensen Archives, Art & Architecture Library (cited as AAL), Genevieve Gillette Papers, Bentley Historical Library (cited as BHL), and Lincoln Highway Association Papers, Special Collections, Harlan Hatcher Graduate Library, all at University of Michigan at Ann Arbor.

1. Jens Jensen, *Siftings* (Chicago: Ralph Fletcher Seymour, 1939), 13–16.

2. Ibid., 18; Thomas Rordam, *The Danish Folk Schools* (Copenhagen: Det Danske Selskab, 1980), 48–59, 68.

3. Jenson to Johannes Tholle, 15 October 1950 (MA).

4. Mertha Fulkerson, "Jens Jensen and The Clearing" *Parks and Recreation,* November 1941, 93–94; Alfred Caldwell, interview by the author, 17 December 1989.

5. Jens Jensen and Ragna B. Eskil, "Natural Parks and Gardens," *Saturday Evening Post,* 8 March 1930, 19.

6. *Twenty-eighth Annual Report of the West Chicago Park Commissioners* (Chicago, 1896), 74, 447.

7. Jensen and Eskil, "Natural Parks," 169.

8. Throughout his career, Jensen's use of native plants became progressively more pure, and he modeled his designs more closely on nature. In his early work he sometimes used native plants simply as substitutes for horticultural varieties; later on he grouped them in natural associations. Stephen F. Christy, "Jens Jensen: The Metamorphosis of an Artist," *Landscape Architecture* 66 (January 1976), 63.

9. See the responses to Jensen's paper given at the Twenty-seventh Annual Meeting of the American Society of Landscape Architects, 21–23 January 1926, Chicago, in the published proceedings (Boston: ASLA, 1926), 3–4.

10. Ruth Dean, "Landscape Vegetable Gardening," *Country Life in America* 31 (March 1917), 45–47.

11. Jens Jensen, letter to Camillo Schneider, 11 March 1937 (MA).

12. Bernard Eckhart, a prominent businessman, was appointed commissioner of the West Parks and charged with cleaning up the system's corruption. West Park Commissioners, 1874–93, unpublished notes (CPD); Dwight H. Perkins, *Report of the Special Park Commission to the City Council of Chicago on the Subject of a Metropolitan Park System* (Chicago: Special Park Commission, 1904); Leonard K. Eaton, *Landscape Artist in America: The Life and Work of Jens Jensen* (Chicago: University of Chicago Press, 1964), 18, 29; "Reforms in the West Park System of Chicago," *Park and Cemetery* 15 (August 1905), 329–30.

13. Jensen and Eskil, "Natural Parks," 18.

14. Among those with offices at the hall were Dwight Perkins and Robert Spencer. H. Allen Brooks, *The Prairie School: Frank Lloyd Wright and His Midwest Contemporaries* (Toronto: University of Toronto Press, 1972), 28; Genevieve Gillette, interview by Patricia Frank, 1973, tape no. 16c:14 (BHL).

15. Jens Jensen, "Beauty and Fitness in Park Concrete Work," *Park and Cemetery* 18 (November 1908), 435–36. Wim de Wit and William H. Tippens, "Prairie School in the Parks," in *Prairie in the City: Naturalism in Chicago's Parks: 1870–1940* (Chicago: Chicago Historical Society, 1991), 33, 36–40. For a more detailed discussion of a "prairie" regional style of landscape design, see Robert E. Grese, *Jens Jensen: Maker of Natural Parks and Gardens* (Baltimore: Johns Hopkins University Press, 1992), 44–51.

16. Jens Jensen, "The Naturalistic Treatment in a Metropolitan Park," *American Landscape Architecture* 2 (January 1930), 34–35.

17. William E. Golden, "History of Columbus Park—formerly Warren Woods," 1920 (CPD); ibid., 34–38.

18. Thomas McAdam, "Landscape Gardening under Glass," *Country Life in America* 21 (December 1911), 11–13.

19. Jens Jensen, *A Greater West Park System* (Chicago: West Park Commission, 1920); Grese, *Jens Jensen,* 87–94.

20. Jensen wrote several articles on plant distribution and soil types around Lake Michigan, and from botanist friends such as Henry C. Cowles and George D. Fuller at the University of Chicago he learned about the emerging science of plant ecology. Jens Jenson, letter to Camillo Schneider, 15 April 1939 (copy lent to the author by Darrel Morrison); Malcolm Collier, "Jens Jensen and Columbus Park," *Chicago History* 4 (Winter 1975), 228; Malcolm Collier, "Prairie Profile: Jens Jensen and the Midwest Landscape," *Morton Ar-*

boretum Quarterly 13 (Winter 1977), 51. Jensen also wrote several articles on plant distribution. See Jens Jensen, "Soil Conditions and Tree Growth around Lake Michigan," *Park and Cemetery* 14 (April 1904), 24–25, and 14 (May 1904), 42. Jensen's relation to larger efforts in plant ecology and the use of native plants in landscape design is explored in Grese, *Jens Jensen*, 52–61.

21. During World War II, Jensen moved his office from Steinway Hall to what had been his summer home in Ravinia. Gillette/Frank interview.

22. Wilhelm Miller, "What Is the Matter with Our Water Gardens?" *Country Life in America* 22 (June 1912), 24–26, 54.

23. Alfred Caldwell, interview by the author and Julia Sniderman, 31 January 1987.

24. On Jensen's plans this meadow is shown as a golf link—part of a small nine-hole course probably intended for Ford's son, Edsel. Shortly after the Fords moved into the house, however, Edsel married and moved away, and it is doubtful that the golf course was ever built.

25. When Jensen was hired by Henry Ford, in fact, Ford had already ordered a trainload of pine to reforest his estate. Jensen did use a few evergreens to mark special places in the landscape: the backdrop to a quiet pool, a hillside bubbling spring source, and the edges of a woodland grotto. But the general framework of the garden used deciduous trees and shrubs native to this area of Michigan. Alfred Caldwell, interview by Malcolm Collier, January 1979, 4:7 (MA)

26. Jensen, *Siftings*, 81–85; Jensen, "Naturalistic Treatment," 37.

27. Wilhelm Miller, "Bird Gardens in the City," *Country Life in America* 26 (August 1914), 46–47, 74.

28. Julia E. Rogers, "Bringing Back the Birds," *Country Life in America*, 1 September 1911, 27–29, 58, 60; Julia E. Rogers, "The Scientific Feeding of the Birds in Winter," *Country Life in America*, 1 December 1911, 55–56, 84; ibid, 46–47.

29. Robert E. Grese and Miriam Rutz, "History and Management Plan for the Grounds of the Edsel and Eleanor Ford House," report, Ford House, Grosse Pointe Shores, Mich., 1988, 47–48.

30. Robert E. Grese, "A Process for the Interpretation and Management of a Designed Landscape: The Landscape Art of Jens Jensen at the Lincoln Memorial Garden, Springfield, Illinois" (Master's thesis, University of Wisconsin, 1984), 109–11, 166; Jensen, *Siftings*, 86–87.

31. "Seedling Oaks Will Be Transplanted Soon," *Garden Glories,* September 1938, 15–16. For more on the Lincoln Memorial Garden, see Grese, *Jens Jensen,* 113–20. Jensen's work serves as an important model for current efforts to incorporate ecological principles into the practice of landscape design. Some of his later projects, such as the Lincoln Memorial Garden, also hold timely lessons for current ecological restoration efforts. Parts of this garden now function as a natural landscape; other areas are severely compromised by the invasion of weedy non-native plants from off the site and the absence of the fires that American Indians used to maintain the region's complex of woodlands, savannas, and prairies. Studies of the Lincoln Memorial Garden and other Jensen-designed landscapes indicate the need for on-going management programs. Merely reintroducing native plants into the landscape is not enough; landscape processes must also be restored.

32. J. Ronald Engel, *Sacred Sands: The Struggle for Community in the Indiana Dunes* (Middletown, Conn.: Wesleyan University Press, 1983), 200–201.

33. Jensen (*Siftings*, 66) claimed that the first ring he built was at his summer home in Ravinia, Ill. An earlier version, however, with a semicircular seat around a council fire, was constructed at the Rubens estate, which he began designing in 1903. (Jensen bought the property in Ravinia in 1908, so its council ring would have been built well after his work at the Rubens property.) At The Clearing, his later home and school in Ellison Bay, Wis., Jensen included two such rings. The more intimate of them was located on a prominent point overlooking the waters of Green Bay; a much larger one was situated in the

woods nearby. The larger was apparently intended for dance performances and was originally built for Sybil Shearer, a dancer from Chicago who brought her students to The Clearing. Shearer, interview by the author, January 1991.

34. Edsel Ford to Jens Jensen, 17 June 1925 (AAL).

35. *Forty-seventh Annual Report of the West Chicago Park Commissioners* (Chicago: West Park Commission, 1915), 18–24.

36. Jensen, *Siftings*, 66; Jens Jensen, "Report of Mr. Jens Jensen, Consulting Landscape Architect, on the Design of Columbus Park," in *Forty-ninth Annual Report of the West Chicago Park Commissioners* (Chicago: West Park Commission, 1917), 17; Frank A. Waugh, *Outdoor Theaters* (Boston: Richard G. Badger, 1917), 125–30; Genevieve Gillette, interview by Scott Hedberg, 27 March 1978 (tapes lent to the author).

37. Jens Jensen, "Object Lesson in Placing Park Sculpture," *Park and Cemetery* 18 (November 1908), 438.

38. "The Sculpture Show in Humboldt Park, Chicago," ibid., 440.

39. "Chicago's Park Sculpture Show," *Park and Cemetery* 19 (October 1909), 127–30.

40. Will H. Tippens and Julia Sniderman, "The Planning and Design of Chicago's Neighborhood Parks," in *A Breath of Fresh Air: Chicago's Neighborhood Parks of the Progressive Reform Era, 1900–1925* (Chicago: Chicago Park District, 1989), 25–26; Julia Sniderman, "Bringing the Prairie Vision into Focus," in *Prairie in the City: Naturalism in Chicago's Parks, 1870–1940* (Chicago: Chicago Historical Society, 1991), 28.

41. Paul B. Riis, "Poetic Park Trails," *Parks and Recreation* 15 (September 1931), 63–65.

42. Jens Jensen, "Report of Mr. Jens Jensen, Consulting Landscape Architect, on His Plan for the Greater West Park System," in *Fiftieth Annual Report of the West Chicago Park Commissioners* (Chicago: West Park Commission, 1918), 16–20; Jensen, *Greater West Park System,* 45–53.

43. Some of these features were used at other school sites designed by Jensen, such as the Helen C. Peirce School in Chicago (1917), the Roosevelt School in Mason City, Ia. (1924), and the Manitowac High School in Manitowac, Wis. (1920–25).

44. Malcolm Collier, "Organizations and Ideas in the Life of Jens Jensen," paper presented at the annual meeting of the National Association of Olmsted Parks, Chicago, 1982, 8–10 (MA).

45. Among those Jensen invited to its first meeting were Riverside businessman Avery Coonley; Harold Ickes, later secretary of the interior under President Franklin D. Roosevelt; Stephen Mather, who become the first director of the National Park Service; the poet Harriet Monroe; Dwight Perkins; and Augusta Rosenwald, the wife of Sears & Roebuck magnate Julius Rosenwald. Other notable members included Henry Cowles, George Fuller, and the writers Vachel Lindsay and Carl Sandburg.

46. The masque, titled *The Spirit of the Dunes,* was written by Mrs. Jacob Abt. Engel, *Sacred Sands,* 11–42; Kay Franklin and Norma Schaeffer, *Duel for the Dunes: Land Conflicts on the Shores of Lake Michigan* (Urbana: University of Illinois Press, 1983), 43–46.

47. Stephen K. Mather, *Report on the Proposed Sand Dunes National Park, Indiana* (Washington, D.C.: National Park Service, 1917).

48. Engel, *Sacred Sands,* 249.

49. Carol Doty, "About the Masque," *Morton Arboretum Quarterly* 7 (Spring/Summer 1971), 8.

50. Friends of Our Native Landscape, *Proposed Park Areas in the State of Illinois: A Report with Recommendations* (Chicago: Friends of Our Native Landscape, 1921), 15; John E. Trotter, *State Park System in Illinois,* Research Paper no. 24 (Chicago: University of Chicago, Department of Geography, 1962), 97–100.

51. Jensen, *Siftings,* 91–92.

52. Lincoln Highway Association, *The Lincoln Highway: The Story of a Crusade That Made Transportation History* (New York: Dodd, Mead, 1935), 203–11.

53. Mertha Fulkerson and Ada Corson, *The Story of The Clearing* (Chicago: Coach

House Press, 1972); Grese, *Jens Jensen,* 140–50. In his work and teaching at The Clearing, Jensen left a legacy of ideas about education and an approach to learning which he believed was essential for training people involved in the design and management of the landscape. His teaching style blended learning directly from nature with an appreciation of and involvement with the arts. Present-day classroom-based systems of education for designers are often narrow in their focus. The level of artistry Jensen advocated requires an intimate understanding of landscapes and a thorough knowledge of the natural processes and materials relating to their design. Jensen believed that designers of parks and gardens must understand a landscape's comprehensive history, not only the post–European settlement phase but earlier Native American activities and values as well. For him it was critical that landscape designers devote years to observing and learning about the regional environment and be capable of reading the landscape—that they be able to see land not only from their own limited perspective but through the eyes of many generations.

54. Jensen, *Siftings,* 109–10.

EIGHT

Warren H. Manning and His Minnesota Clients

DEVELOPING A NATIONAL PRACTICE IN A LANDSCAPE OF RESOURCES, 1898–1919

Lance M. Neckar

AT THE TURN OF THE CENTURY Minnesota was a microcosm of the possibilities and problems of the modern, progressive nation. Rich in natural resources, the state had been rapidly developed by Yankee immigrants who knew the business and technology of farming, logging, milling, and transporting goods and by European immigrants who saw in their work the possibility of a better life in this country. Landscape architect Warren H. Manning recognized its industrial and recreational potential, rail connectivity, and scenic beauty, which today are hallmarks of the state. Aggressive marketing yielded over seventy-five commissions for Manning in Minnesota, ranging from home grounds and estate designs to park, university, and industrial location plans, the latter concentrated on the Iron Range in the northern part of the state.[1] His clients, particularly in Minneapolis, the state's largest city, comprised an extraordinarily influential group of transplanted New Englanders and others who aspired to traditional "yankified" taste. Over the course of twenty years, beginning in 1898, Manning expanded his landscape architecture practice from its Boston base through the Midwest, and particularly in Minnesota, Wisconsin, and Illinois. It would soon become one of the country's largest, most successful firms; at the time of Manning's death, he had recorded over 1,600 commissions.

As Manning began to see and understand more of the Midwest, his response was to conceive of the region as a landscape resource, part of a constellation of national landscape resources. This was a period of progressivism, a culturally pervasive movement founded on faith in progress. Manning, perhaps naïvely, saw himself as an agent of transformation, harnessing individual wealth through landscape architectural projects to benefit the com-

Warren H. Manning,
c. 1920–25. (Courtesy of
the University of Massa-
chusetts Lowell, Center
for Lowell History)

monwealth. In the alliances he forged with his midwestern clients, many of
them "captains of industry" and their wives, Manning's strategy was to de-
mocratize wealth without substantially undermining its societal foundations.
Through his Minnesota projects, Manning tried to instill in his wealthy clients an understanding of the need to sustain human and natural resources—
the real sources of wealth. Manning's Minnesota work was also a microcosm
of his evolving larger vision for managing natural resources, a vision he articulated in his remarkable National Plan.[2]

Manning's interest in a comprehensive view of the nation's resources was
singular among landscape architects at this time. His mapping of large, complex landscapes to depict specific resources, such as forest cover in combination with roads, represented the first systematic attempt to develop an
analytical geographic information system. A progressive ideology under-
pinned Manning's emerging national vision: he saw the development of re-

sources as a vehicle for a better-balanced world economy and social order. In the final sentence of the National Plan Study Brief of 1923, he stated: "There can be no higher patriotism than this planning and working to help the United States of today and of our children's children to lead the world in its progress." The National Plan also articulated Manning's vision of a Euro-American nation in which governmental control of natural resources would check "the economic exploitation of the majority by a minority," which Manning postulated would lead to a more equitable sharing of profits among labor and industry.

Manning's ambitious evolving vision was a direct expression of his background and character. Like his mentor Frederick Law Olmsted Sr., Manning was a driven man. He went to work for his father, nurseryman Jacob Warren Manning, when he was six years old, packaging seeds on Saturdays. As he grew older he developed even more determined work habits. The trait served him well as a member the Olmsted firm in the 1880s and early 1890s, when all of the principals traveled extensively in the service of furthering a national practice that demanded their frequent presence on-site. Manning traveled with them and on his own, meeting clients, taking notes, sketching, and walking the project sites.[3]

Like Horace W. S. Cleveland, his predecessor in the Midwest, Manning was most successful when he traded on his New England roots, reinforced with personal client contact. His approach to work undoubtedly appealed to hard-headed midwestern businessmen, who might easily have written off a less attentive consultant—even one from Boston, the city that immodestly claimed to be the hub of the universe. These men dominated the public life of the young city of Minneapolis and, to a lesser degree, the more diverse, older city of St. Paul. Some of Cleveland's clients became Manning's; however, the passing of pioneering industrial leaders in the region coincided with Manning's more practical appeal to an eager younger generation.[4]

Manning extended his practice into the Midwest within the first years of setting up his office. His extensive horticultural experience on private estates with the Olmsted firm gave him a logical point of departure as he launched his own practice. The Olmsted experience also provided him with a model for establishing a national practice. In many ways, Manning's Midwest work can be viewed as a successful, pragmatic updating of the Olmsted model. He left his position as superintendent of planting for the Olmsted firm after eight years, in 1896, taking a significant group of midwestern client contacts with him. Among them were James H. Stout, a lumberman and U.S. senator from Menomonie, Wisconsin, and Frank H. Peavey, a Minneapolis grain magnate.[5] He secured additional clients through his work at the World's Columbian Exposition and other jobs for the Olmsted firm, particularly in Wisconsin and Illinois.

Warren Manning was not completely unfamiliar with the Midwest before his professional involvement there in the 1890s. At midcentury, two of his uncles had settled on opposite banks of the Mississippi River at Lake Pepin, seventy miles southeast of the Twin Cities, and Manning had spent one summer there as a boy, botanizing in western Wisconsin and Minnesota.[6] Manning saw the region's rapid growth late in the century against the backdrop of this early experience. His knowledge grew as he worked for the Olmsted firm in the heady period of 1892–93, when he assisted with the planting design and implementation at the World's Columbian Exposition in Chicago and on the Milwaukee parks system.[7] At the time, Manning had briefly contemplated relocating or expanding his practice to Chicago, and had broached the issue with his colleague O. C. Simonds, with whom he thought he might develop a partnership.

In a letter to his wife Nettie, in early December 1893, Manning described the situation, which seemed fairly advanced: "Will go out to see Mr. Simmonds [sic]—you remember he was a cemetery superintendent and Landscape Gardener I met while at the Fair. I want to talk landscape gardening with him. I think that the outcome of this trip may be very important in some ways to me. . . . It is possible that it may result in my staying permanently with the firm. . . . Do not hint to anyone however that there may be a change for there may be none."[8] In part, Manning's stratagem was a response to the extraordinary pressures of the grueling work in the Olmsted firm during this period. Manning was also under considerable pressure from his wife to spend more time at home. Undoubtedly he was considering forming his own practice as a way to control his schedule. Nothing came of the partnership idea, but Manning and Simonds remained friends for a long time.

When Manning embarked on his solo practice, he already had experience both with wealthy private clients and those who were operating with a larger civic vision and purpose. He was well positioned to succeed in the Midwest. Among his first midwestern clients were Cyrus and Harriet Hammond McCormick, who commissioned Manning to develop an arboretum and to stabilize the Lake Michigan shoreline at their estate, Walden, in Lake Forest, north of Chicago.[9] (Manning also designed the McCormicks' winter estate in Montecito, California.) His treatment was featured in Wilhelm Miller's *Prairie Spirit in Landscape Gardening* (1915) as an example of appropriate "lake bluff restoration" in its use of largely native plantings.[10] The McCormick commission was a large one, and Manning worked on it over many years. Harriet McCormick, in part through Manning's encouragement, became an enthusiastic promoter of landscape design. She was active in the American Park and Outdoor Art Association (APOAA), which Manning had been instrumental in founding in 1896, and also underwrote *Billerica,* one of Manning's magazine ventures.

Highcroft, the Peavey summer home in Lake Minnetonka, Minnesota, c. 1904. (Courtesy of the Minnesota Historical Society, St. Paul)

Manning's work for his Minnesota clients, with their public and private networks, reflected even more clearly his ideal of a progressive national practice, one that had both local and national consequences. He concentrated his work first in the Twin Cities, which, as he later wrote, were "notably attractive to visitors, residents, and for business by reason of location, historic, and landscape values. . . . The falls, the steep cliffed gorges of the river, the hundred or more lakes about the city with infinitely varied outline, bays, channels, shores, islands, and the much varied high lands within the cities gives unrivalled residential and institutional locations."[11]

Manning's first important Minnesota client was Frank H. Peavey, a Maine native and the owner of a colossal network of grain elevators and terminals that stretched across the entire region. In 1896 he was hired to complete the design of Highcroft, a summer estate on a high bluff above Lake Minnetonka, west of Minneapolis.[12] For this large, vaguely Colonial Revival house designed by William Channing Whitney, Manning developed a grand design of gardens, greenhouses, and agricultural fields and buildings. On the lake side of the house he created an open clearing that yielded a broad prospect over a belt planting along the main road to the water below. From the side porch, a vast formal flower garden set up views to the lake. This naturalistic open prospect style combined with formal gardens near the house was reminiscent of British prototypes and served as an ideal model for future estate development in his practice.

By spring 1898, work at Highcroft was far enough advanced that Manning, then secretary of the APOAA, arranged for the annual meeting to be held in Minneapolis and to include a visit to the garden hosted by Peavey. Manning also went on to work for Peavey's extended family, neighbors, employees, and colleagues—these clients were among the most emulated (and rich) families in Minnesota. In this way, Peavey provided an important entré to a network of midwestern clients. Manning capitalized on these contacts by providing his new clients with a style of service that suited their (real or presumed) Yankee lineage and their economic position in the evolving Minnesotan social hierarchy.

Manning's service with the APOAA also facilitated his work on civic projects in Minnesota. It brought him into contact with the principal public figures of Minneapolis and led to ties with two local visionaries, William Watts Folwell and Charles M. Loring.[13] Folwell, the first president of the University of Minnesota, and Loring, a miller and telephone company executive, had been early principal promoters of H. W. S. Cleveland's work in the development of parks in the Minneapolis metropolitan area. In no small measure, Manning's relationships with Folwell and Loring were critical to

Formal garden at Highcroft, c. 1904. (Courtesy of the Minnesota Historical Society, St. Paul)

his finding park work in the city. Since 1895, when Cleveland had become too aged to serve, the park commission had been without a landscape architect. Manning was clearly the kindred spirit, cut from the same New England cloth as his predecessor.

In 1899 Manning was commissioned to design Interlachen Park, a stretch of marshy ground with a low ridge between Lake Calhoun and Lake Harriet. The site was a gift to the city, some seventy acres from each of the two adjacent properties, Lakewood Cemetery and Colonel William S. King's Lyndale Farm.[14] Manning was also hired to work on a section of the East River Parkway and Powderhorn Park. The three projects were critical links in the parks scheme that Cleveland had envisioned and may have held symbolic value in the community as the first major works undertaken since his retirement.

Manning also outlined the proposed improvements to other parks in a "Report on the Minneapolis Parks" in early 1901. In the introduction, he recalled Cleveland's vision for the park system, quoting the elder landscape architect's revered sentiments: "I would have the city itself as such a work of art as may be a fitting abode of a race of men and women whose lives are devoted to a nobler end than money-getting and whose efforts shall be inspired and sustained by the grandeur and beauty of the scenes in which their

Central (Loring) Park in Minneapolis, Minnesota, c. 1905. (Courtesy of the Minnesota Historical Society, St. Paul)

Loring Park, c. 1906. (Courtesy of the Minnesota Historical Society, St. Paul)

lives are passed."[15] Cleveland's inspiration had been nurtured in the meadows, poetic and literal, of New England. His idea for Minnehaha Park, specifically, was born in the *Song of Hiawatha,* Henry Wadsworth Longfellow's poem about the overtaking of the native landscape by European American culture.[16] Cleveland saw the large river parks as emblems of nature, the ultimate engineer. This vision was the transcendentalist article of faith by which Folwell, Loring, and their generation had proceeded with the park system work.

When he invoked his predecessor's grand vision, however, Manning was also aware that a younger generation was ascendant, and that the old visionary spirit must give way to the new practicality of an era of problem-solving and progress. He knew that his clients were the generation attuned to the financial and commercial aspects of the public landscape. And so Manning was careful to add to the invocation of Cleveland's lofty sentiments that "there is also commercial value to beauty which is appreciated in one form or another by every individual."[17] Aesthetics—in this case, landscape beauty—was, in short, good business. It was a sentiment that undoubtedly spoke to more than a few pragmatic predispositions in the milling community.

Manning's 1901 report noted the work needed in each segment of the continuous park system and in most of the city's public squares, and gave more extended, eloquent treatment to four major projects: the proposed

Minnehaha Parkway (along Minnehaha Creek from Lake Harriet to the Mississippi) and Minnehaha Park; the Eastside Park and Parkway, which Manning had recommended be relocated to the quarry lands directly along the river rather than on an existing residential street; Powderhorn Park, originally planned and laid out by Cleveland in 1892 but not yet completed; and the Interlachen site, later renamed for the King farm, Lyndale.[18] The report had influenced the park commissioners, who hired Manning to draw up plans. Dire financial circumstances, however, abruptly ended Manning's work on the Minneapolis system in 1904.[19]

Through the same network of "insider" connections Manning landed commissions for the design of the Minnikahda Club, a golf course on Lake Calhoun, and the Lafayette (or Minnetonka) Club, a private club on the grounds of the old, mammoth Lafayette Hotel on Lake Minnetonka to the west of the city. William Channing Whitney, the architect of Frank Peavey's Highcroft, also designed the Lafayette.[20] Both Peavey and his Park Avenue neighbor Charles M. Harrington were members of the club. Harrington, a New York–born grain merchant and president of the chamber of commerce, would have had considerable influence on the decision to retain Manning (he hired Manning himself for a private commission in 1903). T. B. Janney, one of the older generation of Yankee businessmen, was a member of both clubs; he became a Manning client in 1902.[21]

Although the park and club work heralded Manning's arrival on the Minnesota scene, clearly he was most confident with residential projects. Between 1902 and 1913 Manning secured forty-five commissions to design private grounds for Twin Cities clients. He was not only attracting scores of clients, but, as a congenial and masterful salesman, was able to negotiate the region's complex and often treacherous intersections of business and social networks. For example, among the grain entrepreneurs he worked not only for four of the seven directors of the Washburn Crosby milling company, the precursor to General Mills, but also for a direct descendant of the rival Pillsbury line.[22] He focused on two areas, the rapidly urbanizing residential belt of palatial homes that ringed the southern edge of downtown Minneapolis and those clustered along the intricate shoreline of Lake Minnetonka.

Through the most fashionable neighborhoods of Minneapolis, Manning catered to the carriage trade. From Lowry Hill, where the streetcar tsar Thomas Lowry had erected his Hennepin Avenue mansion in the eighties, to nearby Groveland, where pioneer miller William H. Dunwoody, then vice president of Washburn Crosby, built his residence at the turn of the century, to Park Avenue, home of the Peavey clan and his company men, Manning garnered one commission after another. He seems to have secured these clients largely by word of mouth or through the architects involved. In the Park Avenue neighborhood, connections among the Peavey family and business associates link the commissions and those at the same clients' summer estates on Lake Minnetonka. J. S. Bell, another Washburn Crosby executive, for example, hired Manning to design both his Park Avenue estate grounds in 1903 and, in the next year, the landscape at Ferncroft, his summer retreat near Peavey's Highcroft.

Manning took an eclectic approach to these projects. His experience with the Olmsteds on private estates, at the World's Columbian Exposition, and to a lesser degree in park work had prepared him well to deal with the variety of situations he encountered in Minneapolis, and he was able to tailor his designs to his clients' needs and budgets. Manning never considered himself a stylistic purist; his work varied according to the circumstances of the client, the site, and, as his office grew, his staff. Manning never adopted a comprehensive regional design aesthetic in the sense that some of his colleagues, such as Simonds, did. He relied on his ability to read the specifics of the landscape and, more particularly, the client—to respond to the situation at hand—with an attentive facility. This process meant that, in some instances, he glossed over the fine points of the inherent genius loci of the re-

J. S. Bell summer house in Wayzata, Minnesota, c. 1907. (Courtesy of the Minnesota Historical Society, St. Paul)

gion, drawing instead on a well-crafted understanding of the organization and planting design of traditional landscape spaces.

A comparison of four commissions from 1902 to 1904 illustrates this variation and response to site. At the Lowry mansion in town, Manning adapted his design to the soft curves of the existing nineteenth-century garden. For Lowry's unusual brick Italianate summer house at Monticello, on the flat terraces above the Mississippi flood plain, Manning designed an extravagant walled formal garden. For Charles J. Martin, a Washburn Crosby executive, Manning provided a modest formal entrance court to the Renaissance Revival house designed by William Channing Whitney; the remainder of the dramatic steep site, where a fully developed villa garden might have been expected, was set out in an informal manner without significant reference to the architectural style. In contrast, for Penhurst, the in-town Dunwoody residence—featuring a Tudor Revival structure, also by Whitney—Manning adopted a formal style with a balustraded terrace scheme; as an interpretation of Tudor Renaissance precedent, the design brought the house and garden into aesthetic harmony.[23]

Manning remembered another commission from these early years in his autobiography, which he wrote in the thirties. Recounting his first visit to Red Oaks, the estate of T. B. Janney, one of the founders of Excelsior, Minnesota,

Grounds of the Thomas Lowry summer house in Monticello, Minnesota, c. 1905. (Courtesy of the Minnesota Historical Society, St. Paul)

Charles J. Martin House in Minneapolis, Minnesota, c. 1915. (Courtesy of the Minnesota Historical Society, St. Paul)

Manning described how, when he arrived on the site, the house was still under construction, though "framed and covered." Janney asked Manning where the landscape architect would have placed the house if he had been called in before it was built, and "I gave my reasons for another location. They led [Janney] to move the house to my site and grade over the first one."[24] Clearly, Manning had developed considerable authority with his new clientele.

Manning's connection to Sarah Pillsbury (Mrs. E. C. Gale), daughter of Governor John S. Pillsbury, was even more significant to his practice. He worked on her Upland Farm, in St. Bonifacius, between 1902 and 1908 and returned to it in 1919—it was one of the few private commissions in Minnesota that he carried into the latter half of the decade. During the first period of Manning's work on her estate, Mrs. Gale actively and successfully promoted Manning for the commissions that resulted from the university's campus expansion, which her father, one of the university's original regents, had inaugurated in 1889. Manning landed commissions not only to design plantings for two new halls but, more important, to develop a site plan for new buildings, to study the entrances to the campus, and to design a road along the campus edge bordering the curving valley of the Mississippi River.[25] However,

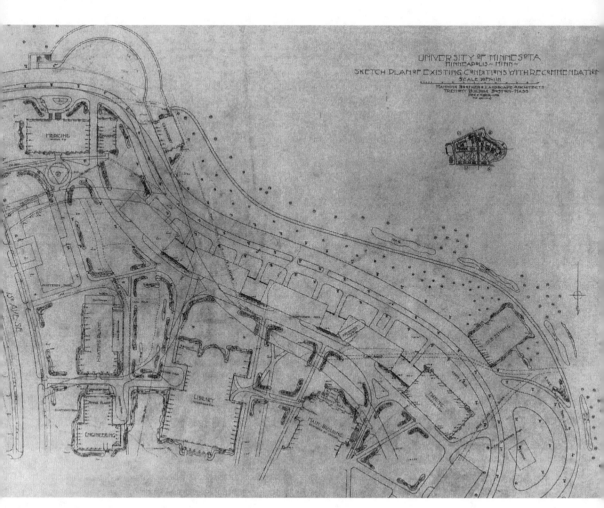

Expansion plan for University of Minnesota, 1902. (Courtesy of the Special Collections Department, Iowa State University, Ames)

Manning's firm disappeared from the scene after Cass Gilbert won a competition to design a mall to extend the campus southward to the Mississippi.

In 1918–19, Manning was hired by William Gwinn Mather, president of the Cleveland Cliffs Iron Company, for nine commissions. He had designed the Michigan company town Gwinn, for Mather and had done the planting designs for his Cleveland estate of the same name. Iron ore had been discovered in 1890 on the Mesabi Range in northern Minnesota. Across a wide territory, development was literally chopped out of the forest. The towns of Hibbing and Virginia were built first, but soon mining encampments and smaller towns were needed to bring workers closer to the vast open pits. By the first decade of the new century, the region was booming. Manning recorded these jobs as "industrial grounds," and although they likely were for relatively small-scale designs, grounds around offices, for example, some may also have been larger in scope—improvements around the vast pit sites in Hibbing and Kinney, for instance.[26]

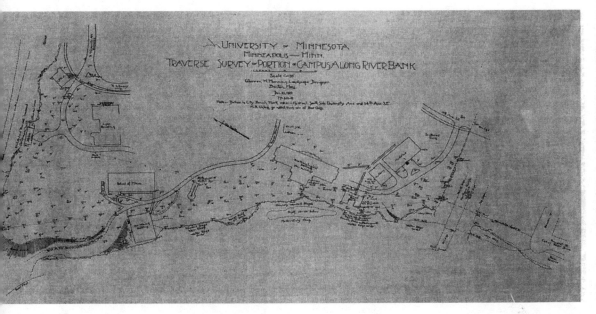

University of Minnesota traverse survey for an extension of the campus along the Mississippi River Road, 1905. (Courtesy of the Special Collections Department, Iowa State University, Ames)

As Manning undertook the Iron Range work, the United States had emerged victorious from World War I but was uneasy as a society with ongoing unresolved economic and cultural changes. These last Minnesota projects brought Manning far from the polite precincts of Minneapolis's finest neighborhoods and the glittering shores of Lake Minnetonka to an immediate confrontation with the resource bases of Minnesota's wealth. The Iron Range projects mirrored the realities of the country's social and economic inequities, and Manning's work in this region further developed his progressive model for landscape architecture.

By this time, Manning was carrying the responsibilities of a booming, expansive practice, as well as serving as president of the ASLA. He had become involved with national issues—the National Parks Act, housing for soldiers, and his own project, the monumental National Plan. Forseeing the necessity, he had several years earlier established one of his "boys," Charles Ramsdell, in Minneapolis to represent the Manning firm.[27] Manning himself had to quit the Minnesota scene.

❖

In the twenty years that he was involved with projects in Minnesota, Warren Manning developed a practice that allowed him to work on both large- and small-scale projects in nearly every state of the Union. While he remained a horticulturally grounded specialist in the design of relatively small private and public landscapes, he also became a land planner of much grander scope. During the period he developed commissions for Minnesota's most

Wade Mine in Kinney, Minnesota, c. 1915–18. On the far left is the "dry building" where minors changed their clothes. The large building is the power house. The four poles support the electrical substation. (Courtesy of the Cleveland Cliffs Mining Services Co., Ishpeming, Mich.)

Wade Mine, c. 1915–18. On the left is the repair shop for maintenance work. The Wade Mine office is the building on the right. (Courtesy of the Cleveland Cliffs Mining Services Co., Ishpeming, Mich.)

influential entrepreneurs and public figures, sometimes shaping its most important landscapes. As he gained experience he began to better understand Minnesota's place in the national picture. Although the scale of Manning's projects did not grow, his concerns and his vision did.

Notes

1. Warren H. Manning, "Record of Undertakings," ca. 1928, Manning Collection, Center for Lowell History, Lowell, Mass. (hereafter cited as MC).

2. Warren H. Manning, "National Plan Study Brief," *Landscape Architecture Quarterly* 13 (1923).

3. See Manning Letters and Business Records, MC.

4. See Lance Neckar, "Fast-Tracking Culture and Landscape: Horace William Shaler Cleveland and the Garden in the Midwest," in *Regional Garden Design in the United States,* ed. Marc Treib and Terese O'Malley (Washington, D.C.: Dumbarton Oaks, 1995), for an interpretation of Cleveland's role in defining a regional landscape aesthetic in the Midwest. See also an item in the Cleveland files of the Ramsey County Historical Society, St. Paul, Minn., which records that Manning and Cleveland corresponded during the period of the founding of the APOAA and that Manning visited Cleveland in Hinsdale, Ill.; this information is attributed to Charles Ramsdell, a landscape architect-in-training in Manning's Minneapolis office at the time.

5. Stout is the only one of the three which Manning recalled in his "Autobiography," ca. 1935, see pages 116–17; Stout is also noted in Manning's diary entry of 7 January 1896. The 1897 diary has many entries for the Peavey commission. Diaries and autobiography in MC.

6. William Manning, *The Genealogical and Biographical History of the Manning Families of New England and Descendants; From the Settlement of America to the Present Time* (Salem, Mass.: Salem Press, 1902); "Autobiography," 131; see also MC for manuscripts related to Lake Pepin.

7. The work in Milwaukee is liberally documented in MC; also see "Autobiography" and Manning Letters to Nettie (Henrietta), MC.

8. Manning, letter to Nettie, 2 December 1893, MC.

9. The link to the McCormicks and to Lake Forest may have developed as early as 1893, with the Olmsted work on the Chicago fair and simultaneous work on the Milwaukee parks system. Early notes on the McCormick work can be found in "Jobs, Journal Notes (1897)," vol. 39, MC.

10. Wilhelm Miller, *The Prairie Spirit in Landscape Gardening,* University of Illinois Agricultural Experiment Station Circular, no. 184 (Urbana, 1915).

11. "Autobiography," 131.

12. Horace B. Hudson, *A Half Century of Minneapolis* (Minneapolis: Hudson Publishing, 1905), 357–58; "Autobiography," 118–20; also see William Grundmann, *The Warren H. Manning Collection* (Ames: Iowa State University, Department of Landscape Architecture, 1985), 15–16, for citations of other Highcroft materials.

13. Jeffrey Hess, *Their Splendid Legacy: The First 100 Years of the Minneapolis Society of Fine Arts* (Minneapolis: Society of Fine Arts, 1983), 5. Also see William Watts Folwell Papers and Charles Loring Collection, c. 1897–1904, Minnesota Historical Society, St. Paul, for records of both men's involvement in the APOAA and local park system development.

14. See Manning, "Record"; also David Lanegran and Ernest Sandeen, *The Lake District of Minneapolis: A History of the Calhoun-Isles Community* (St. Paul: Living Historical Museum, 1979), 26–29; Minneapolis Board of Park Commissioners, *Annual Reports, 1899–1905;* and Warren H. Manning, "Report on the Minneapolis Parks," 13 January 1900 (Boston), 13–18.

15. "Report," 1.

16. Cleveland had known Longfellow as a youth. Also, the transcendentalist Ralph Waldo Emerson, author of the essay "Nature," had been among his first clients in the design of Sleepy Hollow Cemetery in Concord, Mass. See Neckar, "Fast-Tracking," 74–76.

17. "Report," 2.

18. To solve the complex convergence of traffic at Interlachen, Manning proposed a seemingly preposterous three-tiered grade separation of pedestrians, bicycles, and through traffic (including an existing streetcar track), and parkway traffic. The proposal was never built, and the bottleneck Manning had foreseen is one of the principal points of traffic congestion in the system.

19. In his "Record," Manning reported that he had prepared plans for Interlachen Park (1899–1904), Eastside Park (1899), Powderhorn Park (1899), and two commissions in 1903, the planting of the Lake Harriet pavilion site and of Loring Park. He also noted that he had prepared a plan or design for the St. Paul–Minneapolis Metropolitan Park System (1904–7), but no client was indicated, and the document has not been found. Manning was never hired for an official design commission on the St. Paul municipal park system. Theodore Wirth, *Minneapolis Park System: 1883–1944* (Minneapolis: Board of Park Commissioners, 1945), briefly mentions Manning; he also notes that the park commission was in dire financieal straits when it began the Manning commission and that Manning's plans outlined in the "Report" were "held in abeyance" (68).

20. Lake Minnetonka Garden Club, "Historical Reminiscences of Lake Minnetonka" (1945), 5, Minnesota Historical Society, St. Paul; Thelma Jones, *Once upon a Lake: A History of Lake Minnetonka and Its People* (Minneapolis: Ross and Haines, 1957), 253–54, 280–84. Whitney and Harry Wild Jones, a longtime member of the park board, are the two Minneapolis-based architects listed in Manning's promotional materials, MC.

21. Hudson, *A Half Century,* 358, 387, 431, treats various members of the Peavey and Heffelfinger clans but gives no clear indication of direct involvement of either in either club. See also Grundmann, *Manning Collection,* 15–16. See Hudson, *A Half Century,* 370, on Harrington; 438–39, on Janney. Whitney is credited with the Lafayette design in contemporary pamphlets found in the Minneapolis Municipal Collection and the Minneapolis Public Library.

22. "Record"; also see City Directories for the period, and Hudson, *A Half Century,* 154, for specific references to the Pillsbury line.

23. Photographs of the Lowry garden are in the Manning Collection, Iowa State, and the Audio and Visual Files of the Minnesota Historical Society; of the Martin garden, in A and V Files, MHS, and the Minneapolis City Reference Library; of the Dunwoody garden, in Lanegran and Sandeen, *Lake District.*

24. "Autobiography," 132.

25. Hudson, *A Half Century,* 94–97. Manning's drawing for the university projects of 1902–8 are held by the Manning Collection, Iowa State; see also the University Archives for a selection of copied images of these drawings and for early photographs of the drive.

26. Federal Writers Project, *Minnesota, the WPA Guide* (reprint; St. Paul: Minnesota Historical Society, 1945), 318–19. Photographs, c. 1915–20, archives of the Cleveland Cliffs Iron Company, Cleveland. See also Arnold Alanen, *The Planning of Company Communities in the Lake Superior Mining Region* (Madison: University of Wisconsin, Department of Landscape Architecture, 1979), 22–24c.

27. Beginning in January 1919, typical daybook records show expenses for the "Minneapolis Office"; three people are noted: W. Clarkson, F. J. Otis, and Charles Ramsdell.

NINE

The Olmsted Brothers in the Midwest

NATURALISM, FORMALISM, AND
THE CITY BEAUTIFUL MOVEMENT

William W. Tippens

THE LEGACY OF THE OFFICES established successively by Frederick Law
Olmsted Sr. and his sons, Frederick Jr. and John Charles Olmsted, remains
unparalleled in the history of American landscape architecture.[1] Over the
course of nearly a century these firms were involved with projects from Maine
to California and from Michigan to Florida. None was better known than that
of New York's Central Park, designed in 1858, where Olmsted Sr. and Calvert
Vaux incorporated the polarities of naturalistic and formal landscape design
to great and lasting effect. By the end of the century, however, any approach
to park design had to be realized within the overarching context of the pervasive City Beautiful movement.

The concept of the City Beautiful grew out of a desire to control the diversity and chaos of rapidly growing industrial cities by applying Beaux Arts
principles of classical order and monumentality to the design of urban spaces.
These principles were potentially at odds with those of the parks movement,
which was based on a belief in the salutary effect of nature on the human
spirit. Nowhere was the formalism/naturalism debate more vigorously carried on than in the Midwest. There architects such as Louis Sullivan and Frank
Lloyd Wright and landscape architects such as Jens Jensen and O. C. Simonds
were developing the Prairie School style, abandoning the formal precedents
so important to the City Beautiful movement and championed by the architect Daniel Burnham, among others. It was in the essential reconciliation of
these different approaches in urban park design—incorporating both naturalistic and formal elements—that Olmsted Brothers made one of their most
significant contributions. Their midwestern work, much of it accomplished
between 1895 and 1905, is especially interesting in this regard.

❖

The Olmsteds' lengthy association with the Midwest began in 1868 with Olmsted Sr. and Calvert Vaux's work on the new town of Riverside, Illinois. One year later, the team accepted the commission to design Chicago's South Parks. The Olmsted firm returned to Jackson Park two decades later, first when Olmsted Sr. was hired to supervise the transformation of its swampy lakefront into the setting for the Columbian Exposition, and then again in 1895, during the removal of the exposition's "White City," when Olmsted, Olmsted and Eliot were recalled to implement the park's original design.[2]

Olmsted and Vaux's 1871 plan for the South Parks (what came to be Jackson Park, Washington Park, and the Midway Plaisance) encompassed an open space system of more than one thousand acres. In the report accompanying that plan, Olmsted Sr. had envisioned the transformation of Jackson Park's swampland into a reserve of lagoons, islands, and glades; his description of the site revealed that Lake Michigan had had an extraordinary effect on the proposed design: "There is but one object of scenery near Chicago of special grandeur or sublimity, and that, the Lake, can be made by artificial means no more grand or sublime. By no practical elevation or artificial hills . . . would the impression of the observer in overlooking it be made greatly more profound. The Lake may, indeed, be accepted as fully compensating for the absence of sublime or picturesque elevations of land."[3] Washington Park, smaller than Jackson, was built on higher and drier ground, with a large open meadow in the center. The mile-long Midway Plaisance provided a wide, straight connecting ribbon between the two. Olmsted proposed a canal within the Midway to connect the lagoons in Jackson and Washington Park. The Great Fire of 1871 precluded construction of the planned system, although work on Washington Park proceeded under the supervision of the local landscape gardener H. W. S. Cleveland.

In 1891, the Olmsted, Olmsted and Eliot firm returned to the Midwest to design another lakeshore commission, Lake Park in Milwaukee. The sublimity of Lake Michigan, which had earlier so moved Olmsted Sr., once again impressed the designers, who in their proposal considered the untamed water of the lake a major design element. While Olmsted Sr. was somewhat chagrined that the park was not closer to the city's downtown, where the middle and lower classes would have had easier access to it, its bluffs, ravines, and lakeshore offered many opportunities for developing dramatic views and vistas.

The design of Lake Park incorporated many of the components that have become familiar attributes of Olmsted landscapes: a concert grove, a carriage concourse, and a system of drives to serve active park users, and for times of contemplation and more passive activities, paths and secluded glades. A

meadow was also proposed, for which one of the site's many ravines would have to be filled. On the whole, however, the ravines were valued and preserved.[4]

Somewhere in each of his parks, Olmsted Sr. liked to provide a mystery-laden wilderness, or "ramble"—the term he used for such an area in Central Park. Lake Park's thickly wooded ravines and bluffs offered a natural and uniquely "wild" landscape; their abrupt vertical surfaces could not have been replicated artificially. Dramatic views could be had from both footpaths and drives at the bottom of the ravines or from the bridges that spanned them. These diverse vantage points offered visitors different perspectives of the same landscape. Moreover, each ravine also connected the park to the adjacent great lake. The primary carriage drive was laid out to enhance the experience of the dramatic body of water. As visitors entered the park from the south, they saw the vast lake below the bluff to the right of the carriageway. Passing the lighthouse, they followed the drive into the park's interior. As the view of the lake closed, another opened across the meadow, in the opposite direction. Thus, when the lake began to recede from view behind the carriage, the sea of water was replaced by a sea of verdure. The carriageway then turned away from the meadow, and drivers could follow either the upper road or the ravine drive, which dropped toward the lake. Lush vegetation on the adjacent slopes enclosed this curving roadway until the view ahead burst open to an endless horizon over the ever-changing water. Lake Park's natural attributes offered Olmsted, Olmsted and Eliot a dramatic opportunity to

Lake Michigan shoreline in Milwaukee, Wisconsin, where Lake Park was developed. Note the steep ravines running to the waterfront. (Courtesy of William H. Tishler)

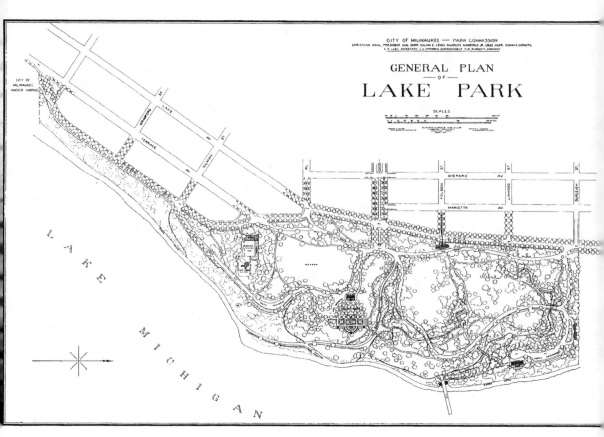

General plan for Lake
Park prepared by
Olmsted, Olmsted and
Eliot in 1895. (Courtesy
of the National Park
Service, Frederick Law
Olmsted National His-
toric Site, Brookline,
Mass.)

explore in a new and distinctive midwestern landscape the design ideas introduced by Olmsted and Vaux in New York's Central Park.[5]

In 1891 Olmsted Sr. returned to Chicago to help lay out the Columbian
Exposition, conceived as a temporary construction. After its partial demise
in 1894, Olmsted, Olmsted and Eliot were retained by the South Parks commissioners to redesign the site as a park. Their new plan returned to ideas
from Olmsted and Vaux's original 1871 design. When Daniel Burnham, formerly director of works for the exposition, saw that it called for the removal
of Grand Canal in Jackson Park, he was shocked and wrote to a friend: "The
scheme of Jackson Park is very poor and uninteresting. I was utterly aston-
ished to find them destroying the canals and the grand basin; this seemed to
me a bloodless proceeding." He could not believe that the plan came from
"the Frederick Law Olmsted of old."[6]

But the desire to return to the intentions of the original Olmsted, Vaux
plan is understandable. The site was no longer the setting for monumental
buildings that displayed the technological prowess of mankind but was once
again a windswept area far from the city center, on the shore of the lake. The
setting called for a naturalistic design—with one exception, the north end,

South entrance to Lake Park showing an ornate iron bridge and an early lighthouse that is still in the park. (Courtesy of William H. Tishler)

One of Lake Park's early rustic wooden bridges spanning a steep, densely vegetated ravine. (Courtesy of William H. Tishler)

where the Fine Arts Pavilion of the fair had been located and remained. (Here Olmsted, Olmsted and Eliot introduced a great lawn on the north side of the building and a reflecting pond to the south, which complemented the structure's formal, civic character.) The project reflected the Olmsteds' fundamental approach to designing largely outlying urban parks: a use of predominantly naturalistic design with the inclusion of some City Beautiful elements, such as civic buildings.

These principles were significant in the redesign of the Midway Plaisance after the fair, in which Olmsted, Olmsted and Eliot dramatically altered the original Olmsted, Vaux proposal. In the 1871 plan, the Midway was to be an entirely fenced, closed ground with a series of intimately spaced outdoor rooms delineated by masses of shrubbery surrounding the canal. The 1894 redesign conceptualized the Midway as an unfenced park with open expanses of lawn divided by a rigorously straight canal and formal plantings lining the straight boulevard. This dramatic shift can be attributed, in part, to the designers' consideration of the changing neighborhood that bordered the park. To the north, an academic city was emerging; the Midway was becoming the front yard of the University of Chicago. Unlike the southern portion of Jackson Park, where the naturalistic feature of Lake Michigan dominated, the Midway (like the northern section of Jackson Park in the precinct of the Fine Arts Pavilion) was dominated by the architecture of the university.

The principle that landscapes should respect their surrounding built environment is clearly articulated in the Olmsteds' writings. In remarks about the landscape of the University of Chicago, they clarified what they believed to be distinct characteristics and appropriate use of the formal and the informal. Asked by the university trustees to review O. C. Simonds's plan, the Olmsteds acknowledged their colleague's ability but indicated that his design was inappropriate for the formal campus: "Mr. Simonds has failed to realize that the buildings are many times more important than the grounds and that their layout and massive, imposing architectural style absolutely demand, from an artistic point of view, a corresponding simplicity, formality and dignity in the treatment of the ground [sic]. We feel obliged, therefore, to advise that the drives which remain to be constructed be laid out on straight lines or where it is necessary to have curves that the curves be radial and distinctly formal."[7]

Where the public interest was best served by sylvan or pastoral landscapes in outlying parks such as Jackson, the Olmsteds believed that the integrity of such an environment should be protected from buildings or monuments that might disrupt the tranquillity these landscapes were intended to engender. This philosophy was tested in the southern section of Jackson Park when it was selected as the site for a monument dedicated to General John Logan, a Civil War hero. The designers were deeply troubled by the proposal, which

Cascading steps lead
down the slope from the
pavilion in Lake Park.
(Courtesy of William H.
Tishler)

A pond in West Park
(now Washington Park),
one of the three parks in
Milwaukee planned by
Olmsted's office. (Cour-
tesy of the State Historical Society of Wisconsin,
Madison)

they felt to be contrary to the philosophy of a naturalistic park, and waged a campaign to have the monument put in a more suitable location. "In our opinion," they wrote,

> no important military monument ought to be erected in a park of such size and design that is essentially a piece of landscape, because the sentiment and character of a great military leader in time of war is incongruous with those sentiments and ideas which any successful piece of rural park landscape, whether sylvan or pastoral, is designed to call forth in the mind of the beholder. The accomplishment of great results in war can only be attained through an appalling loss of life and property, or in other words, though bold destructiveness, and while this dark side of the persons or events to be commemorated may be obscured by the glory and brilliance of the results accomplished, still it is characteristic and any one of a sensitive mind must necessarily suffer in his enjoyment of a rural park from the contemplation of such a subject.[8]

The Olmsteds did believe, however, that formal parks in more urban locations could be appropriate for such memorials and suggested Grant Park, which was being constructed on the lakefront next to downtown Chicago.

> It seems to us that the appropriate place for a military monument is in the heart of the finest part of the city, in the midst of the busy, stirring life of the community, not among their quiet homes and surely not amidst the peaceful quiet scenery of a rural park. . . . The finest opportunity for placing this splendid work of art among appropriate surroundings will be found in the development of the new Lake Front, where it will be accessible to vastly greater numbers of people, especially to strangers, who are usually in the receptive mood for appreciating the magnificent and artistic features of the City. If we look for suggestions in such a matter to what has been done in Europe, we find that almost always the monuments to the great leaders of men are placed in city squares, rather than in rural parks. That is not due to accident or to tradition, but to the sense of appropriateness.[9]

Grant Park began as a thin strip of land between Michigan Avenue and the Illinois Central train trestle along the lake's edge. By the 1870s the lake was being filled with debris from the Great Fire and other refuse. Eventually the landfill became part of an intentional program to create additional parkland. Immediately adjacent to the business district, traversed by a rail line, and protected from the lake by a series of breakwaters, the new park was a product of and completely surrounded by bold features representing the triumph of man's technology.

Although they began their association with Grant Park in 1895 (and through their persistence Logan Memorial was constructed there in 1897), it was only in 1903 that Olmsted Brothers were officially hired to develop a comprehensive plan for it.[10] Everyone who had been involved with the park since its inception, including Daniel Burnham, agreed that the landscape should be formal, subservient to the architectural environment that surrounded it.[11] Olmsted Brothers followed the design philosophy they had expressed in regard to O. C. Simonds's University of Chicago campus plan. Framed by the principles of the City Beautiful movement, their plan acknowledged the importance of the great public edifices that were to occupy the space. At the park's center, on new landfill beyond the tracks, was the Field Museum of Natural History. Congress Boulevard was laid out on axis with the building, culminating in a grand plaza at Michigan Avenue, from which the stately building, set high on a plinth, could be seen. Two spacious meadows were placed symmetrically on either side of the museum, and a grand boulevard bordered the lake. The Art Institute of Chicago had occupied a site in Grant Park along Michigan Avenue since 1893. To balance it to the north, the John Crerar Library was sited equidistant south of Congress Boulevard. The park's roads and paths defined the symmetry and balance of the buildings while subordinating the landscape to them.

However, litigation prevented construction of the Field Museum in the park, and the Olmsted Brothers' plan was never implemented. The building's eventual relocation at the southern end of the park required a new design. Although the Olmsteds made several new plans, the one undertaken was by Edward Bennett, formerly with D. H. Burnham's firm. Nevertheless, the park's overall spatial composition, formalism, and strict symmetry relate directly to recommendations in the Olmsteds' 1903 plan.

Lake Park, Jackson Park, and Grant Park were all designed in general for passive recreation. As active recreation became more important and the requirements of recreation changed over time, park design had to respond accordingly. Olmsted Sr. had defined two types of recreation: receptive, which included walking, concerts, and seasonal festivals, and exertive, which included not only ball games and other sports but activities such as chess which stimulated the mind.[12] Few parks at this time, naturalistic or formal, were designed to include athletics and facilities for active sports. But Olmsted, Olmsted and Eliot proposed a track and playground for the western edge of Jackson Park as early as 1895, and their design revision for Grant Park included an athletic center at the park's southern boundary.

A new series of neighborhood parks for the South Parks commissioners gave Olmsted Brothers an opportunity to further develop their design philosophy. There they carried the influence of the City Beautiful movement beyond the city centers and into the neighborhoods.[13] Communities nationwide were influenced by the example of civic and recreational facilities appearing in neighborhood parks.

Program elements for the neighborhood parks were articulated by J. Frank Foster, the visionary general superintendent of the South Parks com-

Sketch of Davis Square, one of the proposed new series of South Park neighborhood playgrounds that emphasized active recreation. (Reprinted from the *Chicago Tribune,* 5 Feb. 1904; courtesy of the Chicago Park District Special Collections, Chicago, Ill.)

missioners, who has been referred to as the "father of the small park."[14] Early in 1903 Foster proposed that neighborhood parks should include a ball field, a running track, sand pits, a swimming pool, a wading pool, outdoor gymnasiums, and areas with shade trees and shrubs for desperately needed green space in the densely populated neighborhoods. Foster wanted these parks to provide health-enhancing athletic areas and green areas for rest and relaxation.[15] Thus, Olmsted Brothers were charged with synthesizing program elements defined by the playground movement with those of traditional park landscapes—the same task that had been addressed in the late 1880s and early 1890s in Boston by F. L. Olmsted and Company.[16]

Because of Chicago's bitter winters, indoor gymnasiums were necessary to extend neighborhood park benefits beyond six months of the year, and assembly halls and club rooms were needed.[17] Including all such facilities in the same building gave rise to the field house, a new type of civic building that became the most prominent built element in the South Parks Commission neighborhood parks. Their classical Beaux Arts design, by D. H. Burnham and Com-

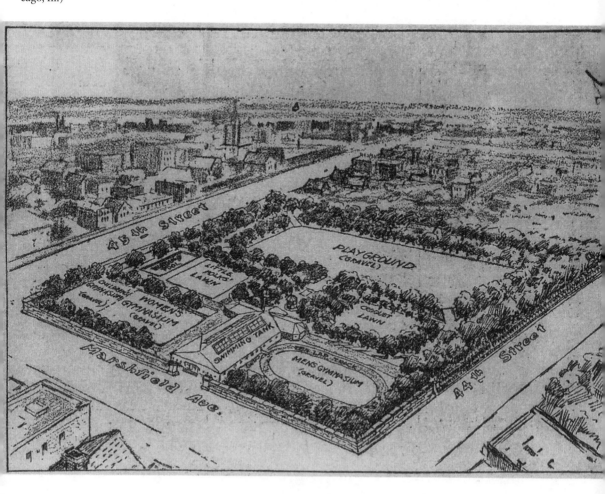

pany, strongly influenced the landscape design of Olmsted Brothers. Regardless of the size of the new parks, the Olmsteds organized the components of each to create appropriate settings for the field house.

The young architect overseeing Burnham's commission was Edward Bennett, who also helped Burnham with the 1909 Chicago Commercial Club plan of Chicago and was instrumental in seeing its implementation after his death. Bennett's designs fit the orderly mold of the Burnham office, although they varied in the details depending on the respective site and makeup of the surrounding neighborhood. The president of the South Parks Commission, Henry Foreman, was proud to write that "the field houses reflect in miniature the architectural beauty of the world's fair buildings."[18]

In December 1903, John Olmsted sketched on a sheet of hotel stationery a prototype design for the South Parks Commission's neighborhood parks.[19] All park activities were divided by type of facility needed and placed in different zones of the park. Women's activities were separated from men's. Facilities requiring supervision were clustered along a single edge of the park. The front entry court, children's playground area, running track, wading pool, men's and women's open-air gymnasiums, swimming tank, and changing booths were symmetrically arranged around the field house. The remaining portion of the park was devoted to a ball field and areas for passive pursuits. A border of trees, shrubs, and grass delineated the latter, which the Olmsteds referred to as the "usual location for shade trees in a playground."[20] Immediately within this boundary planting was a promenade. In the 1903 sketch, this walkway echoed the orthogonal city grid, turning right angles at the corners of the ball field. The promenade terminated at the field house entrance court, which looked out over the ball field. The entrance court, ball field, and promenade played an important role in creating a suitable field house setting. Viewed from the promenade opposite the field house, the trees became the framing foreground, the ball field, the middle ground, and the field house, the focal point in the background. Various manifestations of these elements occurred in each of the neighborhood parks. The squares—parks under ten acres—were formal in design because they were dominated by a large field house. Heavy demand on these landscapes to accommodate many activities restricted passive uses to the promenades and surrounding grassy areas. The larger parks, too, were dominated by formal elements. One exception was Sherman Park, whose original plan was altered to create an intricate landscape comprising primarily naturalistic areas. Initially, Olmsted Brothers developed a formal design consisting of a rectangular island within straight canals with hard edges. The plan resembled a Beaux Arts building complete with central and end pavilions connected by curtain wings.[21] John Olmsted wrote of Burnham's delight with it and his desire for even stronger formalism: "Burnham was particularly pleased with No. 7. He criticized the

Children in a wading pool at Chicago's Mark White Square neighborhood park (now McGuane Park), c. 1905. (Courtesy of the Chicago Park District Special Collections, Chicago, Ill.)

pair of water shelters or summer houses not being on axis of the men's running track. I said we could easily adjust that. Also he suggested that the two footbridges be on axis of the two field houses. I agreed we could easily adjust that."[22]

But neither Henry Foreman nor Frank Foster was enthusiastic about the initial proposal, primarily because of the construction costs of the rigid canals. As a result, the Olmsteds redesigned the park with a wandering canal and a soft-edged island. Although both John Olmsted and Burnham continued to fight for the earlier design, the two commissioners eventually prevailed. In the new design, however, the Olmsteds did maintain a formal landscape in the northern third of the property around the field house and active recreation facilities. The field house, with its auditorium, library, lunch room, and club rooms, was separated from the athletic buildings by a large outdoor court defined by a series of pergolas, which had a tree-lined esplanade running through it. The entire building complex was sited on an earthen island terraced down to the meandering lagoon. The park perimeter was bermed to separate the pastoral scenery from the surrounding busy neighborhood, and the paths and road encircling this area curved informally among masses of vegetation.

Subtle elements were used to enhance the transition between the formal and informal portions of the park. These included the style and detailing of four bridges that connected the island to the edge of the park: the two in the southern, pastoral section of the park were rustic in character, while the two in the northern section, adjacent to the recreation complex, were refined, with classical details. Vegetation along the interior roadway also played a part: within the southern section of the park the trees and shrubs were massed in informal clusters; where the road curved and became the esplanade through the recreation complex, the trees were formally planted in double rows. The resulting Sherman Park landscape combines the informal design pioneered by Olmsted Sr. with the formalism that his successors deemed important to the context of civic buildings, while they maintained a clear separation between the zones of influence of each.

The desire for a beautiful and efficient city led to the design of environments that served distinctive purposes and were clearly made for given activities. In an address he gave in 1910, Frederick Law Olmsted Jr. referred to the planned city as having "complex unity": "The idea of city planning is one in which all these activities—all the planning that shapes each one of the fragments that go to make up the physical city—shall be so harmonized as to reduce the conflict of purpose and the waste of constructive effort to a minimum, and thus secure for the people of the city conditions adapted to their attaining the maximum of productive efficiency, of health, and of enjoyment of life."[23]

Following this theory, Olmsted Brothers designed landscapes of retreat in a naturalistic manner while advocating that civic areas be formal and subservient to the architecture that represented the icons of the industrial city. Burnham and Bennett's 1909 plan of Chicago clearly articulated these concepts. It included a design for Grant Park showing several elements that appeared in Olmsted Brothers' earlier plans as well as several scenes from the neighborhood parks they designed and the plan of Sherman Park. As a result of the Chicago Plan and of others by Burnham, Bennett, and Frederick Law Olmsted Jr., the distinctive use of landscape design as part of the City Beautiful movement influenced the development of many cities. The work of Olmsted Brothers on the shores of Lake Michigan nurtured this significant role for landscape design.

Notes

1. In 1859 Frederick Law Olmsted Sr. married his brother's widow and adopted her children, young John Charles among them. Eleven years later, Frederick Law Olmsted Jr. was born. The stepbrothers' most influential training for their future career came from their early life experiences. John watched the construction of Central Park and camped in the Sierra Nevada, where his stepfather managed a gold mine. He also worked in the rugged West with the 40th Parallel survey team. This training was supplemented with a formal education at Yale's Sheffield Scientific School, and he joined his stepfather's firm in 1875. Frederick Jr. worked in Chicago during construction of the World's Columbian Exposition and in North Carolina on his father's commission at George W. Vanderbilt's estate, Biltmore. He officially entered the firm as an apprentice in 1895. After the senior Olmsted retired that year, the firm's work passed into the hands of Charles Eliot and the two stepbrothers. A year following Eliot's untimely death in 1897, John and Frederick Jr. formed Olmsted Brothers.

2. The day after the selection of Jackson Park as the site for the fair, in July 1890, South Parks commissioner Richard Ellsworth made plans to visit Olmsted and secure his services for the design of the grounds (Ellsworth to Daniel Burnham, 22 November 1893, Burnham Papers, Burnham Library, Chicago Art Institute; hereafter cited as BP). Ellsworth maintained a relationship with the Olmsted firm during his tenure as commissioner.

3. Olmsted, Vaux and Co., "Report Accompanying Plan for Laying Out South Park," Chicago, 1871.

4. Christian Wahl, "Public Park System of the City," in *History of Milwaukee from Its First Settlement to the Year 1895,* ed. Howard Louis Conard (Chicago, 1895), 5.

5. Owing to the constant vigilance of Christian Wahl, a member of the first Milwaukee board of park commissioners, the intent of Olmsted, Olmsted and Eliot was carried out with few alterations; Diane M. Buck, "Olmsted's Lake Park," *Milwaukee History* 5, no. 3 (1984), 57–58.

6. Undated correspondence between D. H. Burnham and Mr. Ware, BP.

7. Olmsted Brothers to C. L. Hutchinson, 20 March 1902; copy in Olmsted Papers, Manuscript Division, Library of Congress; hereafter cited as OP.

8. Olmsted Brothers to Mr. James Ellsworth, 25 August 1896; copy in OP.

9. Ibid.

10. Following the Olmsteds' letter to Ellsworth, Daniel Burnham was requested to complete sketches of the piece in Grant Park, which he sent to Mrs. John Logan, to Olmsted, Olmsted and Eliot, and to the sculptor, Augustus Saint-Gaudens. Mrs. Logan approved the new location on 31 October 1896. D. H. Burnham to Mrs. John Logan, 30 September 1896; Burnham to Olmsted, Olmsted and Eliot, 1 October 1896; Burnham to Augustus St.-Gaudens, 1 October 1896; Mrs. John Logan to South Parks Commissioners, 31 October 1896; copies in BP.

11. Despite the significant sentiment in favor of constructing the new park on the lakefront, Ellsworth was reluctant to commit public funds to it before he had received a strong mandate from the public that it was a project worth pursuing. Burnham agreed to complete the sketches on a pro-bono basis in order to facilitate discussion. Burnham speech to Merchants Club, 16 April 1896, 1; copy in BP.

12. Frederick Law Olmsted Sr., *Public Parks and the Enlargement of Towns* (Cambridge, Mass., 1870), 17.

13. The Playground Association of America held its first annual convention in Chicago in 1907. Before the meeting President Theodore Roosevelt had issued a statement encouraging people from around the country to attend "to see the magnificent system that Chicago has erected in the South Park[s?] district, one of the most notable achievements of any American city." *South Parks Commission Annual Report, 1909,* 37.

14. Tributes to J. Frank Foster, private publication, 28; copy in Chicago Park District Special Collections.

15. J. Frank Foster, "An Article on Small Parks," paper read before the Chicago Society for School Extension, c. 1903, 16 pp.; copy in Pamphlet Collection, Chicago Historical Society.

16. Cynthia Zaitzevsky, *Frederick Law Olmsted and the Boston Park System* (Cambridge: Harvard University Press, 1982), 95–108.

17. Ibid.

18. Henry G. Foremen, "Chicago's New Park Service," *Century Magazine* 69 (February 1905), 610–20.

19. Sketch for a ten-acre playground by John Olmsted, 30 December 1903. Olmsted site, Brookline, Mass.

20. Olmsted Brothers to H. Foreman, 7 December 1903; copy in Job Files, OP.

21. Olmsted Brothers, Brookline, Mass., "Preliminary Design for Park No. 7," 1904; copy in Chicago Park District Special Collections.

22. John C. Olmsted, "Field Notes on Chicago Parks," 1 February 1904; copy in Job Files, OP.

23. Frederick Law Olmsted Jr., "City Planning," in *Proceedings of the Second National Conference on City Planning and the Problems of Congestion,* 2–4 May 1910 (Cambridge: Harvard University Press, 1912), 15.

TEN

Wilhelm Miller

PRAIRIE SPIRIT IN LANDSCAPE GARDENING

Christopher Vernon

THE PRAIRIE SCHOOL, named for the region's definitive ecological phenomenon, is the most readily identifiable landscape design legacy of the Middle West. The Chicago-based movement was initiated in landscape architecture by O. C. Simonds and later championed by the flamboyant, outspoken Jens Jensen. These designers, like their architectural counterparts, sought to establish a middle western cultural identity, and crusaded for fresh regional expressions.[1] Avoiding the New England landscape imagery and Italianate gardens tentatively introduced into the prairie by many of their eastern contemporaries, Simonds and Jensen worked within the context of the open, indigenous middle western landscape—with its omnipresent horizon—and allowed it to inform their designs.[2] The movement coalesced in what Wilhelm Tyler Miller termed the "prairie spirit in landscape gardening," or the "Prairie School." Miller was a celebrated horticultural writer and editor for *Country Life in America* and *The Garden Magazine* who defined and intensively promoted a comprehensive awareness of the prairie and its inspirational potential for landscape gardening. Miller's efforts culminated in the publication in 1915 of his manifesto, *The Prairie Spirit in Landscape Gardening*. The work provided an ideological catalyst for the Prairie School.[3]

Born on 14 November 1869 in King William County, Virginia, Wilhelm Tyler Miller was raised in Detroit, Michigan.[4] In keeping with the family tradition, Miller attended the University of Michigan, graduating in 1892. At the suggestion of his uncle, the literary historian Moses Coit Tyler, Wilhelm "harnessed his sentimental interest in nature" and pursued graduate studies at

Wilhelm Miller (lower left) and his wife, the nature-study writer Mary Rogers Miller (with camera), at Starved Rock, c. 1913, during an outing of Jens Jensen's conservation group, The Friends of Our Native Landscape. (Photograph by Jens Jensen; courtesy of the Jens Jensen Collection in the archives at the Morton Arboretum, Lisle, Ill.)

Cornell University under the direction of the renowned botanist and horticulturalist Liberty Hyde Bailey.[5] Miller later received both his master's and a doctorate from Cornell.

In 1896, while still a "special student in horticulture," Miller was hired as Bailey's assistant at the university's agricultural experiment station.[6] It was the beginning of a friendship that would prove lifelong. At Cornell Miller became involved with studies of chrysanthemums and dahlias and efforts to popularize them and wrote experiment station bulletins on these subjects.[7] As early as 1897 Bailey recognized Miller's abilities. In his preface to Miller's bulletin *A Talk about Dahlias,* he remarked, "Although Mr. Miller may not agree, I do not consider the dahlia to be the chief merit of this bulletin. The best thing in it is the personal point of view."[8] Miller's personal point of view would emerge as a hallmark of his publications. In 1897 Bailey appointed Miller associate editor of his monumental, and now classic, publication, the *Cyclopedia of American Horticulture.*[9] In addition to editing, Miller contributed several essays to the *Cyclopedia.* His survey of American landscape gardening not only was instrumental in expanding his interests from horticultural studies of a single flower to embrace theories of landscape design, but it apparently also stimulated his thinking about what constituted an "American" style of landscape gardening. This idea would come to dominate Miller's writings.

In 1901 Bailey was hired to edit a new magazine, *Country Life in America.* The "growing interest in country life" and the "growth of suburbanism" were cited as the primary factors leading to its creation. Bailey expressed what he believed to be the magazine's progressive mission and audience: "We stand for the elevation and betterment of farming in its best and broadest sense, because the fundamental thing in a self-sustaining country life is agriculture. . . . We shall make sketches of farms and gardens [and] endeavor to portray the artistic in rural life. . . . *Country Life in America* is a country magazine for the country man, and for the city man who wants to know the country; it is not a city magazine that sees the country afar off and takes it for granted. . . . We hope that the smell of the soil will be on its pages." Bailey also emphasized that *Country Life* would "take particular account of horticultural matters." In response to his effort to "enlist the best literary talent of the day" and perhaps at his suggestion, the publisher soon hired Bailey's former pupil and associate Wilhelm Miller as horticultural editor.[10]

The advent of *Country Life in America* did not go unnoticed by the architectural press. The editor of the *Architectural Record,* for example, summarily reported that "[Americans] have decided that they do not take enough interest in the country, and now with perhaps even greater enthusiasm, they are preparing to make themselves more familiar with nature. Bird books are being published by the score and sell as well as romantic novels. Books about all kinds of gardens are almost equally in demand, and a hot fight is on between the advocates of the formal and the so-called 'natural' garden. Within the last six months two periodicals [*Country Life* and *House and Garden*] devoted to different aspects of country life have been started, and will, we hope, have a most prosperous existence."[11] Early on, Miller began writing feature articles for *Country Life* as well as editing the horticultural contributions to the magazine, and he soon joined the "hot fight" between the formal and the informal. Eventually he used the pages of *Country Life* to advocate for the development of an American type of natural garden.

Miller assisted Doubleday and Page with other projects as well. In addition to editing their 1903 publication *How to Make a Flower Garden: A Manual of Practical Information and Suggestions,* Miller contributed two essays, "Scattered Planting versus Masses" and "Pergolas: A Suggestion," indicative of his continuing interest in landscape design.[12] In "Scattered Planting," Miller urged that lawns should be framed and defined with masses of native trees and shrubs, composed in a "nature-like" manner. This view sharply contrasted with the currently popular gardenesque fashion, which he characterized as "the indiscriminate scattering of individual plants throughout the center of the lawn." Miller lamented that the effect of scattered planting was "distracting and bewildering." "There are many plants," he complained, "but there is no picture." Miller favored masses of hardy, native vegetation, which, he noted pragmatically, required minimal care relative to the "rare and costly plants" typically used in gardenesque plantings. His advocacy of the use of native plants in a pictorial or picturesque manner was clearly in place by 1903. It became the foundation of his effort to establish American Prairie School ideals.

One of Miller's first feature articles, "An American Idea in Landscape Art," published in the September 1903 issue of *Country Life*, praised the landscape cemetery as an American phenomenon and O. C. Simonds's design of Graceland in Chicago as exemplary.[13] Landscape design had become the primary focus of his attention, and here, for the first time, he lauded a middle western work. That Miller considered the landscape cemetery an American concept is also significant.

Miller's "American Idea" article was not typical of *Country Life*. In fact, since its inception, the magazine had steadily grown away from Bailey's intended constituency of progressive country men and farmers. By 1903 the magazine was publishing such fare as "Polo, Ancient and Modern" and "Yachting, A Personal Experience."[14] Apparently the smell of "old money," not the "smell of the soil," had come to dominate the pages of *Country Life*. The magazine had found an audience of East Coast sophisticates, those who could afford to live the good country life, at least on the weekends. Within two years, *Country Life* had become almost precisely what Bailey had hoped it would not: "a city magazine that sees the country afar off" and a "vacation journal." He resigned as the magazine's editor in the summer of 1903.[15]

Despite his mentor's departure, Miller stayed with *Country Life*, and the magazine continued to be his primary vehicle for promoting his landscape design aesthetic. In fact, two years later, in 1905, in response to the popular demand for garden-oriented pieces such as Miller's articles, the publishers created *The Garden Magazine*, devoted solely to gardens and horticulture, and asked Miller to edit it.[16] He continued to edit and write for *Country Life*, and so gained a second outlet for his opinions. In contrast to his more technically oriented articles for *Garden Magazine*, Miller's *Country Life* pieces focused on "taste-making" and became inspirational in their intent.

It is evident from his writings that Miller had become preoccupied with the notion that America lacked a national style of landscape design and, further, that the prevailing eclectic styles were derived largely from English sources. With a desire to discover "the causes of English garden excellence" and the "methods by which the most satisfying English effects might be produced in America with American materials," Miller traveled to England in

1908.[17] After one year there, Miller concluded that "the noblest lesson English gardens can teach us is this: Let every country use chiefly its own native trees, shrubs, and vines and other permanent material, and let the style of gardening grow naturally out of necessity, the soil and the new conditions. When we stop imitating and do this, America will soon find herself." For Miller, an American style of landscape gardening would result from the adaptation of the English technique of naturalistic planting to the American needs of privacy, relaxation, and comfort, using chiefly native plants. The theory was a synthesis of his English garden studies and his earlier advocacy of massed, naturalistic plantings. Although Miller's view was grounded in his now characteristic practicality—native plants were hardy and permanent—he was also affected by the idea that the use of native plants contributed to the establishment of an American style. Over the next two years, 1909–10, Miller detailed the results of his English study tour and advocated his American style ideal in a series of *Country Life* and *Garden Magazine* articles. In 1911, in response to their popularity, Miller was asked to revise the articles for publication as a book, *What England Can Teach Us about Gardening*.[18]

In these articles, Miller initially focused on gardens in the eastern United States—apparently home to most of *Country Life*'s readers—which exemplified successful adaptations of English technique. By 1911, however, his crusade for Americanism began to find regional expression. In a September 1911 article otherwise devoted to the description of a Massachusetts rock garden, Miller abruptly shifted his attention "inland" and reported that he had "had a chance to study wild and rock gardening in a very different environment— that of Chicago."[19] He then elaborated: "In the ravines near Lake Forest lovely pictures have been made by saving and intensifying the native arborvitae with witch-hazel, cottonwoods, and meadow-rue. . . . At Humboldt Park I saw a prairie river in miniature, its banks clothed with lush, water-loving vegetation." The landscapes he described were the work of Jens Jensen. In this first printed reference to what he later termed the "Prairie School," Miller described how the "great landscape design artists of the Middle West love the prairie and use its horizontal lines in their art. . . . For instance," he elaborated, "hawthorns and crab apples are full of horizontal lines, and therefore these are used as accent marks on lawns, to frame lake vistas, and to reduce the apparent height of buildings that seem too tall. And these artists love the [stratified] rocks that are occasionally found in the prairie rivers." Although he was actually describing Jensen's work, by using phrases such as "these artists" and the "great landscape artists," Miller promoted the notion of a common bond among a group of designers.

Miller concluded his article by applying his middle western examples to a national context: "In every part of America we should study nature and make garden pictures full of local color." Perhaps this was a concession to

his practicality or, perhaps, the East Coast orientation of the magazine. The use of indigenous plants arranged in pictorial compositions had become the primary means of achieving what Miller termed "local color." Local color, then, could be expressed throughout the country and offered the foundation of an American style. In future essays, Miller would continue to define local color while citing Jensen's work by name.

Within five months of Miller's publication of Jensen's work, the landscape architect himself reviewed Miller's *What England Can Teach Us* for Chicago's *Park and Cemetery* magazine. Jensen urged that Miller's book "should be in the hands—not the library—of every lover of horticulture, as it is the best effort in horticultural literature that has been laid before the American people." As Bailey had been earlier, Jensen was struck by Miller's opinionatedness, noting that he wrote in a "forceful, fearless manner."[20] Without doubt, Miller had made contact with a kindred spirit.

By mid-1912 Miller had come to consider himself a crusader, a missionary for local color, an American style of landscape gardening. His primary target was the gardenesque, a style he had criticized in 1903 for its composition of a too "miscellaneous and meaningless collection of curiosities."[21] In his *Country Life* article of June 1912, "What Is the Matter with Our Water Gardens?" Miller, now a more firmly established arbiter of taste, boldly lamented: "What a pity it is that Americans, who have such good taste in many other matters, have such low standards of beauty in gardening! . . . Men who would never think of wearing clothes with conspicuous stripes or checks will have lines of scarlet sage crossing the lawn or big squares of cannas by the waterside. . . . It is simply that people do not know what is best in gardening. We need higher standards." Once again, he presented his readers an alternative aesthetic—local color: "Now the highest standard of gardening beauty is the pictorial, or artistic, which aims at nature-like pictures. . . . The right way to get variety in this world is to restore and intensify the native beauty of each locality upon which nature has set a peculiar stamp. When you wake up from a night's ride on a train you are most refreshed if you can see a new and endless landscape. . . . If you wake amid endless cornfields you know you are in one of the prairie states." Miller's continuing belief in the use of native plants in naturalistic, pictorial compositions had gained a new, ideological dimension: local color had become synonymous with Americanism. "It goes straight to the heart—this local color," he concluded. "And it builds up patriotism like beef, wine, and iron."[22]

In the same article Miller used the "nature-like" work of Jensen as examples of local color, with illustrations of Jensen's "prairie rivers" in Chicago's Humboldt Park and the private garden of Harry Rubens, at Glencoe, Illinois. Where previously he had only alluded to Jensen's specific designs, Miller's 1912 essay was, in fact, an unabashed promotion of the tough and implacable Dane. Miller's newly formed reverence for Jensen and his work was much in evidence: "I have met a man who knows what is best in gardening, and he has cut and burned out of his heart every trace of the cancerous spirit of show, pretense, display. He is a rough diamond in Chicago, by the name of Jensen. He has the aspect of a Danish Viking and the soul of an artist. . . . I spent with him three days to be marked with a white stone. . . . [Jensen's work] is a sample of the new native art of every kind that is growing right out of the prairie soil, full of local color, absolutely sincere, and tingling with Americanism."[23]

Miller elaborated that Jensen and, by implication, other middle western landscape gardeners were not alone in producing regionally inspired art. Many middle western painters, poets, sculptors, and architects, he asserted, "glory in the very flatness of the prairie"; the architects "repeat [horizontal] lines in their great buildings and they decorate them with conventionalized flowers of the great plains."[24] This "very flatness" was one of the distinctive

Urging his readers to frame and define their lawns with mass plantings of native trees and shrubs, Miller advocated "pictorial," "nature-like" compositions. His ideal is exemplified in this view of Simonds's landscape design for William G. Hibbard Jr.'s home in Winnetka, Illinois. (Reprinted from *Country Life in America*, April 1914, 39)

Jensen's "prairie river," an idealization of its naturally occurring counterpart, at Humboldt Park. (Reprinted from Miller, *The Prairie Spirit*, 2)

qualities of the middle western landscape, but it was a quality that—at least in the East—popularly had a negative connotation. According to Miller, these "daring innovators" had transformed a landscape liability into an asset.

Lest his eastern readers feel excluded, Miller characteristically ended the article with practical suggestions for how the (educated and moneyed) layman might benefit from Jensen's middle western examples in creating uniquely American gardens:

> If you have seen so many showy gardens that you have come to hate them worse than poison, if you believe that the goal of our effort should be an American style of gardening, . . . look about you and see if your land does not represent a disappearing type of landscape. . . . Then try to find out what it was like when the first white man came. Consult the local and state historical societies about the oldest descriptions and pictures of your locality. Ask the nearest botanist to help you evolve a consistent plant society. Go to the art galleries and see all the paintings that deal with your type of landscape. Or engage a landscape designer of Mr. Jensen's type and you will have a garden that is really unique, a garden that will become more precious to you every year, and in centuries to come will be preserved as religiously as any work of the old masters.[25]

Miller's articles for *Country Life* increasingly focused on what had already been accomplished in the Middle West—albeit largely only through the efforts of O. C. Simonds and Jensen. In August 1912 he turned his attention to the prairies and published an article on the work of Simonds, in which he humorously addressed his eastern readership: "See here, my Eastern friends, especially you who have never been west of the Hudson or the Charles, I want to show you that something good can come even from Chicago."[26]

A month later, Miller synthesized his argument for an American style in his article "How the Middle West Can Come Into Its Own." In the opening paragraph he revealed his increasingly strong personal bias: "Nobody can love more than I do the Middle West—the runway of the winds and ideas . . . no barriers to human thought like the complicated mountain systems which have produced such a bewildering variety of languages, customs, and governments in Europe." Miller perceived the Middle West to be less laden with European landscape gardening traditions than the East. Considered by many of his literary contemporaries to be the "most American" region of the country, the Middle West would be more in sympathy with his aesthetic quest. "If Boston is not a geographical entity but a 'state of mind,'" he wrote, "then the Middle West is a 'state of soul' and its spirit is progressiveness."[27] Middle western regionalism had become, for Miller, synonymous with "Americanism."

In October 1912, likely as a result of his national reputation, Cornell education, and association with Liberty Hyde Bailey, Miller was offered a position in landscape horticulture at the University of Illinois. Already attracted

Miller's house in Urbana, Illinois, shortly after it was built and three years later, demonstrating his ability to practice what he preached. (Reprinted from *The Garden Magazine* 24 [Oct. 1916], 86)

to the Middle West and perhaps seeking the opportunity to participate more actively in the development of a regional aesthetic, he accepted. Although he no longer had time to serve as editor of two magazines, Miller did continue to write articles for both *Country Life* and *Garden*. As a faculty member, Miller's primary responsibility was to further the university's "Country Beautiful" programs (which were an extension of the "City Beautiful" program of D. H. Burnham and Charles Mulford Robinson), primarily through publications and public lectures.[28] There is no evidence that Miller actually taught classes.

Following the passage of the Smith-Lever Act (which provided funding to land-grant universities for the development of agricultural extension agencies and related programs), in 1914 Miller was appointed head of the newly created Division of Landscape Extension at Illinois. With this additional funding, he aggressively expanded the scope of the university's extension services to include the preparation of landscape designs (free to Illinois residents), intended as object lessons in beautification.

In his publications and lectures, Miller continued to develop and promote what he considered a proper regional, middle western design style. He introduced the concept of a state style, "The Illinois Way."[29] After it failed to take hold, he abandoned the political boundary of the state for a natural, ecological one—the region. *The Prairie Spirit in Landscape Gardening,* published in 1915, represented the culmination of his efforts. In it, Miller synthesized his previously published tenets regarding Americanism. He defined the Prairie style as "a new mode of design and planting, which aims to fit the peculiar scenery, climate, soil, labor, and other conditions of the prairies, instead of copying literally the manners and materials of other regions . . . [which is] based upon the practical needs of the middle-western people and is characterized by preservation of typical western scenery, by restoration of local color, and by repetition of the horizontal line of land or sky which is the strongest feature of prairie scenery."[30]

For Miller, the work of Simonds, Jensen, and Walter Burley Griffin was inspired by the "prairie spirit" and expressed in the "prairie style."[31] Miller saw this spirit manifested in the ecological use of indigenous plants, particularly those with horizontal branching patterns, and striated or "stratified" rock work, echoing the rock outcroppings along middle western rivers.[32] The resulting landscape designs were not literal imitations but rather idealizations or symbolic representations of nature, evocative of the spatial characteristics of the groves and prairies of the native landscape.

Miller's claim of regional inspiration, however, was inaccurate. The Prairie style was actually derived from English picturesque principles, and Miller's advocacy of hardy native plants, reminiscent of William Robinson's idea of the English "wild garden."[33] In the end, Miller's Prairie style actually had little to do with a novel or alternative mode of design. Rather, its distinction lay in its horticultural program: the use of plants indigenous to the Middle West. Despite his one-sentence palliative that "the prairie style can be executed in the formal manner," Miller presupposed that indigenous plants would be grouped in informal, naturalistic compositions. "To summarize it all," he concluded, "people generally pass in their appreciation from the temporary to the permanent, from the spectacular to the restful, from the showy to the quiet, from the artificial to the natural, from rare to common, from foreign to native."[34] The Prairie style, then, was a regional, primarily horticultural, expression of Miller's American, local color crusade begun four years earlier.

Beyond his call for the use of native plants in pictorial compositions, what did, in fact, distinguish Miller's Prairie style from his earlier local color campaign? Its distinctiveness was rooted in its use of regional, physical settings. By viewing the Illinois landscape through a lens derived from ecological plant societies and geomorphology, Miller divided the state into eight "natural units" or "scenery types," aside from prairie: lake bluffs, ravines, riverbanks, ponds, rocks, dunes, woods, and roadsides. He examined this last type because "it is an asylum for the wild flowers, and it has immense possibilities for beauty thru [sic] planting." He suggested that the beauty of these "eight minor types is of the obvious and popular sort, because of their romantic or picturesque character." The prairie, however, was another matter, for its beauty is "harder to understand."[35]

In an effort to make the more subtle beauty of the prairie comprehensible, Miller deconstructed its composite elements: "You begin to study the main features of the scenery and find that there are usually five—land, sky, woods, crops, and water. Next you notice that the distant woodlands have level or gently rounded tops; that the corn crop is level, as well as the ground; and if there be a lake or river, that, too, is level. If the prairie looks its best there will be fleecy clouds in the sky, sailing toward the horizon like fleets of flat-bottomed ships. Then it gradually dawns upon you that the essence of the prairie's beauty lies in all these horizontal lines."[36]

Miller also attempted to reduce the prairie landscape into a series of vignettes or views—perhaps to help locate the viewer psychologically in the seemingly infinite landscape. Miller contended that "all prairie scenery" could be "reduced to two units, the broad view and the long view." By his definition the broad view suggests "infinity and power" and is "more inspiring for occasional visits." The long view, on the other hand, is "more human and intimate, and often more satisfactory to live with." Miller believed that these views could be integrated into landscape design, defined and accentuated with foreground plantings of indigenous trees and shrubs. Through their creation the "fearful Infinite" could be transformed into the "friendly finite."[37]

Miller espoused a distinctive approach to landscape conservation, too, which he believed consisted of more than simply "intensifying, preserving, and restoring" natural features. His vision embraced both nature and culture. For example, he urged Illinois citizens, to "save every historic feature [such as pioneer cabins] and give it a proper setting!" "It will do little good to bewail the beauty that has been destroyed in Illinois," he warned, asserting that even "cultivated" prairies—that is, the ubiquitous agricultural fields—were beautiful and had "scenic value."[38] This scenic value, however, was to some degree dependent on landscape gardening: in Miller's opinion, undifferentiated views to the cultivated prairie ought to be transformed into long and broad ones.

Miller's effort in *The Prairie Spirit* to link landscape gardening with ecology, "a new and fascinating branch of botany," and the concept of plant societies, was pioneering. Miller defined plant societies as "combinations of plants that are far more effective in restorations than any which can be invented by man, because Nature has evolved them by ages of experiment." He suggested that his audience read Henry Cowles's *Plant Societies of Chicago and Vicinity* as "an introduction to the science," and to learn how native plants could be grouped in ecologically sound combinations.[39]

Miller defined the "broad view," framed here by stratified honey locusts, as being evocative of the prairie's "infinite extent" and "more inspiring for occasional visits." (Reprinted from Miller, *The Prairie Spirit*, 16)

Miller defined the "long view" as more intimate, human, and suggestive of hope. (Miller, *The Prairie Spirit,* 17)

Perhaps the most distinctive contribution of Miller's Prairie School crusade is the term itself, as it applied to both architecture and landscape gardening.[40] The label first appeared in an essay titled "The New Prairie School"—replete with a quotation from Jensen—in the May 1914 issue of *Country Life in America.*[41] (Although the article was unsigned, it is most likely that Miller himself was the author. Miller's long association with *Country Life* continued during his years at the University of Illinois.) A letter from Frank Lloyd Wright to Miller, dated 24 February 1915, lends further credence to Miller's authorship of the term. In it Wright informed Miller that he did not consider himself to be a part of the "'school' you would name."[42]

A long view to cultivated prairie, and the ubiquitous agricultural fields, has been established through selective cutting of indigenous growth. (Reprinted from Miller, *The Prairie Spirit*, 17)

Shortly after publication of *The Prairie Spirit*, Jens Jensen wrote to a client that "Miller is the greatest writer on landscape gardening that is living today. . . . I think he has that stuff in him to pound his gospel into the minds of people . . . but," he concluded, "I am not sure that a University is the right place for a man of progressive thoughts."[43] His doubt, it turns out, was well founded. *The Prairie Spirit* proved to be Miller's undoing in academia. His university colleagues did not share his zeal for the promotion of the Prairie School. J. C. Blair, head of the department of horticulture, wrote, "We have gone too far as an educational institution with this sort of inspirational stuff."[44] Furthermore, Miller's gratis design projects brought him into conflict with practitioners and the professional Division of Landscape Gardening (newly created in 1907). As a result of dramatically reduced federal and state funding, the university disbanded its Division of Landscape Extension in the summer of 1916. Miller's employment was terminated.

After his departure from the university, Miller tried unsuccessfully to establish a landscape architectural practice in Chicago, and then returned to his hometown of Detroit with the same objective in 1918.[45] Unfortunately, World War I had forestalled the demand for landscape architectural commissions. In 1920 Miller retired to Los Angeles, where he died in obscurity on 16 March 1938. At the time of his death, Miller's publications numbered in the hundreds, but neither *Country Life in America* nor *The Garden Magazine* published an obituary.

Although the scope of Wilhelm Miller's brief career as a landscape architect has never been examined, the significance of his writings has secured him a prominent place within the history of the discipline. It was largely through Miller's articles and books that a Prairie School of landscape architecture came into being at all. O. C. Simonds and Jens Jensen maintained a collegial relationship, but it is unlikely that they consciously perceived themselves to be members of a school or partners in advancing the ideals of one. It was Wilhelm Miller who observed the commonalities of their work and "forged the links" in print and theory.

Notes

I gratefully acknowledge the assistance of the University of Illinois Scholar's Travel Fund and the College of Fine and Applied Arts Dean's Fund. I am especially indebted to Walter L. Creese, for his limitless inspiration and encouragement.

1. Although images of the "gently sloping roofs, low proportions, quiet skylines, suppressed heavy-set chimneys, and sheltering overhangs" of the "prairie houses" of Frank Lloyd Wright come readily to mind, the Prairie School expression in landscape design is more obscure. Frank Lloyd Wright, "In the Cause of Architecture," *Architectural Record* 23 (1908), 157. On the Prairie School of architecture, see H. Allen Brooks, *The Prairie School: Frank Lloyd Wright and His Midwest Contemporaries* (Toronto: University of Toronto Press, 1972). On Simonds, see Mara Gelbloom, "Ossian Simonds: Prairie Spirit in Landscape Gardening," *Prairie School Review* 12 (1975), 5–18. On Jensen, see Leonard K. Eaton's pioneering study, *Landscape Artist in America: The Life and Work of Jens Jensen* (Chicago: University of Chicago Press, 1961), and Robert E. Grese, *Jens Jensen: Maker of Natural Parks and Gardens* (Baltimore: Johns Hopkins University Press, 1992).

2. Many of the landscape architects who first practiced in the Midwest were originally from the Atlantic seaboard. Unlike the undulating, thickly wooded land of the eastern states, midwestern states such as Illinois were flat and dominated by agricultural fields, if

not remnant prairies. It was this landscape that inspired Simonds and Jensen and that Frederick Law Olmsted Sr., in contrast, bleakly assessed as "not merely uninteresting, but during much of the year, positively dreary." *The Papers of Frederick Law Olmsted* (Baltimore: Johns Hopkins University Press, 1992), 6:276. The Victorian gardenesque, which lingered in the Midwest well into the twentieth century, and the Italianate gardens of Charles A. Platt are examples of the European-inspired design aesthetic rejected by the Prairie School.

3. Wilhelm Miller, *The Prairie Spirit in Landscape Gardening: What the People of Illinois Have Done and Can Do toward Designing and Planting Public and Private Grounds for Efficiency and Beauty,* University of Illinois Agricultural Experiment Station Circular, no. 184 (Urbana, 1915). Beginning in 1958—only two decades after Miller's death—architectural historians were the first to recognize Miller's instrumental role in chronicling the origin and progress of the Prairie School. See Grant C. Manson, *Frank Lloyd Wright to 1910: The First Golden Age* (New York: Reinhold Publishing, 1958), 102; Eaton, *Landscape Artist;* Mark L. Peisch, *The Chicago School of Architecture: Early Followers of Sullivan and Wright* (New York: Random House, 1964), chap. 6; Brooks, *Prairie School,* 10–11; and Walter L. Creese, *The Crowning of the American Landscape: Eight Great Spaces and Their Buildings* (Princeton: Princeton University Press, 1985), 212–14. However, despite this limited recognition, which he achieved almost exclusively from his *Prairie Spirit* circular, the details of the genesis of Miller's ideas as well as the particulars of his career have remained obscure and largely unexamined.

4. For a chronology of Miller's career, see L. H. Bailey, ed., *R[ural].U[plook].S[ervice].: A Preliminary Attempt to Register the Rural Leadership in the United States and Canada* (Ithaca, 1918), 196; also see the 1920, 1925, and 1930 editions.

5. Quotation from Wilhelm Miller, *What England Can Teach Us about Gardening* (New York: Doubleday, Page, 1911), dedication. See Andrew Denny Rodgers III, *Liberty Hyde Bailey: A Story of American Plant Sciences* (Princeton: Princeton University Press, 1949); this source is especially valuable as it was prepared in cooperation with Bailey.

6. L. H. Bailey, preface to *The 1895 Chrysanthemums,* Cornell University Agricultural Experiment Station Bulletin, no. 112 (Ithaca, 1896).

7. See, for example, Wilhelm Miller, *Fourth Report upon Chrysanthemums,* Cornell University Agricultural Experiment Station Bulletin, no. 147 (Ithaca, 1898).

8. L. H. Bailey, preface to Wilhelm Miller, *A Talk about Dahlias,* Cornell University Agricultural Experiment Station Bulletin, no. 128 (Ithaca, 1897).

9. Bailey, *R.U.S.* (1918), 196. L. H. Bailey et al., *Cyclopedia of American Horticulture: Comprising Suggestions for Cultivation of Horticultural Plants, Descriptions of the Species of Fruits, Vegetables, Flowers, and Ornamental Plants Sold in the United States and Canada, Together with Geographical and Biographical Sketches,* 4 vols. (New York: Macmillan, 1900–1902). Also important is the retitled and much revised 1914–17 edition, *The Standard Cyclopedia of Horticulture.*

10. *Country Life in America: A Magazine for the Home-maker, the Vacation-seeker, the Gardener, the Farmer, the Nature-teacher, the Naturalist* (New York: Doubleday, Page, 1901). [Liberty Hyde Bailey], "What This Magazine Stands For," *Country Life in America* 1 (1901), 24–25. Rodgers elaborated, "That Bailey's utterances were always regarded as words of authority and that he led both scientific and popular opinion, may be inferred from the fact that *Country Life in America* in its first year attained, it is said, a larger circulation than any magazine in the field ever had" (*Bailey,* 303). Also see Bailey, *R.U.S.* (1918), 196.

11. "American Country Life and Art," *Architectural Record* 11 (1902), 112.

12. Wilhelm Miller, ed., *How to Make a Flower Garden: A Manual of Practical Information and Suggestions* (New York: Doubleday, Page, 1903), 52 and 107–8 (the author of these essays was identified by the initial "M").

13. W.M., "An American Idea in Landscape Art," *Country Life in America* 4 (1903): 349–50.

14. "A Snift [*sic*] at Old Gardens: Memories and Remnants of Gardens Aforetime . . . the Old Hudson River Manors" appeared in February 1901; "Polo" followed in August, and "Yachting, a Personal Experience: An Account of a Country Life Experience on the Tide-Water Region of Virginia—Suggestions to Those Who Like the Water" in October 1902.

15. According to Rodgers, Bailey resigned because "the purpose of the magazine—which was to portray wealthy estates and the nation's most famous gardens, a city man's country life—did not coincide with his own. He was afraid that this association might impair his relationship with the trades and the schools . . . and also felt that it was not furthering his ideal of gradually improving by science and practice all simple agrarian life" (*Bailey*, 297).

16. *The Garden Magazine: A Monthly Magazine on Practical Gardening;* the first issue appeared in February 1905.

17. Review of *What England Can Teach Us about Gardening* by Wilhelm Miller, *Country Life in America* 22 (1912), 10–12.

18. Wilhelm Miller, "What England Can Teach Us about Gardening," *Country Life in America* 15 (1909), 265–68 (quote); Miller, *What England Can Teach Us about Gardening* (Garden City, N.Y.: Doubleday, Page, 1913), v.

19. Wilhelm Miller, "Successful American Gardens VIII: The Higginson Garden at West Manchester, Mass.," *Country Life in America* 20 (1911), 35–38; following quotations are from page 38.

20. Jens Jensen, review of *What England Can Teach Us about Gardening* by Wilhelm Miller, *Park and Cemetery* 21 (1912), 779.

21. Miller, *How to Make a Flower Garden,* 52.

22. Wilhelm Miller, "What Is the Matter with Our Water Gardens?" *Country Life in America* 22 (1912), 23–26, 54.

23. Ibid., 24.

24. Ibid., 25.

25. Ibid., 54. Miller did not mention that his use of the term "plant society" was a reference to the pioneering work of Henry Chandler Cowles, a University of Chicago botanist. Both Cowles and Miller were charter members of the Friends of Our Native Landscape, a conservation organization founded by Jensen in 1913. Later, Miller would incorporate the nascent science of plant ecology and its potential application to landscape gardening into his Prairie School aesthetic. But, ultimately, his argument remained focused on the use of native plants instead of a more novel and exotic "style." See also Grese, *Jens Jensen,* 120–36.

26. Wilhelm Miller, "How to Multiply Your Grounds by Four," *Country Life in America* 22 (1912), 34–36.

27. Wilhelm Miller, "How the Middle West Can Come Into Its Own," *Country Life in America* 22 (1912), 11–14. For more on contemporary views of the Midwest, see James R. Shortridge, *The Middle West: Its Meaning in American Culture* (Lawrence: University Press of Kansas, 1989).

28. See Charles Mulford Robinson, "City Planning Course at the University of Illinois," *Landscape Architecture* 3 (1913), 97–100.

29. See Miller's *The Illinois Way of Beautifying the Farm,* University of Illinois Agricultural Experiment Station Circular, no. 170 (Urbana, 1914).

30. Miller, *Prairie Spirit,* 5.

31. A former apprentice to Frank Lloyd Wright, Griffin is remembered primarily as a Prairie school architect and the designer of Australia's federal capital city, Canberra. For Griffin as a landscape architect, see Christopher Vernon, "Expressing Natural Conditions with Maximum Possibility: The American Landscape Art of Walter Burley Griffin," *Journal of Garden History* 15 (Spring 1995), 19–47. Of these three designers, the majority of Miller's text and illustrations was devoted to the work of Jensen, by then his personal friend. See also my "Frank Lloyd Wright, Walter Burley Griffin, Jens Jensen, and the

Jugendstil Garden in America," *Die Gartenkunst* 7, no. 2 (1995), 232–46; "Wilhelm Miller and 'The Prairie Spirit in Landscape Gardening,'" in *Regional Garden Design in the United States,* ed. Teresa O'Malley and Marc Treib (Washington, D.C.: Dumbarton Oaks Research Library and Collection, 1995), 271–75; and "The Landscape Art of Walter Burley Griffin," in *Beyond Architecture: Marion Mahony and Walter Burley Griffin, America, Australia, India,* ed. Anne Watson (Sydney: Powerhouse [Museum] Publishing, 1998), 86–103.

32. It is likely that many of these defining design features originated with Jensen, not Miller.

33. Miller was quite familiar with Robinson's work. While in England in 1908, he met with Robinson at his Gravetye Manor. See Miller, *What England Can Teach Us.*

34. Miller, *Prairie Spirit,* 4, 32.

35. Ibid., 12.

36. Ibid., 19.

37. Ibid., 17–18, 20.

38. Ibid., 6, 17.

39. Ibid., 18. Henry C. Cowles, *The Plant Societies of Chicago and Vicinity,* Geographic Society of Chicago Bulletin, no. 2 (1901); see note 25 above.

40. The architect and critic Peter B. Wight, in a review of Miller's circular in the *Architectural Record,* gave Miller credit for the concept of the "prairie spirit": "It is one of the natural results of his study of landscape art, horticulture, and arboriculture. He perceived the influence of the prairie on the design of many buildings, the erection of which had come under his observation, and he bore witness to it." Peter B. Wight, "Country House Architecture in the Middle West," *Architectural Record* 40 (1916), 590–92.

41. I am grateful to T. Paul Young for bringing this source to my attention.

42. Miller offered his view that the architect Louis H. Sullivan might be considered the founder of the "Prairie School," to which Wright responded, "I cannot see how he could figure in any form other than grotesque as the founder of a 'Prairie School of Architecture.'" Even though Wright did not share Miller's view, his response suggests that Miller coined the term. Wright's letter is reprinted in Bruce Brooks Pfeiffer, ed., *Frank Lloyd Wright: Letters to Architects* (Fresno: Press at California State University, 1984), 49–52.

43. Jens Jensen, letter to Mr. A. H. Lake, 3 November 1915 (University Archives, University of Illinois at Urbana-Champaign).

44. J. C. Blair, letter to J. Horace McFarland, 6 January 1916 (University Archives, University of Illinois at Urbana-Champaign).

45. See Wilhelm Miller, "The Prairie Style of Landscape Architecture," *Architectural Record* 40 (1916), 590–92, and Bailey, *R.U.S.,* 196. Apparently to avoid anti-German sentiments engendered by the war, Miller changed his first name from Wilhelm to William that same year.

ELEVEN

Elbert Peets

HISTORY AS PRECEDENT IN
MIDWESTERN LANDSCAPE DESIGN

Arnold R. Alanen

ELBERT PEETS (1886–1968) emerges as an anomaly in comparison with other landscape architects who practiced in the Midwest during the late nineteenth and early twentieth centuries. The two best-known midwestern practitioners of the period, O. C. Simonds and Jens Jensen, emphasized a "naturalistic" approach that was directly inspired by the prairie itself—its plants, horizontality, and cultural traditions.[1] Peets, by contrast, looked to the neoclassical traditions of Renaissance Italy and Colonial America for inspiration and applied historical ideas to a range of midwestern landscape projects, including the modern suburb.

Peets's knowledge and understanding of urban design history was particularly thorough, and, as a result, he was able to make inspired use of historical models in his contemporary city plans. Yet Peets's viewpoint was pragmatic and "typically American in its inclusive and functional character," according to one historian. It provided the "necessary balance" to the more theoretical approaches of Europeans.[2]

Born in Hudson, Ohio, on 5 May 1886, Peets was the son of a cabinetmaker who had emigrated from England. He was introduced to his future profession as a high school student, working for H. U. Horvath, a landscape architect, nurseryman, and consultant forester to the city of Cleveland.[3]

Immediately after graduating magna cum laude from Cleveland's Western Reserve University in 1912, Peets enrolled in the masters program in landscape architecture at Harvard University. Already an excellent plantsman and

Elbert Peets. (Courtesy of the Rare and Manuscripts Collection, Carl A. Kooch Library, Cornell University, Ithaca, N.Y.)

arboriculturist by the time he entered the program, Peets taught horticulture during his final year there.

Peets's early writings revealed a keen interest in urban forestry: his 1915 Harvard thesis was titled "Some Design Aspects of City Street Trees," and during the same year he published his first article, "Street Trees in Built-up Districts of Large Cities," in *Landscape Architecture.* In 1916 his book *Practical Tree Repair* was published. In contrast to the philosophical and historical essays that Peets wrote several years later, *Practical Tree Repair* was a textbook and how-to manual. In it the young landscape architect dramatically chronicled the protection and salvation of specimens damaged from physical injuries "caused by wind and ice-storm, the ignorance or carelessness of men, the attacks of boring insects, and of that silent destroying host, the rot-producing fungi."[4]

Peets secured his first job with the landscape architecture firm of Pray, Hubbard, and White in Cambridge, Massachusetts, where he was primarily responsible for the preparation of subdivision plans.[5] Sometime during 1915 or 1916 he met the famous city planner Werner Hegemann, with whom he would collaborate for many years.

Werner Hegemann (1881–1936) was a prolific author and world traveler and played an important role in the exchange of ideas about urban planning between Europe and America. A native of Mannheim, Germany, he made several stays in the United States during which he lectured and became acquainted with a number of prominent early planners, including John Nolen, George P. Ford, and Charles Mulford Robinson.[6] Hegemann eventually settled in Milwaukee (a city with a high proportion of German residents) and remained in the Midwest for the duration of World War I. Before returning to Europe in 1921, Hegemann, with Peets functioning as his junior partner, completed several planning projects in Wisconsin, at Sheboygan, Milwaukee, and Madison.[7]

Hegemann and Peets's first Wisconsin project was a plan for Kohler, a small company town situated just west of Sheboygan, where before the turn of the century John Kohler had begun to move the operations of his plumbing fixtures manufacturing firm.[8] Walter Kohler, who had assumed the presidency of the company after his father's death, guided the firm for several decades and was instrumental in converting the community from a typical company town into a model village. Deeply concerned over the nondescript appearance of the residential settlement that was developing adjacent to the family's enterprise, the younger Kohler had become interested in community planning in the early 1900s.[9]

In 1915 Kohler hired Walter Hegemann on the basis of his international reputation. He requested that Hegemann work with two other professionals who previously had been commissioned to prepare plans for various phases of community expansion and development in Kohler: Richard Philipp, a Milwaukee architect, and J. Donahue, a Sheboygan civil engineer. Soon after, Hegemann asked Kohler if Elbert Peets could join the planning team as landscape architect. Kohler agreed, and during the summer of 1916, Hegemann and Peets began to work on plans to convert the settlement into a model village.[10]

In appraising the Kohler family's 3,000-acre holding, Hegemann commented on its beauty and natural features, noting that the site included "rolling land, fine trees, a most surprisingly winding stream, high ravine, with perfectly formed views, in short, an ideal location for a garden city." The team recommended that residential lots of adequate size be provided so that each residence could be situated where it would both receive sun and be protected from the wind. They also included proposals for cultural activities and cooperatively run institutions, such as banks, home rental plans, stores, and insurance programs. The application of these guidelines, Hegemann maintained, would establish Kohler as a national model and "an important factor for the civilization of the country."[11]

Hegemann appears to have provided most of the philosophical direction for the Kohler plan, while Peets worked out the physical details. Their design for the section of the village located adjacent to the factory and its headquarters had to incorporate several existing residences and streets. In 1916 numerous preliminary plans were readied for the overall extension and layout of roadways, the development or redesign of lots for new dwelling units, and the design of a residential block.[12]

Throughout, Walter Kohler held complete control over all planning activities and their implementation. During the summer of 1916, he grew especially critical of the time Hegemann and Peets were devoting to planning projects elsewhere. Particularly damning was his criticism that Hegemann had spent so much time learning drafting skills from Peets that the realization of their proposed plan for the village neighborhood had been delayed.[13] These disagreements culminated in the dissolution of the business relationship between Kohler and the Hegemann-Peets team by late that year.[14]

Following Hegemann and Peets's departure, the village continued to develop over several years under the direction of Richard Philipp. In the mid-1920s Olmsted Brothers of Brookline, Massachusetts, was commissioned to design another neighborhood in the development. The network of American landscape professionals was still surprisingly small: the Olmsted Brothers partner who oversaw most of the planning activity for the village at this time was Henry V. Hubbard, one of the people who had hired Peets to work in Cambridge shortly after the young landscape architect graduated from Harvard.[15]

Walter Kohler certainly had been correct in claiming that Hegemann and Peets were involved with several other Wisconsin projects in 1916. That year and again in 1919–20 the team was commissioned to prepare an extremely ambitious scheme for Lake Forest, a planned community in Madison.

The origins of Lake Forest can be traced to 1911, when two developers, Chandler Burwell Chapman and Leonard Gay, decided that a suburban community could be built on an 840-acre parcel of marshland, wooded area, and pasture situated along the southern shore of Lake Wingra. Although the site was just a mile from the University of Wisconsin campus and only somewhat farther from the state capitol building, the wet, uneven topography had isolated it from the built-up area of the city for decades. Nonetheless, Chapman and Gay believed that the tract could be developed profitably since it was the only large untouched parcel with lake frontage still to be found within several miles of Madison.[16]

Before construction began, various drainage schemes were developed. Most of the land was soft and spongy with subsoil of peat and marl, some of it hundreds of feet deep. In fact, thirty years earlier the Illinois Central Railroad had decided not to run a line through the area, concluding that road-

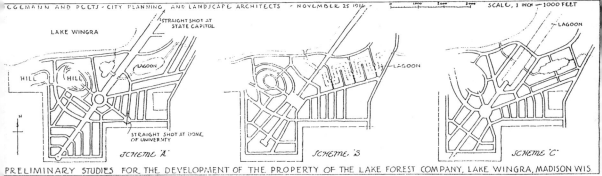

In late 1916, Peets and Hegemann prepared three possible schemes for the central area of Lake Forest, a large subdivision proposed for Madison, Wisconsin. (Reprinted from Hegemann and Peets, *The American Vitruvius*, 283)

beds and trestles would sink. It is not surprising that when Chapman and Gay began to promote their property in 1917, they neglected to mention the problem but elaborated instead on "beautifully wooded hills on the northwest, the rolling meadow to the south, the beautiful terraces to the east and the water front on the north."[17]

By November 1916 Hegemann and Peets had prepared at least three preliminary designs for Lake Forest. All provided a "straight shot" of the state capitol building to the northeast and a view northward toward the landmark dome of Bascom Hall on the university campus. In two of the schemes, a broad avenue provided the link to the capitol; in the third, the axis was a linear lagoon. Residential areas were conceived as distinct neighborhood units; some were to have their own square and provide residents with self-contained areas free of through traffic.[18]

The three proposals each suggested a different setting for the town's civic center, though all borrowed directly from classical models. In one, the major organizational element was a circular form; another utilized a rectangular plaza; the third, an ellipse. The plan that was selected—the circular arrangement—displayed radiating streets and avenues; it was at least partly inspired by the Piazza di San Pietro in Rome and bore some similarities to Washington, D.C.[19]

The team also prepared studies for the civic center itself.[20] Their design intent "was to fix upon some means of immediately, economically and definitely marking out the shape of the large round plaza in such a way that shops and small public buildings could be built later without breaking the uniformity of the frame." To accomplish this they recommended that a high pergola be built around much of the circle; any buildings later constructed behind it would be lighted by clerestory windows placed just above the structure. Preliminary plans also included a massive athletic field, a thousand-foot-long mall lined with willow trees, and recommendations for a large open-air theater and a nine-hole golf course.[21]

Engineering and financial problems bedeviled the project, however. When

CIVIC CENTER FOR LAKE FOREST — MADISON WIS.   HEGEMANN AND PEETS · 1920

The plan for the proposed civic center at Lake Forest, prepared by Hegemann and Peets in late 1920, displayed a familiarity with classical formalism and motifs that Peets would demonstrate throughout his career. (Reprinted from Hegemann and Peets, *The American Vitruvius*, 198)

dredging began during the summer of 1917, the water level in Lake Wingra dropped two to three feet below normal and the recently created lagoons in the adjoining park became "stagnant and offensive"; the shoreline of the lake was deemed "unsightly and unsanitary." The developers were eventually forced to restore the lake to within one foot of its original level. One year later, forty-eight of the nine hundred lots had been sold, but no houses built.[22]

In 1920 the Lake Forest Company began aggressive promotion efforts, which included publication of a semimonthly bulletin, the *Lake Forester*. By November, sixty-one lots had been sold, five houses constructed, and twenty-three people were residing in the tiny community. Capitol Avenue, the long axis, had been laid out across the marsh (although as a regular street, not a double boulevard); a bridge provided access to the Madison street system; an artesian well had been drilled; a one-story brick pumping station built; and electricity brought to the site. During the next year, shade trees were planted, a water system was provided, and telephone service was installed linking the area to Madison.[23]

Very quickly, however, a new set of serious problems emerged. The spongy land beneath Capitol Avenue started to shift, causing the roadway to buckle. Some of the partially dredged canals became clogged with mud and dead leaves. Even more disastrous, in 1922 the mortgage loan company that had been formed to provide the developers with financial support failed.[24] Ultimately, only two relatively small neighborhoods were built within the 840-acre Lake Forest plat.

The ill-conceived scheme was eventually redeemed when, in the 1930s, most of the tract was purchased by the University of Wisconsin for its new arboretum. Perhaps this more appropriate use of the land had already been envisioned by Franz Aust, a university landscape architect whom the Lake Forest Company commissioned in 1920 to design the Council Rock Spring Garden. Aust proposed a place of dignified natural beauty, with the theme of restoration: "restoration of the spring to its boiling, bubbling, untamed condition and restoration of the native plants and wildflowers found there before the advent of civilization."[25]

Another Wisconsin suburban project that Hegemann and Peets began in 1916 found greater success. Washington Highlands, a large subdivision situated near Milwaukee in Wauwatosa, was located on 133 acres of hilly land known as the Pabst Farm (after its former owner, the brewer Gustav Pabst). Hegemann was particularly proud of the design scheme, which avoided the "monotonous checkerboard" pattern that characterized traditional approaches.[26] Primary access to the development was provided by a continuation of a city boulevard in nearby Washington Park. The new roadway bridged a creek valley that served as the informal cross axis in the plan. This primary artery terminated in a cluster of large houses sited at the high point of the tract. Additional access was provided by streets adapted to the rather rugged topography; the broad arc offered by another route, Washington Circle, provided an easier climb up the hill to the houses. Hegemann touted the curvilinear forms for their economic advantages—for example, reduced grading costs—and enumerated his aims in the overall scheme: "to avoid cutting and filling, to bring the streets at easy grades up or around the hills, to make the hills points of vantage crowned by highly desirable building sites, to organize the whole area as a secluded residential park and by a visual relation to bring it in close connection with Washington Park."[27]

The plan also incorporated existing trees, including two ancient specimens that were preserved by manipulating the roadway to create a small plaza around them. Innovative solutions were devised to accommodate the elevation changes and access to individual house sites. Several streets that passed in front of the hills, for example, were designed to appear as terraces. In the steepest areas the houses were situated close to the street; wide lawns gave residences in the flatter areas larger set backs. Split-grade boulevards were used in several sections, providing some homes with access to adjacent streets at both the upper and lower ground levels.[28]

Development of the Highlands was curtailed in 1917 when America entered World War I. Peets left for Washington early that year to serve as a civilian planning engineer. In January 1919, two months after the Armistice was signed, he returned to Wisconsin and joined Hegemann in preparing the final plans for Washington Highlands. Hegemann is credited with the general plan, Peets as author of a scheme for the development of small parks, proposals for street grading, and designs for the bridges spanning the creek. His influence is also evident in specific details such as the hedges bordering the entire property and the principal axis, the posts that identified the Highlands' entrance, and the hedge plantings and clipped lindens of varying sizes planted throughout the community. Peets undoubtedly provided significant input into the development of proposals that protected the site's natural features, especially the many fine trees and existing vegetation.[29]

Only eight houses were constructed before 1920, but 281 residences were built during the following decade. The Washington Highlands Homes Association, organized in 1919, adopted several covenents, ostensibly to preserve the enclave's "countrified" atmosphere. Most of the restrictions addressed open space and architectural concerns, although one covenant contained a glaring prescription for racial prejudice, stating that "at no time shall the land included in Washington Highlands or any part thereof or any building thereon be purchased, owned, leased or occupied by any person other than the white race." (Such covenants were common in elite developments built throughout the United States at the time, but Hegemann and Peets almost certainly would have disagreed with these restrictions.) Since the regulation excluded domestic servants, it subsequently was modified to accommodate the non-white individuals employed by some residents. The vast majority of the Highlands' covenants remained intact until some were modified in 1987. Today, the development retains the character of the physical planning proposals that Hegemann and Peets formulated more than three-quarters of a century ago.[30]

Facing page: The 1916 plan for the 133-acre suburban subdivision of Washington Highlands, developed by Peets and Hegemann for an area of Wauwatosa, Wisconsin, reflected the designers' sensitive awareness and recognition of local terrain features and vistas. (Reprinted from Hegemann, *City Planning for Milwaukee*, 29)

With most of the planning for Washington Highlands completed by 1920, Peets was finally able to use the Charles Eliot Traveling Fellowship that Harvard had awarded him in 1917. He toured Amsterdam, Berlin, London, Paris, Rome, and Vienna among other cities. He was especially impressed with the urban squares, piazzas, and parks that he saw on foot, once visiting more than sixty sites in London during a single hyperactive day. The countless planning insights that Peets absorbed during the trip were later incorporated into designs for parks, gardens, new towns, and the revitalization of existing cities in America.[31]

To establish his European itinerary, Peets corresponded regularly with James Sturgis Pray, chairman of the School of Landscape Architecture at Harvard. Interactions between the two men, which continued by letter when Peets was in Europe, remained cordial until the young landscape architect

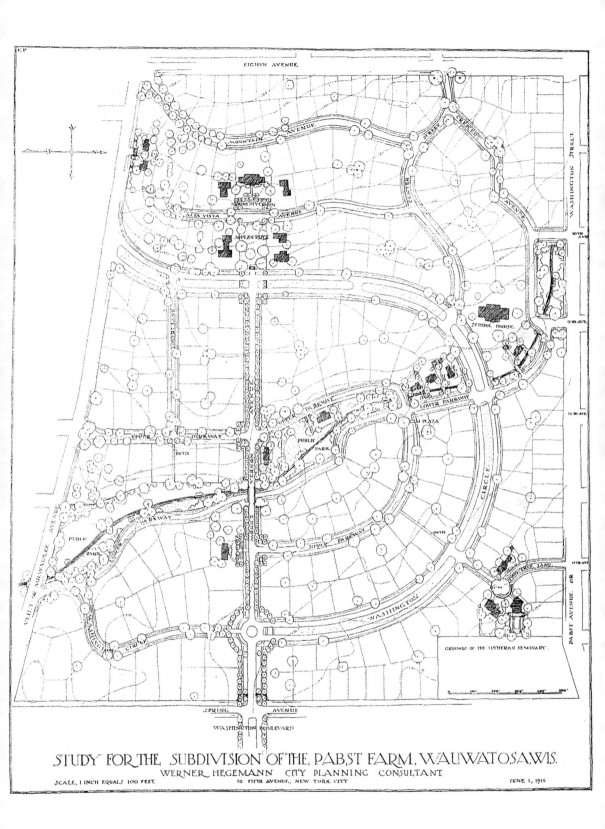

STUDY FOR THE SUBDIVISION OF THE PABST FARM, WAUWATOSA, WIS.

WERNER HEGEMANN CITY PLANNING CONSULTANT

SCALE, 1 INCH EQUALS 100 FEET.   70 FIFTH AVENUE, NEW YORK CITY   JUNE 1, 1916

ELBERT PEETS   201

The extensive areas of open space that Peets and Hegemann proposed for Washington Highlands continue to define the community today. (Courtesy of Arnold R. Alanen)

returned to the United States in February 1921. Shortly thereafter the relationship soured because of misunderstandings over the report that Peets was to submit to the university. When Peets refused the chairman's offer to have the School of Landscape Architecture publish the report (probably because he wanted to use some of the material in a book that he and Hegemann were developing), Pray had the final payment of the travel stipend withheld until the document was submitted. Pray acerbically observed that the issue was a "disgrace which has never had to come to any of our Fellows before, [yet it] is as nothing compared with the fact that you are willing to place yourself in such relation as you are doing to the School and me."[32] Peets remained highly critical of Harvard's School of Landscape Architecture for the remainder of his life.

A few weeks after returning from Europe, Peets rejoined Hegemann in Milwaukee, where the two men finished the manuscript that became their magnum opus, *The American Vitruvius: An Architect's Handbook of Civic Art*. This massive, copiously illustrated volume, published in 1922 and twice reprinted (in 1972 and 1988), proclaimed an "allegiance to the classical ideals associated with the Vitruvian tradition." The authors cautioned that they did not intend to write a complete history of civic design, but instead sought to provide "a thesaurus, a representative collection of creations in civic art, so grouped and so interpreted in text and captions as seemed best suited to bring out the special significance of each design." Although it was noted that the text represented the judgment of both men, Hegemann claimed primary responsibility for it and rather condescendingly concluded that Peets was "not to be held accountable for every detail of the opinions expressed." Only the last chapter, which featured an assessment of Peets's beloved Washington, D.C., was written primarily by the younger author.[33]

Peets's key contributions to *The American Vitruvius* were a number of the plans and drawings—rendered in his accomplished hand—and the detailed captions for the book's 1,200 illustrations, which included, in addition to Peets's work, many photographs and other archival materials. Several illustrations were based on Peets and Hegemann's collaborative projects; others were plans and oblique views that had been redrafted and adapted to fit the book's format or to illustrate particular design concepts and details.[34]

Peets and Hegemann's collaboration ended in 1921 when Hegemann returned to Germany. The thirty-five-year-old Peets then established an independent landscape architecture practice in Cleveland. He remained in the city for about ten years, primarily designing gardens, parks, and subdivisions. Most of the major essays that established his reputation as a landscape critic and essayist date from this period. Peets was an uncommonly good writer who exhibited "taste, elegance, wit, and a readiness to swipe at the pompous or banal." No less a talent than H. L. Mencken edited the articles that Peets published in the *American Mercury*.[35]

Among the best known of Peets's articles from this time is his scathing essay "The Landscape Priesthood," published in 1927. In it he criticized the work of numerous colleagues, including many members of the American Society of Landscape Architects, some of whom, he claimed, were "fitted to teach no art higher than pitching horse-shoes." Peets also lambasted his alma mater. Noting that the chairman expressed great pride in the maturity of students (who averaged twenty-eight years of age), Peets commented: "That is a catastrophe. The brain of such a student is a terminal moraine pushed into his skull by the academic and professional glaciers that have moved over it. Only pedagogical dynamite, not abstention from repression, can open up those minds and start them reworking the treasures of accumulated aesthetic form."[36]

To Peets, however, the "calamity of the first magnitude" was the reverence given by American landscape architects to "the English landscape style of gardening." A proper antidote for the "nature-imitative" design schemes fostered by the English landscape style could be found in "such rudimentary principles of design as straightness, uniformity, economy and equal balance." Blaming much of this Anglophilia on Frederick Law Olmsted Sr., Peets accused the founder of American landscape architecture of having made a religion out of nature, "the holy word of his time." Central Park, according to Peets, could have been New York's acropolis, but since it lacked integration with the greater city, the repose found in the formality of Versailles and Hampton Court was lacking. Olmsted and his colleagues failed in this integration "because they thought of the city as the enemy of the country."[37]

In many of his articles, Peets praised the gridiron, noting that such patterns were convenient, orderly, and simple in design. He traced the origins of the grid to the towns of Greece and the Roman colonies, to the great cities of Renaissance Europe, and to the American colonies. Whether the plan was for a city or a park, Peets maintained, it was "only by a geometric relation of geometric parts" that "the ruling feature of a design [could] establish its dominance over a large area."[38]

During the Depression, Peets gave up a waning private practice to work on government projects. In July 1933 he joined the Cleveland City Planning Commission and later that year prepared site plans for the federal Department of Agriculture at its Beltsville, Maryland, property. Two years later he was called back to Washington to work as the principal planner for the U.S. Farm Resettlement Administration's community of Greendale, Wisconsin.[39]

The land for the project was acquired by late 1935 and surveying had begun when Peets visited the site shortly before Christmas, but severe cold and heavy snow delayed most of the engineering work until spring 1936.[40] Nevertheless, Peets and his staff had soon developed their preliminary proposals. The initial plan called for two thousand acres of permanent open space encircling the residential districts. Greendale was unique among the three federal towns under development (the Greendale staff was also responsible for

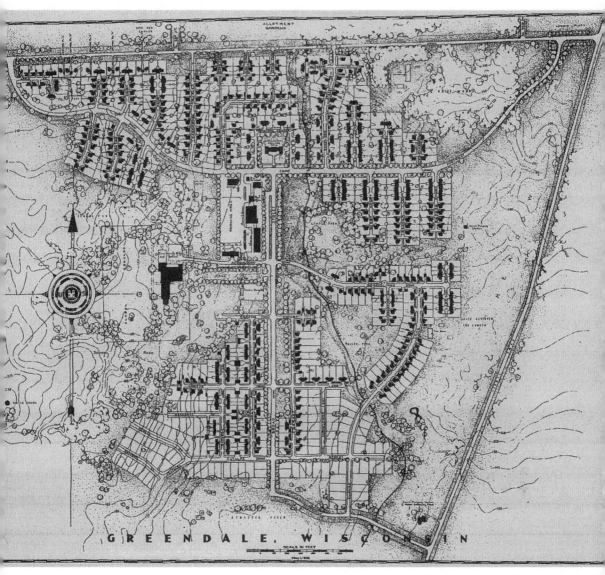

G R E E N D A L E ,   W I S C O N S I N

Greenbelt, Maryland, outside Washington, D.C., and Greenhills, near Cincinnati, Ohio) since its greenbelt included exceptionally productive agricultural land—seventeen dairy farms and twenty-three small truck and poultry farms. Besides providing for some continuation of farming, Peets planned for hiking and cross-country ski trails through much of the greenbelt. Moreover, "in the planting of outlying parks and wildlife reservations," he assured, "we shall do whatever we can to preserve and create communities of native plants." His plan also called for "a boundary-line walk, with other lanes running between the farms of the greenbelt so that our people may have close contact with the land and its plants and also with farm life and work."[41]

For certain elements of his Greendale plan, Peets turned to Radburn, New

The 1936 plan that Peets prepared for Greendale, Wisconsin, was based on European Renaissance planning and the layouts of American colonial and midwestern villages but especially displayed his fondness for Williamsburg, Virginia. (Courtesy of the John S. Lansill Papers, Special Collections and Archives, University of Kentucky Library, Lexington)

Jersey, a planned community built in 1928–29, which had become the most influential model of urban design in the mid-thirties. Peets acknowledged Radburn's impact when he described the ideal city as multi-cellular, dispersing the population in "a new texture . . . that preserves much of the countryside . . . keeps land open for the gradual movement of industry, and groups the people into neighborhoods having a stimulating autonomy in many social ways." Greendale was most closely related to Radburn in its pedestrian scale, its central grouping of public buildings, and its street hierarchy: main streets were widest, then "collector" streets, and then residential lanes, most of which terminated in culs-de-sac.[42]

But several elements of Radburn were not appropriate, Peets believed, to the midwestern setting. The contours of the terrain did not lend themselves to Radburn-type superblocks, and Peets also assumed that midwesterners would prefer housing lots that were "definitely bounded and privately controlled." Radburn's parks and pedestrian underpasses were too expensive to replicate at Greendale, which Peets described as "a workingmen's town"— "in actuality and in appearance it must be direct, simple, and practical, free of snobbishness, not afraid of standardization."[43]

In many ways, the Greendale plan represents the essence of Peets's style and approach. He disliked the curvilinear suburban streets and sweeping lawns then in fashion. Greendale was to be "built around a line instead of a point," with its street pattern delineated by a central boulevard, Broad Street, laid along a north-south linear depression in a shallow valley floor. Peets drew heavily from the layouts of Renaissance cities and American colonial villages that he had studied for many years, particularly Williamsburg, which at the time was undergoing massive restoration. Walter Thomas, one of Greendale's architects, also borrowed directly from Virginia's colonial capital for the village hall and other public buildings. The resulting architectural character of the village so incensed Jens Jensen that he remarked, "The buildings are lost. Frank Lloyd Wright, a true son of Wisconsin, should have been the guiding hand, but a profit [sic] is always stoned in his own country."[44]

Even more upsetting to Jensen than the architecture, however, was Peets's planting plan, which called for the introduction of non-native plants—about one-quarter of the total. From his home at Ellison Bay, Wisconsin, Jensen wrote to the secretary of agriculture, Henry Wallace, in 1937, asking why foreign plants were being used in projects such as Greendale when the local flora of southeastern Wisconsin were so rich and diverse. He decried their use as "a tragedy" and urged that the planting plan be altered from "utter mediocrity" before it was too late.[45]

Peets responded by acknowledging Jensen's mastery of "garden art," but claimed that his colleague's plant repertory was too limited and that certain plants, although non-native, were appropriate to the setting. Greendale resi-

dents, he maintained, "will want to see the trees and shrubs that have been made dear to them by familiarity. The golden-twig willows that were planted by the pioneers to cheer the winter landscape, apple and cherry trees, lilacs and hollyhocks—all of these came from other continents, but we want the people who come out to their new homes in Greendale to find these old friends."[46]

Other members of the Greendale planning staff were also at odds with Peets.[47] James Drought, a recent graduate of the University of Wisconsin, criticized Peets's planting scheme for much the same reason that Jensen had: its inclusion of non-native plants. "These departures from natural grace," he wrote, "point to the eclectic nature of the plan—the result of compromise."[48]

Despite these criticisms, Peets's planting list prevailed. Plants were chosen not only for beauty but for their screening potential. Protection and lot boundaries on all sides would be created with plantings. Hedges or small trellises with vines would provide a barrier between the entrance court and the street. Between the garage drive and the neighboring structure, vines, high-growing shrubs, and small trees would "better the appearance of the substantially blank wall which normally bounds the entrance court of a detached house at the southerly side." Backyards, Peets believed, should have central open areas for recreation and clothes drying which would be bounded at the rear by plants. These generous plantings of trees, vines, and shrubs

In 1936, along with
Harry Bentley, Peets
designed a variety of
exterior spaces for
Greendale through the
judicious placement of
houses, garages, vegeta-
tion, and gardens.
(Courtesy of the John S.
Lansill Papers, Special
Collections and Ar-
chives, University of
Kentucky Library, Lex-
ington)

linked the houses and garages with the narrow courts and culs-de-sac, co-
hering the street into a unified, yet varied, visual experience. Peets so believed
in the importance of closure in the streetscape that he nearly eliminated side-
walks altogether, placing houses only a few feet from the street.[49]

Greendale's planning staff paid a great deal of attention to keeping down
costs. Cinderblock, stucco, whitewash, and drab-colored paints could be purchased locally and inexpensively; once in place the materials were regarded
as providing a "gracious functionalism" to the workingmen's village. Peets
and Bentley disavowed any intention to imitate European villages, and were
somewhat bewildered when early visitors commented on the similarity.[50]

By the time the first residents moved into Greendale, in spring 1938, Peets's
intensive involvement with the community had ended. Immediately after
World War II, however, he was hired to serve as a consultant to the federal
Public Housing Authority and returned to Greendale to plan for an additional
three thousand homes and the development of a zoning ordinance. At that
point, the primary planning thrust had begun to shift: rather than just moderate-income groups, a more diverse mix of socioeconomic classes was
sought, together with a blending of urban and rural land use.[51] In addition
there was a move to change from public to private ownership.

To attract private developers to Greendale, Peets dispensed with the more

The limited setbacks that Peets employed along many residential streets in Greendale's original village center remain one of its most distinctive features. (Courtesy of Arnold R. Alanen)

unusual aspects of the 1930s plan, in particular its lot lines and siting of residences. Courts were now replaced with "polygonal" arrangements of streets, in which pairs of parallel roadways terminated at a connector loop. Such innovations emphasized Peets's long-held desire to preserve the villagelike character of the community. The new houses were to be clustered into three or four discrete neighborhoods that would be surrounded by a 1,330-acre greenbelt, including 820 acres of working farms.[52]

Peets's updated plans were shelved for several years, however, as an often rancorous debate over the transition from public to private ownership raged among Greendale residents, Milwaukee-area politicians and developers, and federal officials. Finally, an agreement was forged in 1952, and a plan was built on the proposals that Peets had made just after World War II.[53] Streets and lots were laid out with minimal disruption of the natural contours, and each neighborhood was left with 10 to 20 percent of its area in parkland. Unfortunately, the large greenbelt that Peets had so strongly sought to maintain and protect was reduced in size; today, only a small version exists as part of the Root River Parkway.[54]

The community, located within the expanding Milwaukee metropolitan area, with its attractive natural features and wide range of housing types, grew rapidly.[55] From 1950 to 1960, the population increased from 2,750 to 6,845 residents; then it exploded, approaching a total of 15,100 in 1970, a level it has basically maintained ever since.[56]

Today, people move to Greendale primarily for the ample open space and its high level of amenities. Indeed, it is ironic that a community initially intended for moderate-income groups now comprises several neighborhoods

The earliest conceptual plans that Peets prepared for Greendale included a pathway system linking the community's residential areas to the commercial district and surrounding greenbelt. As seen here, by the late 1930s the pathways were clearly identifiable features in the incipient settlement. (Photograph by John Vachon; courtesy of the Farm Security Administration Collection, Library of Congress, Washington, D.C.)

that cater to some of the wealthiest people residing in the Milwaukee area. In addition, Greendale's population remains almost entirely white, reflecting the racial segregation that is so evident throughout metropolitan Milwaukee.[57]

During 1946–47, Peets was involved in the development of another major midwestern community, the new town of Park Forest, Illinois—one of the first planned communities to emerge in post–World War II America.[58] Situated in the southern reaches of the Chicago metropolitan area, Park Forest was divided into five neighborhoods. Peets once again modified his classical preferences and provided a scheme that was more reflective of postwar suburban planning tastes. A large shopping and recreation area was centrally located within the enclave; the street system was laid out on an informal ring pattern; and the main thoroughfares surrounding the residential neighborhoods were adapted to fit the rolling site. In many ways, Park Forest's appearance was (and is) typically suburban, especially in its housing styles, ample lawns, and large areas of public open space. Outside of the Levittowns, few places better visualize the postwar American dream. Park Forest was the focus of William Whyte's classic study, *The Organization Man,* and the setting of some of his earliest explorations of the relation between physical design and social interaction. Park Forest also achieved notoriety for its residents' experimental approach to solving local social problems.[59]

Poor health severely curtailed Peets's activities by the early 1960s, and the veteran landscape architect died in Ohio in 1968. Some ten years after Park Forest was built, however, other planned communities such as Columbia, Maryland, and Reston, Virginia, were developed, for which Greendale and Park Forest served as prototypes. In this way, the legacy of Elbert Peets continued to influence community planning efforts in the United States late into the twentieth century.

Some critics might dismiss Peets as a lonely voice, a man out of step with his time, especially in comparison with those other landscape designers who celebrated the midwestern prairie landscape. Certainly, Peets differed from Simonds, Jensen, and others in his vision of the Midwest, but his career reveals a constant search for universal design principles that could be interpreted and applied within any regional context. Peets's contribution, therefore, was to blend in a unique way classical design elements with those components of the midwestern landscape and its social and cultural traditions which he deemed important. Talented, philosophical, opinionated, and iconoclastic, Elbert Peets represents the breadth and diversity that distinguished the field of landscape architecture in America and the Midwest during the first half of the twentieth century.

Notes

1. For a recent interpretation of the "natural style" from Frederick Law Olmsted to O. C. Simonds and Jens Jensen, see Robert Grese, *Jens Jensen: Maker of Natural Parks and Gardens* (Baltimore: Johns Hopkins University Press, 1992), 10–61; also refer to Robert E. Grese, "The Prairie Gardens of O. C. Simonds and Jens Jensen," in *Regional Garden Design in the United States,* ed. Therese O'Malley and Marc Treib (Washington, D.C.: Dumbarton Oaks Research Libarary and Collection, 1995), 99–123.

2. Christiane Crasemann Collins, "Hegemann and Peets: Cartographers of an Imaginary Atlas," introduction to Werner Hegemann and Elbert Peets, *The American Vitruvius: An Architects' Handbook of Civic Art* (1922; New York: Princeton Architectural Press, 1988), xx; Paul D. Spreiregen, "Elbert Peets," in *American Landscape Architecture: Designers and Places,* ed. William H. Tishler (Washington, D.C.: Preservation Press, 1989), 108.

3. Paul D. Spreiregen, ed., *On the Art of Designing Cities: Selected Essays of Elbert Peets* (Cambridge: MIT Press, 1968), 226; Collins, "Hegemann and Peets," xiv. Additional biographical information was derived from the biographical summary prepared by Spreiregen and the index to the Peets papers, both in the Elbert Peets Papers, Department of Archives, Cornell University, Ithaca, N.Y.

4. Elbert Peets, "Some Design Aspects of City Street Trees" (MLA thesis, Cambridge: Harvard University, 1915); Elbert Peets, "Street Trees in the Built-up Districts of Large

Cities," *Landscape Architecture* 6 (October 1915), 15–31; Elbert Peets, *Practical Tree Repair: The Physical Repair of Trees—Bracing and the Treating of Wounds and Cavities* (New York: Robert M. McBride, 1916), i–iv, 1 (quote, i); Caroline Shillaber, "Elbert Peets, Champion of the Civic Form," *Landscape Architecture* 72 (1982), 54–59, 100. Shillaber states that *Practical Tree Repair* appeared in 1913, but I could find no verification of this earlier date.

5. Spreiregen, *On the Art of Designing Cities,* 226.

6. For further information on Hegemann's life and career, see Collins, "Hegemann and Peets"; also see her "A Visionary Discipline: Werner Hegemann and the Quest for the Pragmatic Ideal," *Center* 5 (1989), 74–85, and "Werner Hegemann (1881–1936): Formative Years in America," *Planning Perspectives* 11 (1996), 1–21.

7. These included the preparation of a report for the state's largest city, *City Planning for Milwaukee: What It Means and Why It Must Be Secured* (Milwaukee: Wisconsin Chapter of the American Institute of Architects, 1916), which has been praised not only for its "extraordinary range and substance" but also for the "vigor and candor with which it was delivered." Landscape Research, *Built in Milwaukee: An Architectural View of the City* (City of Milwaukee, 1981), 128.

8. Most of the transition was completed by 1912. Walther H. Uphof, *The Kohler Strike: Its Socio-Economic Causes and Effects* (Elkhart Lake, Wis.: privately published, 1935), 3.

9. Before the outbreak of World War I, Kohler visited several industrial communities in America and Europe seeking ideas and inspiration. In 1912 he toured industrial-residential settlements built by the Krupp family at their massive steelworks close to Essen, Germany. But of even greater importance were the two English settlements of Port Sunlight (developed by the Lever brothers outside of Liverpool in 1897) and Letchworth (the first garden city to emerge under the auspices of Ebenezer Howard in 1904). Apparently the Wisconsin businessman was especially impressed by the appearance of Letchworth, for he met with Ebenezer Howard on a subsequent tour of England, praising his "most valuable contribution to the intelligent process of municipal development." Walter J. Kohler to G. L. Geiger, 4 November 1931, in Kohler Company Archives, Kohler, Wis. For more information on Walter Kohler and the model village, see Kohler of Kohler, *Kohler Village: A Hopeful and Stimulating Example of American Community Life* (Kohler, Wis.: Kohler Company, 1925).

10. Walter J. Kohler to Werner Hegemann (not sent), 15 January 1917, in Kohler Company Archives.

11. Werner Hegemann to Walter J. Kohler, November 1916, in Kohler Company Archives.

12. Kohler to Hegemann, 15 January 1917.

13. Ibid.

14. In one of his last communications to Kohler, Hegemann expressed dismay that planning costs had been incorporated into the price buyers would have to pay for land and housing. Such expenses, he contended, should be considered a personal expenditure—analogous to buying a work of art—since they contributed to the industrialist's "education for that very important role of a tasteful and practical builder of a new city." To this, Kohler responded that Hegemann did not possess a consistent attitude when evaluating economics and paternalism within America. Hegemann to Kohler, 20 December 1916, in Kohler Company Archives.

15. Arnold R. Alanen and Thomas J. Peltin, "Kohler, Wisconsin: Planning and Paternalism in a Model Industrial Village," *Journal of the American Institute of Planners* 44 (April 1978), 150–51.

16. C. B. Chapman, "The Madison of Tomorrow: Its Demand for New Building Sites and the Lake Forest Plat (1917), 1, University of Wisconsin–Madison Archives, Series No. 38/6/1, Box 1; Jeffrey Groy, "Men and the Marsh: Lake Forest II," *Arboretum News: University of Wisconsin–Madison* 30 (Winter 1981), 2; David V. Molenhoff, *Madison: A History of the Formative Years* (Dubuque, Ia.: Kendall/Hunt Publishing, 1982), 362.

17. Chapman, "Madison of Tomorrow," 6.

18. *Lake Forester* (Madison), 1 September 1920, 3; Hegemann and Peets, *American Vitruvius*, 198, 283; John Bordsen, "Madison's Lost City," *Wisconsin Regional*, January 1979, 67.

19. *Lake Forester*, 1 September 1920, 3; Bordson, "Madison's Lost City," 67.

20. During 1919–20, the two men were joined by Leonard Smith, who served as their local planning consultant; Smith taught town planning and civil engineering at the University of Wisconsin.

21. Hegemann and Peets, *American Vitruvius*, 198, 223.

22. Madison Park and Pleasure Drive Association, *Annual Reports of the Officers of the Madison Park and Pleasure Drive Association for the Years Ending January 1, 1917, and January 1, 1918, Respectively* (Madison, Wis.: M. Cantwell Printing Company, 1918), 26 (quote); Mollenhoff, *Madison,* 362; Bordsen, "Madison's Lost City," 68.

23. *Lake Forester,* 15 November 1920, 4; 1 July 1921; *Capital Times* (Madison), 14 October 1920, 3; Groy, "Men and the Marsh," 5–6; Mollenhoff, *Madison,* 362.

24. The bankruptcy led to a series of legal actions that were not completely resolved until 1948. "Final Report: Lake Forest Company," 29 December 1948, University of Wisconsin–Madison Archives, Series No. 38/6/2, Box 2; Bordsen, "Madison's Lost City," 67–68; Mollenhoff, *Madison,* 362.

25. *Lake Forester* (quoting Frans Aust), 15 December 1920, 2; Mollenhoff, *Madison,* 362.

26. Hegemann, *City Planning for Milwaukee,* 29.

27. Ibid. (quote); Hegemann and Peets, *American Vitruvius,* 280.

28. Hegemann, *City Planning for Milwaukee,* 29; Bruce E. Lynch and Cynthia D. Lynch, "Nomination of the Washington Highlands to the National Register of Historic Places" (Madison: Historic Preservation Division, State Historical Society of Wisconsin, 1989).

29. Spreiregen, *On the Art of Designing Cities,* 226; Washington Highlands Company, *Washington Highlands* (Milwaukee: the company, 1916); Hegemann and Peets, *American Vitruvius,* 280.

30. Washington Homes Association, *Covenants of Washington Highlands* (Wauwatosa: the association, 1919/1987), 8/3; Lynch and Lynch, "Nomination of the Washington Highlands."

31. Spreiregen, *On the Art of Designing Cities,* 226; Shillaber, "Elbert Peets," 56.

32. The correspondence between Peets and Pray, which has been reviewed by Collins, is summarized in her "Hegemann and Peets," xv–xvi.

33. Hegemann and Peets, *American Vitruvius,* v–vi, 1.

34. Although the School of Architecture at Harvard had provided Peets with the fellowship that enabled him to travel through Europe and James Sturgis Pray had helped to develop and strongly supported Peets's travel proposal, any acknowledgment of the institution or the chairman is conspicuously absent from the book. Ibid.; Collins, "Hegemann and Peets," xvi.

35. Spreiregen, *On the Art of Designing Cities,* vi (quote), 226–27.

36. Elbert Peets, "The Landscape Priesthood," *American Mercury,* January 1927, 94–100 (quote, 97).

37. Ibid., 94, 99 (quotes); Elbert Peets, "Central Park," *American Mercury,* March 1925, 339–41 (quote, 340).

38. Peets, "Central Park," 341.

39. Peets worked most closely with Jacob Crane, a Chicago planner employed half-time by another federal agency, the National Resources Committee. Crane, according to Peets, was the "contact man upstairs," while Peets himself provided site planning directives. Two other major members of the Greendale team were Henry Bentley, the architect responsible for designing Greendale's residences, and Walter Thomas, who designed its community buildings. See Spreiregen, *On the Art of Designing Cities,* 256, and Arnold R. Alanen and Joseph A. Eden, *Main Street Ready-Made: The New Deal Community of Greendale, Wisconsin* (Madison: State Historical Society of Wisconsin, 1987), 8–11.

40. Alanen and Eden, *Main Street Ready-Made,* 26.

41. Ibid., 32–34; W. L. Wilson (quoting Elbert Peets) to Jens Jensen, 15 February 1937, Jens Jensen Papers, Morton Arboretum Archives, Lisle, Ill.

42. Alanen and Eden, *Main Street Ready-Made,* 37–38; Elbert Peets, "Report of the Town Planning Section of the Greendale Planning Staff," in *Final Report of the Greendale Project of the Greenbelt Town Program,* vol. 2 (1938), 5, John S. Lansill Papers, Special Collections, University of Kentucky Library, Lexington.

43. Peets, "Report of the Town Planning Section," 17, 41.

44. Alanen and Eden, *Main Street Ready-Made,* 38–40; Peets, "Report of the Town Planning Section," 49; Jens Jensen to Henry Wallace, 15 February 1937, Jensen Papers.

45. Jensen to Wallace, 15 February 1937.

46. Wilson (quoting Peets) to Jensen, 15 February 1937.

47. Peets had sought advice from Franz Aust at the University of Wisconsin and from Stanley White, a Greendale staff member who taught at the University of Illinois.

48. James Drought, "Landscaping Greendale," *Greendale Review,* 25 January 1940.

49. [Jacob] Crane, [Elbert] Peets, [Walter] Thomas, and [Harry] Bentley to John S. Lansill, "Landscaping," in *Summary Reports and Recommendations: Greendale, Wisconsin* (1936), 1–4 (quote, 1), Lansill Papers; Alanen and Eden, *Main Street Ready-Made,* 42; Peets, "Report of the Town Planning Section," 45.

50. Alanen and Eden, *Main Street Ready-Made,* 42–44; Harry H. Bentley, "Report on Residential and Non-Residential Construction," in *Final Report of the Greendale Project of the Greenbelt Town Program,* vol. 3 (1938), 97–98.

51. Alanen and Eden, *Main Street Ready-Made,* 76–78.

52. Ibid.

53. Existing homes in Greendale were sold to residents and other parties. One year later the remaining undeveloped land was purchased by the Milwaukee Community Development Corporation (MCDC)—a nonprofit organization created specifically to manage Greendale's future development. Almost immediately, the MCDC engaged Peets as a consultant to prepare a master plan for residential development.

54. Alanen and Eden, *Main Street Ready-Made,* 86–88.

55. A range of housing types was available, from $50,000 (in 1960 dollars) estates situated along the parkway to $10,000 prefabs located near the original village.

56. Since most of the undeveloped acreage within Greendale had been subdivided through the 1960s, the size of the resident population began to stabilize during the next decade. Although 1,850 more residents were added to Greendale during the 1970s (giving the village a 1980 count of 16,925 people), a slight decline in numbers was registered during the 1980s—primarily because of smaller family sizes and a general aging of the village's population. Therefore, Greendale's population fell somewhat during the 1980s, to a total of 15,500 by 1990. Alanen and Eden, *Main Street Ready-Made,* 89–92; all population figures have been derived from the federal censuses for 1950, 1960, 1970, 1980, and 1990.

57. Ibid., 93–95.

58. In addition, he worked on the planning and development of Catalina Island in California and prepared a number of reports for Puerto Rico.

59. For more on Park Forest, see the following by William H. Whyte Jr.: "The Future Care of Park Forest," *Fortune,* June 1953, 126–31, 186–96; "The Outgoing Life," *Fortune,* July 1953, 84–88, 156–60; "How the New Suburbia Socializes," *Fortune,* August 1953, 120–22, 186–90; *The Organization Man* (New York: Simon and Schuster, 1956). Also see "American Community Builders," *Architectural Forum* 89 (1948), 70–74, and Delia O'Hara, "The People in Park Forest Sure Have a Lot of Verve," *Chicago Tribune Magazine,* 20 August 1978, 30–40.

TWELVE

Genevieve Gillette

FROM THRIFT GARDENS
TO NATIONAL PARKS

Miriam E. Rutz

Environment was not an everyday word when I was a child but at eight Teddy Roosevelt gave me the word "conservation" and I ran with it. I am pleased with my contribution and cannot be anything but grateful for such a wonderful, long life.
  —*Genevieve Gillette*

GENEVIEVE GILLETTE, landscape architect, conservationist, and lobbyist, dedicated more than sixty years of her life to preserving natural beauty for future generations. Gillette was instrumental in the establishment of two national lakeshores and over thirty state parks in Michigan, the preservation of several wilderness areas, and the passage of bills and the acquisition of funds for parks and recreation areas which benefited not only Michigan but the entire nation. A highly visible and effective lobbyist, Gillette possessed remarkable energy and a vivid, unforgettable personality. Yet when asked about her many accomplishments, she would modestly reply, "I didn't do it alone!"

That endearing and familiar protest is a reminder of the collective nature of many women's activities and achievements, both in Gillette's time and earlier. By the dawn of the twentieth century, when the Progressive era was gathering force, women found channels for their interests and energies in the clubs, leagues, societies, and associations that they organized (or helped to organize) in pursuit of social reform, village improvement, conservation, preservation, and other causes. At that time, women had not yet secured the right to vote. (The idea of women's suffrage was first seriously proposed on 19 July 1848 in Seneca Falls, New York, but not achieved nationwide until 1920.) It is not surprising that the women in the forefront of the suffrage movement were also leaders in the efforts to improve the living conditions of all people, especially the poor, in the industrial cities of the United States. These women were politically astute; they knew how to work with state legislatures, civic organizations, politicians, religious leaders, and businessmen to further their social goals. Today, some of them, including Jane Addams and Susan B. Anthony, are well-known figures. Others such as Genevieve Gillette should be better known for the parks, playgrounds, and other areas of the urban and rural environment that have been preserved or enhanced through their collective efforts.

Born in 1898, Genevieve Gillette was a child of the Progressive era. Early in her life she was exposed to the ideas of humanitarian philosophy and reform in education, labor relations, agriculture, and society. Her grandparents on both sides were farmers in central Michigan, successful, cheerful people who spent time with her, talking about their gardens and farming. Her father was educated at Michigan Agricultural College (now Michigan State University in East Lansing) and managed an agricultural implement business. He enjoyed reading, was interested in government, and liked to discuss politics. Her mother was an intellectual companion for him and supplemented the family's income as a seamstress. Both her parents and her grandparents instilled in her a deep and abiding love of nature.[1]

In 1901, when Genevieve was three years old, her father purchased an attractive 120-acre parcel of land near Diamondale, Michigan. In laying it out for a farm, he carefully incorporated an existing woodlot and stream. Gillette later remembered how, in the spring, her father would hitch up the wagon and drive the family out to enjoy the beauty of the stream. Seventy years later, the image of the place was still vivid in her mind:

> [There were many] sizable trees, probably mostly elm, arched over the stream, and Kingfishers flew up and down and once in a while we were lucky enough to see a Heron wading around, hunting for his breakfast. As we walked through this woods the floor of the woodlot itself was covered with lovely spring flowers. There were spring beauties, violets, trout lilies, dutchmen's britches, cress. . . . It just made a beautiful, lovely carpet all through the woodlot. When we came to the eastern end of the woods, there was a little rise of ground. Over the top of it, when you stood on this little ridge, you looked down into a bowl-like formation and there in the bottom was something that was almost jewel like. It was a cat-tail marsh, but now it was full of golden marigolds, all in bloom.

When their neighbors would visit the scenic retreat to picnic, young Genevieve had the responsibility of gatekeeper—a task she always resented. But her father strongly believed that the family should be grateful for having such a beautiful spot to share with others. His early influence and her

Genevieve Gillette, as she appeared in her twenties when she found work in Jens Jensen's office in Chicago. (Courtesy of the Genevieve Gillette Papers, Bentley Historical Library, University of Michigan, Ann Arbor)

experience of this environment laid the foundation for Gillette's lifelong philosophy, that exceptional landscapes should be made accessible to the public.[2]

Her father, whom Genevieve greatly admired, died when she was an adolescent, and her mother was forced to sell the farm and move to town. In the summer of 1916, following her father's wishes, Gillette enrolled in Michigan Agricultural College, where she began studies in home economics. But she soon tired of lessons in sewing and cooking, and sought out her uncle, president of the college, for advice. He suggested that she study agriculture: "See if you don't like chemistry and botany and things like that," he added.[3]

Gillette was successful in her new course of studies and as a sophomore worked in the pathology laboratory. Rose Taylor, her mentor and teacher, had planned to arrange a job for Gillette in Washington, D.C., but died before she was able to. Shocked and upset by the sudden loss, Gillette enrolled in a course on beautifying the farm home offered by the college's Horticulture and Landscape Program. The instructor, Professor Charles Halligan, immediately recognized Gillette's talent and suggested a career as a landscape architect. He explained that it was a field where women were slowly gaining acceptance as successful professionals.[4]

Ellen Biddle Shipman, for example, was actively promoting women in the field by hiring graduates of the Lowthorpe School of Landscape Architecture, in Groton, Massachusetts, to work in her all-women office. In fact, while Gillette was attending college, Shipman was designing gardens in the Detroit area, and it is possible that Halligan was aware of Shipman's work there. Among the women then practicing, the best known was Beatrix Farrand. A founding member of the ASLA, Farrand had learned about garden design through travel and study in Europe as well as by study under Charles Sprague Sargent, the founder and first director of the Arnold Arboretum in Jamaica Plain, near Boston. Like Shipman, who had received encouragement and some direction from the architect Charles Platt, Farrand had had mentors rather than formal instruction in her field. By contrast, Marian Coffin, another talented landscape architect, earned her professional degree from M.I.T. Nevertheless, throughout the decades before World War II, women would constitute a minority of students and practitioners in the field—despite the resolution passed in 1920 by the National Conference on Instruction in Landscape Architecture that women should be given equal encouragement to study in coeducational institutions.[5]

With good reason, then, Gillette was somewhat skeptical of her prospects, despite the enthusiasm of her professor. At first she thought that the Horticulture and Landscape Program was "grabbing for straws." Finally, however, she decided to change her major.[6] In 1920 she became the first woman to graduate from Michigan Agricultural College with a degree in landscape architecture and subsequently sent out forty-eight job application letters. She recalled that some forty offices responded—telling her they had been closed for the duration of World War I and were not back in business. Jens Jensen wrote back, however, that he would be glad to interview her. She immediately went to Chicago and was hired as his secretary.[7]

In her early twenties at the time, Gillette found working in Jensen's office an exciting experience. "He had all kinds of friends of every description, some very famous," she recalled, "and he always made these people welcome in his office. . . . When they would go he'd stand over by his desk and say, 'Liz (he always called me Liz), did we get anything done today?'" The job resulted in their lifelong friendship. Later she reflected, "He was a great influence in my life . . . maybe more so at the last than at the beginning."[8]

Gillette became enthralled with Jensen's conservation activities. At the time, as president of the Friends of Our Native Landscape, he was deeply involved in promoting a park system for the state of Illinois. "Why don't you

Gillette's naturalistic landscape design style at City Park in Ferris, Michigan, was influenced by Jensen early in her career. (Courtesy of Miriam Rutz)

get up a state park system in Michigan?" he suggested to her. "You've got lots of resources over there and you ought to have a state park system."[9] Intrigued with this concept, Gillette contacted a former classmate, Peter J. Hoffmaster, who in 1922 had been appointed superintendent of state parks in Michigan. She learned that a Michigan state park commission had been created in 1919, then abolished two years later when the Michigan Department of Conservation was established. Hoffmaster managed an assortment of small parks and one two-hundred-acre site near Interlochen, which the legislature had purchased in 1917 to preserve a stand of virgin pine.[10] He shared Gillette's bold dream for a Michigan state park system and encouraged her to volunteer her time to help him identify and secure land for parks.

After two years in Chicago, Gillette returned to Michigan, where she found work at John Brightmeyer and Son's Florists in Detroit, assisting with the landscape work that came from their nursery.[11] Through this job she met many wealthy Detroit residents, who later contributed to her various causes, including parks and conservation. From Brightmeyer's, Gillette moved on in 1923 to the Detroit parks and recreation department, where she served as a garden instructor for the public school system.

Even after she returned to Michigan, Gillette continued to keep in touch with Jensen. He once asked her to organize a Memorial Day weekend meeting in Michigan for the Friends, and she extended an invitation to several influential bankers, lawyers, doctors, and their wives to join the group. As a result of that meeting, 1,276 acres eventually were given to the state for a park at Ludington.[12] Gillette's enthusiasm and organizational skills resulted in the first large state park on the Lake Michigan shore.

During these years, Gillette was volunteering her time to visiting potential state park sites and writing detailed evaluations of them for Peter Hoffmaster. She was never paid for this service, but Hoffmaster was often able to reimburse her expenses, and she loved to travel about in the Model T, camping in the landscapes she was exploring. Occasionally she traveled with her mother or with students from the University of Michigan's landscape architecture program. Although she preferred not to, she often traveled alone, realizing that "Hoffmaster needed my help and my eyes [so] I would somehow manage to fit in a trip." As a member of the Michigan Botanical Club, she organized the Natural Areas Council to assist in her volunteer work; this private organization is still active in recommending properties for state protection.[13]

Gillette was always alert to property that might be available for state park use, but it is difficult to assess the degree of her involvement in these endeavors. One certain example of her effective influence is the establishment of a state park near Grayling, Michigan. One day a young World War I widow, Karen Hartwick, visited Gillette's home, and in the course of conversation her story of a missed opportunity for a park began to unfold. Some time earlier, Hartwick's father had offered to donate a 3,182-acre tract of land to the state of Michigan, as a memorial to her late husband, but it had been refused. When she heard the story, Gillette stepped in and arranged a meeting between Hartwick and Hoffmaster, which resulted in Hartwick's donation of the land in 1927 for the creation of Hartwick Pines State Park.[14]

Because Hoffmaster was interested in Jensen's ideas, Gillette arranged a meeting of the two men while Jensen was in Detroit working on Henry Ford's estate. It may have been the only time they met, but the conversation led to real action. They talked about the need for a park system near the city—consequently, Hoffmaster pursued the idea, and today state parks ring the Detroit metropolitan area.[15]

Other of Gillette's behind-the-scenes efforts resulted in Tawas Point State Park, on Lake Huron. The federal government had declared the land surplus property, and the Audubon Society wanted it preserved as a bird flyway. But the area's state representative was not convinced. When Gillette found out that he had never been to the site, she invited him to visit with the president of the society, and knowing that his son was an avid birdwatcher, she suggested that he go along, too. Several weeks later Gillette learned that the representative had negotiated the state's acquisition of the property.[16]

During the Depression, Detroit's mayor, Frank Murphy, appointed Gillette to the advisory committee that helped thousands of the city's residents with their thrift gardens. When funding for the program was cut, Gillette was able to obtain private money from an anonymous donor (later identified as Michigan state senator James Couzens) to keep the program going for another four years.[17]

Gillette's job with the park and recreation department was eliminated, so she was especially grateful to find work managing the development of Westacres, a low-cost government housing project near Pontiac, begun in 1935. The Depression had not yet ended, and during those years it was particularly difficult for women to find work in the government. Gillette was recommended for the Westacres project by President Franklin Roosevelt and sponsored by Couzens, who asked that Gillette be put in charge based on her work with the thrift garden project in Detroit.[18] She kept this job for eight years, then acted as a consultant with the community for the next seventeen years.

Westacres was an experiment sponsored by Couzens, the Federal Emergency Relief Administration, and Oakland Housing, Inc., to determine whether a nonprofit organization could build affordable homes for the average industrial worker. There were four goals for the project: to provide housing for workers who were seasonally unemployed; to make lots available that were large enough for homeowners to have family vegetable gardens; to encourage the development of residents' enterprises on the corporation's property; and to promote sound and satisfying community life.[19]

Westacres was located on a level tract of 874 acres in an area dotted with small lakes that were used for recreation by Detroit residents. A clubhouse had been built at the northeast corner of the property for an early subdivision and golf course scheme.[20] The Federal Housing Administration developed plans for 150 houses. The rectilinear street plan, with its two rows of widely spaced houses at the front of long, narrow lots, intrigued Gillette, for the lots would provide each homeowner with an ample backyard and additional room for a thrift garden. Moreover, the garden areas, located as they were, could be maintained by collective community initiatives such as plowing and spraying.

Given the responsibility to implement this plan, Gillette decided first to improve the soil and provide proper drainage. After consulting with specialists from Michigan Agricultural College, she proposed that a nearby lake be dredged. The land was then contoured and the rich muck from the lake spread over the poor soil. Giving instructions to the thirty-five construction workers at the beginning of each day required an early start, so Gillette lived close to the project, in the home of the project engineer, R. D. Baker, and his family.[21] Gillette and Baker formed a close working relationship, which made the engineering and landscape development compatible.

Twelve design prototypes for two-story houses offered Gillette considerable flexibility in siting. By varying the tree plantings, she was also able to enhance the identity of individual streets. Selecting and placing plants for the

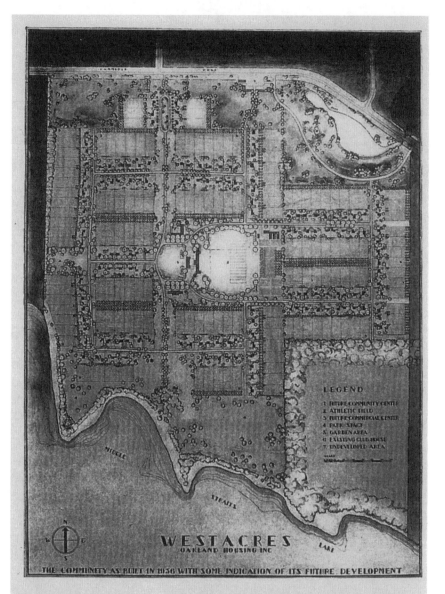

Each family is provided with enough land to enable it to raise fruits, vegetables and poultry for its own consumption. There is also provision for recreation area, a school, community building and stores.

President Franklin Roosevelt recommended that Gillette manage the development of the Westacres housing project during the Great Depression. (Reprinted with permission from *Architectural Record* 80 [Oct. 1936], 257)

thrift gardens at the back of each property, Gillette chose fruit trees, berries, and vegetables that were cultivated, sprayed, and fertilized as a cooperative venture. She developed a nursery at the project, making it possible to implement the landscape design at a cost far below prevailing market prices. The project garnered considerable publicity in the newspapers; in fact, so many visitors came to observe its progress that a chainlink fence had to be erected to prevent vandalism. Thinking back on it, Gillette observed, "Maybe we had more problems with the public than we did with . . . laying out . . . the roads."[22]

After eight years at Westacres, Gillette opened a private practice in the Ann Arbor area in 1943, which she ran for more than thirty years, retaining major clients such as Albion College, Ferris State College, the City of Big Rapids, the sponsors of Westacres, and Star Commonwealth Schools, a nationally prominent educational center for troubled children.[23] She also worked on many private gardens. Clients remember her waving her arms about and drawing with a stick on the ground, leaving the homeowners to create their own landscapes. (She did not like to spend her time drafting.)[24] During these years, her office remained small, operated from her home with the help of one or two full-time employees and a student or two part-time from the University of Michigan.

An imposing figure, Gillette operated with a confidence that came from believing strongly in what she was doing. She was not easily ignored. Many people remember fondly how she would bang her cane on the ground and roar with great gusto and a laugh, "Now, listen here, young man," if she felt the need. Gillette's close friend Vernon Bobbitt, chair of the art department at Albion, recalled another of her methods for getting work accomplished to her satisfaction: "She was with a survey crew, the architect, and the engineer, siting the chapel at Star Commonwealth Schools. The men staked the building at an elevation she thought was too low, and they would not listen to her or change the decision. . . . [A]s soon as everyone had left the site, she went back and moved all the stakes up the hill to the location she felt was best."[25] The workers never realized that the stakes had been changed, and she was able to avoid controversy.

Gillette's design for Bobbitt's home was typical of her residential work. The site was superb, an island in a small river running through Albion. She located the house to avoid flooding in the spring and to catch the morning sun, selecting only native plants and arranging them naturalistically. For several other residences, as well as for a hospital and a park in Big Rapids, Gillette used the same method of design.[26] Her results, which revealed Jensen's influence, were clearly different from the Beaux Arts approach she had been taught at Michigan Agricultural College. Rather than incorporating formal design concepts, she sought to fit structures to the site and used plants to enhance its natural qualities.

Gillette earned a good living from her private practice, but lived frugally and spent considerable time as a volunteer on numerous conservation committees. In the 1950s, as chair of the Michigan Botanical Club's Conservation Committee, she was asked to examine the condition of the state parks. Her old friend Hoffmaster had died suddenly in 1951, and the new director of conservation, a geologist, had little interest in parks. As a result, they had been largely neglected. The Michigan United Conservation Clubs (MUCC) had noticed Gillette's efforts with the Botanical Club and wanted her to join one of their committees. "They were sportsmen and I really didn't want to get mixed up in their things," Gillette recalled; however, as they needed her knowledge of parks, she agreed to work with them. Comparing park programs in other states, the committee concluded that they were all in financial trouble. When Ray Gather, the chairman, died, Gillette held regular meetings at her own home, despite her own poor health.[27]

The Gather Committee (as Gillette referred to it) was interested in parks at all levels—federal, state, county, and city. A support group, the Michigan Parks Association (MPA), was formed to influence legislation. Every organization with an interest in parks was asked to join, including the Automobile Club, the League of Women Voters, the Federated Garden Clubs of the State of Michigan, the Federated Women's Club, the Park and Forestry Associations, the Michigan Botanical Club, and the Natural Areas Council.[28] It was agreed that Gillette would be president of the MPA, a position she held for ten years.

When Gillette discovered a report detailing repair estimates to state park facilities which had been prepared by a conservation department employee, she boldly called it to the attention of the department's director. He agreed with the figures. With the report in hand, the MPA worked with the state legislature and the federal government to secure tax money and determined that a state bond issue would be the best method for obtaining funds. She had rarely been in the capitol, but Gillette did have firsthand knowledge from camping, hiking, or picnicking in almost every park in the state.

She studied the individual lawmakers carefully to determine which were the most effective representatives to contact regarding park issues. She telephoned them directly, introducing herself as "the lady with the hat," so they would recognize her. (Once she used the feathers from one of her hats to make fishing lures for several representatives who were fishing enthusiasts.)[29] The representatives enjoyed working with Gillette, and she never let them forget that she represented a large organization with a worthy cause. She traveled to many of their home districts to talk with them, which she found had a big impact. She also marshaled her friends and contacts to lobby their representatives. Gillette's knowledge of facts and issues earned her the legislature's respect.

In 1961 an interim committee was established in the Michigan senate to study the state parks, and two years later it issued a report revealing a far worse situation than that described by the MPA. Gillette was "delighted." The legislature, finally aware of the dire problems confronting Michigan's parks, called for changes, and eventually the governor was forced to act. But Gillette discovered that the funds he was about to request for the state park system fell far short of the amount she sought. The day before his state of the state message she called the governor and made "it very plain what I wanted and if I didn't get one hundred million dollars for parks, it wouldn't be pleasant." By the afternoon of the day of the speech, her friends were on the phone, shouting, "Genevieve, he went up there and said it . . . one hundred million dollars for parks!"[30]

In 1964 Gillette's lobbying skills were recognized by Michigan's senator Phillip Hart, who invited her to Washington for help with a land and water bill. Hart also introduced legislation to establish Sleeping Bear Dunes and Pictured Rocks as national lakeshores; Gillette lobbied for both successfully and was later asked to assist in developing plans for Sleeping Bear Dunes. Soon after returning home, Gillette received a call from President Lyndon Johnson's office, asking her to serve on a citizen's advisory committee chaired by Laurance S. Rockefeller, that would meet once a month to advise the President's Council on Recreation and Natural Beauty, established in May 1966. Gillette later reflected, "I was floored at the possibilities."[31]

Among other issues, the committee was concerned about the effect of highways on the countryside. Gillette stressed the importance of scenic roads for tourism and organized a conference on the topic. Later she introduced the ideas of using native plants and regulating billboards along the highways—ideas she credited to Jensen. Gillette served on the Citizen's Advisory Committee for several years but finally asked to be removed, believing that she could be more effective working in her home state.[32]

Gillette's lifelong dedication to conservation and parks was formally recognized by the state of Michigan in 1976, when the Genevieve Gillette Nature Center was dedicated. At the moving ceremony, then governor William Milliken and Michigan Natural Resources commissioner Harry Whiteley noted Gillette's impressive list of achievements and awards. Never comfortable seeking fame, she had not contributed money to the building and was adamant about not being so honored. Nonetheless, it was with great pride and a witty sense of humor that she consented to participate in the center's earlier groundbreaking ceremony.

Even after her eyesight failed, Gillette continued to battle the Michigan legislature for greater protection of fragile environments. Travel to Lansing became difficult for her, but she kept up the fight with phone calls and letters. In her last two years, although in poor health, she was able to attend her induction into the Michigan Women's Hall of Fame, where she received a standing ovation.

Gillette remained loyal to her alma mater and left a donation to Michigan State University to underwrite student research. Whenever she could, she stopped in at the university to talk with the students in the landscape architecture program, who would gather around as she recalled her battles with

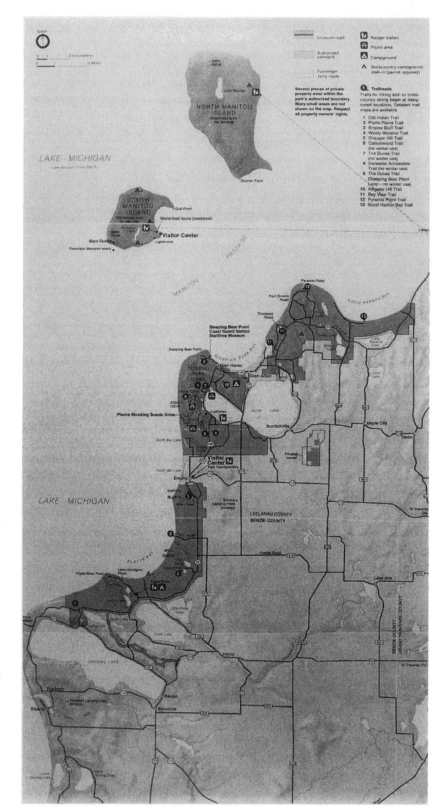

Map of Sleeping Bear
Dunes National
Lakeshore on the north-
western edge of
Michigan's lower penin-
sula. In the 1960s Gillette
successfully lobbied to
have this area (and Pic-
tured Rocks) set aside as
national lakeshores.
(Courtesy of the Sleep-
ing Bear Dunes National
Lakeshore, Empire,
Mich.)

According to Native American legend, the highest of the dunes pictured here represents a sleeping mother bear whose two cubs are swimming to shore after escaping a forest fire on the Wisconsin side of Lake Michigan. (Courtesy of William H. Tishler)

Gillette (with the shovel) participated in the groundbreaking ceremony for the Genevieve Gillette Nature Center at P. J. Hoffmaster State Park in Muskegan, Michigan. (Courtesy of the Genevieve Gillette Papers, Bentley Historical Library, University of Michigan, Ann Arbor)

A trail near the Genevieve Gillette Nature Center. (Courtesy of P. J. Hoffmaster State Park, Muskegan, Mich.)

state legislators and reminisced about how she could "always find a little bit of fun in a situation."[33]

Gillette accepted "not one penny" for her lifetime of volunteer work. Once, when forced by Michigan's Department of Natural Resources to take an honorarium for a talk, she sent back a new picnic table.[34] Her plain way of talking and dressing made her a folk hero to many. She had the extraordinary ability to motivate others and cajole them into action. Gillette gave direction to the conservation movement in Michigan; she saw the state's park system grow from a few small parcels to over eighty parks and lived to see that her efforts had made a difference.

At her death, the *Detroit Free Press* called her "a saving angel to Michigan's natural beauty" and "a miracle worker." "For six decades," the editorial continued, "she haunted lobbyists, legislators and governors with the fervor of an evangel. Her persistence overcame the perennial torpidity of politics, making Michigan a pacesetter among the 50 states for the conservation and popular enjoyment of its natural resources."[35]

Gillette's generosity never ceased. Her will provided a $300,000 trust for "acquiring land exhibiting certain natural and scenic qualities" and giving the property to the public.[36] Thompson's Harbor State Park, near Roger City in Presque Ile County, was Genevieve Gillette's final gift to the people of Michigan.

Notes

1. Biographical information is drawn from transcribed audiotapes of interviews with Genevieve Gillette, 1971–72, edited by Gillette, in the Genevieve Gillette Collection, Bentley Historical Library, University of Michigan, Ann Arbor (hereafter cited as Gillette interview), tapes 16A-3, 3–17, and 16B, 1–13.

2. Ibid., tapes 17A, 2; 16B, 18 (quote); 17A, 2.

3. Ibid, tape 16C, 1–10.

4. Ibid., 16.

5. There is a small but growing body of literature on the early role of women in landscape architecture. See Judith B. Tankard, *The Gardens of Ellen Biddle Shipman* (Sagaponack, NY: Sagapress, 1996), especially Leslie Rose Close's introduction, "A History of Women in Landscape Architecture"; Leslie Rose Close, "Ellen Biddle Shipman," in *American Landscape Architecture,* ed. W. H. Tishler (Washington, D.C.: Preservation Press, 1989), 90–93; Miriam E. Rutz, ed., *Proceedings for Landscapes and Gardens, Women Who Made a Difference* (East Lansing: Michigan State University, 1987); Diane K. McGuire and Lois Fern, eds., *Beatrix Jones Farrand (1872–1959): Fifty Years of American Landscape Architecture* (Washington, D.C.: Dumbarton Oaks, 1982). On the resolution, see *Landscape Architecture* 10 (July 1920), 217.

6. Gillette interview, tape 16C, 16.

7. Genevieve Gillette, interview by Scott C. Hedberg, 27 March 1978, audiotape in the collection of the author.

8. Ibid.

9. Gillette interview, tape 16F, 7.

10. Charles F. Boehler, *State Parks of Michigan: A Report of the Past, A Look to the Future* (East Lansing: Michigan Department of Conservation, 1957), 15.

11. After leaving Jensen's office, Gillette spent part of a year in Lakeland, Florida, working for the chamber of commerce as a consultant on city development. She decided to leave Florida, however, because "winter was like summer and [there] was no fall color and no anticipation of spring." Gillette interview, tape 16E, 1–10, 12.

12. Boehler, *State Parks,* 45.

13. Gillette interview, tape 18A, 6 (quote); Ron Nagel, Director of State Parks, Michigan, telephone interview by the author, fall 1985.

14. Boehler, *State Parks,* 42–43, and Gillette interview, tape 19B, 11.

15. Gillette interview, tape 16E, 12.

16. Ibid., tape 21A, 15–17.

17. Ibid., tape 17B, 25–29.

18. "Westacres," *Architectural Record* (October 1936), 257; Gillette interview, tape 16B, 1–3.

19. Oakland Housing, Inc., "Westacres," 1 July 1945, copy of statement in Gillette Collection.

20. "Westacres," *Architectural Record.*

21. Gillette interview, tape 18B, 14.

22. Ibid., 11–18.

23. *Who's Who in America,* 40th ed., 1201.

24. Member of the Big Rapids Garden Club, conversation with the author, 1986.

25. Vernon Bobbitt, interview by the author, April 1986.

26. Dr. Steven Scholler, letter to the author, November 1969.

27. Gillette interview, tape 19A, 2–13.

28. Ibid., 10.

29. Ibid., tape 20D, 13; tape 21A, 2–22.

30. Ibid., tape 22B, 15; tape 29A, 6; tape 28A, 2.

31. Ibid., tape 28A, 4; tape 25A, 10–11, 16 (quote); President's Council on Recreation and Natural Beauty, *From Sea to Shining Sea: A Report on the American Environment—Our Natural Heritage* (Washington, D.C.: Superintendent of Documents, 1968).

32. Gillette interview, tape 25A, 17–23; tape 25B, 3; tape 20B, 10.

33. Genevieve Gillette in seminar with the author and landscape architecture students at Michigan State University, 1977.

34. Nagel interview.

35. *Detroit Free Press,* 6 June 1984 and 29 May 1986.

36. "New State Park Will Cover 5,000 Acres," *Natural Resources Register* (East Lansing: Michigan Department of Natural Resources, April 1988), 4.

THIRTEEN

Annette Hoyt Flanders

FROM BEAUX ARTS TO MODERNISM

Patricia L. Filzen

IN 1932 THE EDITOR of *House and Garden*, Richardson Wright, praised the "distinction and rare beauty" of the gardens of Annette Hoyt Flanders (1887–1946). Wright was not alone in his admiration of Flanders's talent. That same year, she received the Medal of Honor from the Architectural League of New York and, a decade later, was elected a Fellow of the American Society of Landscape Architects.[1] Norman Newton, author of *Design on the Land*, considered her "among the most able designers of the profession."[2] The quality in Flanders's work that set her apart from many of her colleagues was her ability to balance planting and architecture in garden spaces that were beautiful but also, in Wright's words, "primarily livable." "They are colorful and still are tranquil," he continued. "Mrs. Flanders has kept her architecture well in hand so that Nature might have a chance to complete the picture."[3]

While the gardens of the century's early decades were characterized by ebullience and deliberate stylistic borrowings, the garden spaces of the 1930s tended to be smaller, greener, more intimate, and—at their best—more original. A new generation of clients had both increasingly mature tastes and, because of the Great Depression, increasingly restricted budgets. Annette Hoyt Flanders was one of the few landscape architects first to accommodate the extravagences of the 1920s and then adapt to the restraint of the 1930s and 1940s with smaller, sparer gardens. Flanders's midwestern roots and training, coupled with exposure to East Coast ideas, gave rise to an unusually distinctive style. Identified as a "traditionalist" rather than a "naturalist," Flanders actually blended elements from both an emerging American midwestern style and the more widely used formal Beaux Arts tradition.[4]

Annette Hoyt Flanders.
(Reprinted with permission from *Landscape Architecture* 37 [Oct. 1946], 29)

Born into a wealthy family in 1887, Flanders spent her childhood in Milwaukee. Her father, Frank Mason Hoyt, was one of the state's most successful lawyers, and her mother, Hettie Jones Hoyt, was a painter and short story writer.[5] Flanders spent her early summers in Oconomowoc, Wisconsin, an exclusive resort community on the shores of Lac LaBelle. Perhaps it was here, among the estates of Philip Armour, Patrick Valentine, Gustav Pabst, and Montgomery Ward, that she developed an interest in landscape architecture.

In 1914 Flanders graduated from Smith College, in Northampton, Massachusetts, with a degree in botany, and in 1918 earned a bachelor's degree in landscape architecture from the University of Illinois. She took additional courses in design, architecture, and the history of architecture at the Sorbonne in 1919 and later studied civil engineering at Milwaukee's Marquette University. It was an unusually varied and broad-based preparation for a career in landscape architecture, far exceeding that of most women landscape designers of the period.

Flanders began professional practice in 1920, as an associate with Vitale, Brinckerhoff and Geiffert in New York City, a highly successful firm specializing in estate work, mainly on the East Coast. Among Flanders's projects that received early national recognition during her two years with the firm were the Myron C. Taylor gardens on Long Island and the urban garden of F. E. Drury, known as The Oasis, located in Cleveland, Ohio.

In 1922 Flanders opened an office in New York City while maintaining a second at the family's summer home, The Shelter, in Oconomowoc. The arrangement proved advantageous: her Park Avenue office address carried East Coast status, while visits home were useful in securing commissions. The professional gulf between practitioners of the two regions was pronounced and sometimes contentious. Many midwestern landscape architects of the twenties, thirties, and forties considered the American Society of Landscape Architects and its publications elitist and exclusionary. As an alternative to *Landscape Architecture,* the official journal of the ASLA, many of these practitioners wrote for regional nursery journals and subscribed to them for information about new developments in regional style. Flanders, however, did not participate in partisan politics; throughout her career she promoted landscape architecture with a national rather than regional perspective and continued to work successfully in both the Midwest and the East.

Like most women landscape architects of the period, Flanders specialized in residential landscapes for wealthy industrialists.[6] She supplemented her income and promoted her design services by lecturing and teaching.[7] Flanders always referred to herself as a landscape architect and showed shrewd business sense, actively building a thriving practice.

About one-third of Flanders's projects were located in the Midwest— twenty-two of at least seventy-five that have been documented so far. Although each responded to the idiosyncracies of its site, certain design themes appeared consistently. Flanders would break up space near the residence into clearly defined areas that were structured by stone walls or dense hedges. Often these areas were on different levels, despite the fact that the typically flat midwestern site did not immediately lend itself to this treatment. Flanders had no compunctions about intervening to shape the land.[8] She used fewer flowers than many of her contemporaries, and far fewer than her predecessors, preferring the impact of primarily green gardens to the riotous color of flower borders. She integrated architectural elements (steps, trellises, outbuildings, and ornaments) with restraint. Like most of her contemporaries, she tended to cluster symmetrically balanced areas near the residence and lay out more informal, naturalistic gardens at a distance. None of these stylistic tendencies had regional roots; in fact, all derived from standard Beaux Arts formalism that had structured garden design since the last decade of the nineteenth century. Flanders's plant palette, however, relied primarily on native midwestern trees and shrubs. Her designs also tended to capitalize on local scenery, vernacular—particularly, farm—imagery, and existing woodland.

Among several Milwaukee-area gardens by Flanders, her design for

Kellogg Patton, circa 1930, received considerable national recognition and retains some of its original design to this day.[9] She worked closely on the project with the New York architect Dwight James Baum. (Flanders may have recommended Baum for the job; she collaborated with him on several other projects, both before and after this commission.) Patton, a bachelor and avid gardener, wanted an old-fashioned dwelling for his small, 100-by-120-foot corner city lot: gardens that would appear to be "three hundred years old and surrounding a house of the same apparent age."[10] Baum designed the house as a replica of a 1636 wood-framed example in Dedham, Massachusetts. Construction was completed in 1930, and planting began in March the following year. Patton also insisted on flower gardens, even though the site was shaded by existing trees that were to be kept. But Flanders turned the difficulty to her advantage: the large oaks and lindens added to the sense of age by appearing to have grown up through the flower beds. She also used old "foot worn" flagstones set in grass to form simple, direct paths. Flanders met the second challenge of the commission—the small scale of the space—by laying out two terraces, one off the study, the other adjacent to the dining area, each of which was almost three feet lower than the back of the lot. The change in level increased the sense of distance from the sunken outdoor rooms to the lawn and surrounding gardens. Benches on the terraces faced views over the flower beds, heightening their impact and drama.

Flanders's design for the Patton garden reflected her philosophy of "space and suitability"—the smaller the space, she believed, the greater the degree of formality required.[11] The notion had regional and horticultural implications: according to Flanders, the smaller and more formal the design, the greater the need to grow only what was suitable to the limits of the site. Around each terrace she planted old-fashioned fragrant shrubs, including lilacs (dug from nearby farms), old roses, forsythia, flowering almond, and large native thorn apples. Views to the garden were directed down narrow stretches of lawn to an old apple tree, flowering crabs at each of the corners, and native trees in the background. Ironwood, oak, and linden were interspersed with flowering shrubs, weigela, mock orange, and honeysuckle among others. Small flower beds of old-fashioned varieties repeated the simple geometric pattern of the porch terrace. Two thirty-foot American elms were brought in to lend balance and a sense of age to the front of the house. Dappled light filtered through the foliage of apple and downy hawthorn trees, casting shadows on the terrace and across the lawns and beds, infusing the scene with an air of tranquility.

The same year, 1930, Flanders began a series of gardens around an old farmhouse in Mequon, Wisconsin, for Mrs. Mitchell Young. While Thomas

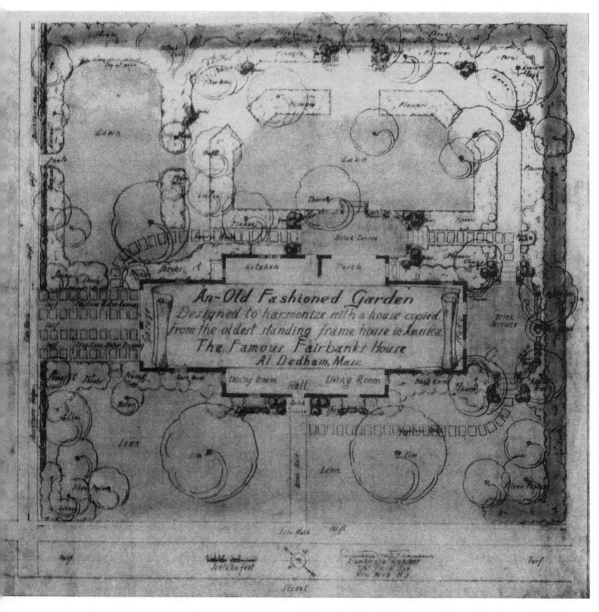

An~Old Fashioned Garden
Designed to harmonize with a house copied
from the oldest standing frame house in America
The Famous Fairbanks House
At Dedham, Mass.

Van Alyea, the architect, was engaged in remodeling and expanding the house, Flanders laid out the flower and vegetable gardens and entertainment areas. Early family photographs show the horse-drawn sleds that were used to move stone and earth for the terraces. Located on a gentle rise, the farmhouse originally faced a county road. With the expansion, the focus was redirected to the new gardens. Four fruit trees, remnants of an old orchard, marked the center. On three sides, the garden was enclosed by lilacs, native cherries, and a stone wall. Broad perennial beds fronted the lilac hedges, and shrub roses

Plan for an old-fashioned garden at the Fairbanks House in Dedham, Massachusetts. (Courtesy of Patricia L. Filzen)

The east and north yards of the Kellogg Patton estate, summer 1931. Flanders's plan and use of vegetation created a sense of age and permanency for the new residence. (Courtesy of Patricia L. Filzen)

tumbled down the fieldstone terraces. Wildflowers bordered a small stream flowing in the background, where the garden was allowed to grow wild.

During this time, Flanders was also engaged in creating a much more grandiose design for Charles W. Wright's forty-acre estate located about five miles from the Young property. A series of formal gardens were planned to complement the house—inspired by a French Renaissance château—including walled rose gardens, a children's playhouse, sports fields, and riding trails. Flanders also created an artificial lake fed by waterfalls and surrounded by hiking paths.[12]

The Mason Phelps's gardens in Lake Forest, Illinois, were among several Flanders designed in Chicago's North Shore suburbs. Her 1937 plan utilized the mature elms on the property and suggested a series of gardens surrounding the house, including an intimate shade garden and a breakfast garden. A tea house proposed for the estate was indicative of Flanders's skill in designing elaborate ironwork garden features.

A sunken terrace off the study of the Kellogg Patton estate was framed by flowering shrubs and an old apple tree. (Courtesy of Patricia L. Filzen)

In each of these designs of the 1930s, Flanders took advantage of opportunities to capitalize on the native beauty of the site, using indigenous plants when possible in layouts that provided satisfying intimacy in clearly defined outdoor rooms and terraces. Throughout the next two decades, she continued to work on similar projects in the Midwest.

From 1934 to 1937, Flanders was commissioned by Ronald Mattox to design several garden areas for the family's Madison, Wisconsin, estate, situated on five acres in The Highlands, a new subdivision originally planned by O. C. Simonds.[13] Flanders's design responded to the dual effect she sought: inward orientation of enclosed space coupled with expansive, outward vistas. She created formal terrace gardens near the house, intimate outdoor rooms directly off the living and dining rooms. A spectacular vista to Lake Mendota, framed by large sugar maples, overlooked an alfafa meadow beyond the formal grounds, revealing the area's natural beauty.[14] A long walk bordered by wide perennial beds led from the back terrace to an informal woodland walk at the property's edge. Mattox especially appreciated the border walk, an informal grass path designed to surround the property, en-

Sketch of a green garden teahouse originally intended for the Phelps estate but actually built on the C. B. Clark estate in Neenah, Wisconsin, in the early 1940s. (Courtesy of Patricia L. Filzen)

closed on both sides with native cherry and plum trees interspersed with roses and lilacs.[15]

A decade later, Flanders was at work on the Francis W. Magin residence, built in 1941 at River Hills, Wisconsin. The Milwaukee architect Thomas Van Alyea Sr. worked with Flanders on this and several other properties in the area. Here she designed a rustic garden house and gardens that created a setting "distinctive in its form and its intimate connection with the charming early American house."[16] The lawn contained specimen hawthorns, elms, and oaks of great size. The property, bordered by willows and framed by open views, extended to the farmland beyond. The Magins' garden house was built of hand-hewn timbers, like the ones that formed the loggia at the front of the main house. Covered by a shake-shingle roof, it was open on all sides. Climbing roses were planted around the timbers, a feature also repeated at the front entrance to the main house. From the garden house, the flower borders could be seen reflected in a rectangular lily pool.

Flanders tried her hand at modernist design in her sketches for the dazzling and futuristic demonstration garden "Century of Progress" at the Chicago World's Fair of 1934. This garden and its dramatic adjacent pavilion were the highlight of the popular "Classic Modern" exhibition sponsored by *Good*

Sketch of a proposed
garden house for the
F. W. Magin estate in
River Hills, Wisconsin.
(Courtesy of the owner's
private collection)

Housekeeping magazine, a project intended to showcase both architectural
and landscape design.[17]

Approaching the massive gateways on Leif Erickson Drive and the board-
walk bordering the Lagoon, visitors entered the 175-foot-long rectangular
garden that fronted on a pavilion at the south end. The striking white stucco
pavilion, by Flanders's frequent collaborator Dwight James Baum, stepped
down to a rectangular terrace of paving units and grass that surrounded the
garden. In a skillful combination of both classical and modern forms, the
design featured four corner pools and a series of planters containing white
flowers bordering a sunken central green space, highlighted by a large
reflecting pool. Long allées of poplars and groups of elms bordered the wall
around the entire site. At the north end, directly opposite the pavilion, a dense
hedge of hawthorn created the background for a large statue. The garden's
simple forms, combined with its color emphasis on calming green and white,
was imbued with a feeling of tranquility and respite from the surrounding
bustle which was characteristic of many Flanders gardens.

Annette Hoyt Flanders died of cancer on 7 June 1946, at the age of fifty-eight.
Her unusually broad understanding of art, art history, architecture, botany,

A "modern garden," sponsored by *Good Housekeeping* for the 1934 Chicago World's Fair. (Courtesy of Patricia L. Filzen)

and engineering informed all her designs. Flanders also used natural settings to best advantage and, whenever possible, relied on native plants. As a result, screen plantings, allées, and shrub walls that she chose more than sixty years ago continue to stand up to the extremes of the Midwest climate, and new generations of garden owners can still follow the outlines of once beautiful flower beds, stone walls, and footpaths she so aptly designed.

Notes

1. Completed in four months, the gardens for which Flanders received the award were estimated to have cost Mrs. Charles E. McCann, a Woolworth daughter, $3,500,000. "Gardens: A Portfolio of Paintings by George Stonehill," *Fortune,* August 1933, 67–74. The most remarkable features, the treillage forms that provided the background for several of the gardens, were designed by Flanders to appear "as handsome as a piece of lace." Herbert C. Cutler, letter to author, 28 January 1987; Cutler was a landscape engineer and draftsman in Flanders's New York office during the early 1930s.

Flanders had joined the ASLA in 1923; during the winter of 1933, she chaired a newly formed committee of the New York chapter members to provide services free of charge during the Depression to help to aid unemployment.

2. Norman T. Newton, *Design on the Land: The Development of Landscape Architecture* (Cambridge: Harvard University Press, 1971).

3. Richardson Wright, foreword to Annette Hoyt Flanders, *Landscape Architecture* (New York: privately printed, 1932).

4. Three other Country Place era designers were identified in a home landscape course developed in 1936 by the University of Wisconsin Extension Division. Flanders, along with Fletcher Steele (who did little work in the Midwest), was flagged as a "traditionalist"; Jens Jensen and O. C. Simonds were defined as "naturalists." Department of Debating and Public Discussion, University of Wisconsin Extension Division and Department of Horticulture, *The Home Landscape* (Madison: University of Wisconsin, 1936).

5. "Hoyt, Veteran Lawyer Dies," *Milwaukee Sentinel,* 5 July 1934, 1, and "Mrs. Hoyt, 86, Artist, Is Dead," *Milwaukee Journal,* 25 November 1942, L-2.

6. Flanders also designed cemeteries. For Fred Pabst, the Milwaukee brewing magnate, she laid out a plot in the rural Summit Cemetery, near Oconomowoc. During construction, friends of the Pabst family made picnic excursions to watch the work. Dory Vallier (daughter of Flanders's friend), interview by author, 17 November 1986, Milwaukee. Today, the Pabst plot remains much the same, although the vegetation is overgrown and the stone steps leading into the area are covered by the aging junipers.

7. Posters and glass slides from her personal collection, which were apparently part of a lecture series, indicate that she taught "A Brief and Practical Course in Landscape Architecture." One slide used a musical analogy to describe the art form. It showed a series of notes and staff lines with the statement: "These notes can be developed to create a great symphony. This line can be developed to create the gardens of Versailles." Private collection of Reuben Getschow, Milwaukee. Analogies drawn by other landscape architects, including Jens Jensen, between landscape design and music were also found in Flanders's notes.

8. Many of Flanders's commissions were for estates being created on the new subdivisions just north of the rapidly expanding city of Milwaukee. Flat farmlands were graded, ravines developed, and drainage patterns rerouted to create a sculptured effect. To further establish an appearance of age, large trees were moved to the sites. This practice of transplanting large trees and converting the countryside into estates that resembled venerable places in Europe had been popular since the 1890s, and Flanders's early gardens followed this trend. See "A Tree Gets a Ride," *Milwaukee Journal,* 22 March 1931, sec. 1, 1; Thomas McAdam, "Transplanting Large Trees," *Country Life in America* 8 (September 1905), 537; and George H. Dacy, "Landscapes to Order," *Country Life in America* 65 (November 1933), 56, 80–81.

9. The Patton gardens, the Ronald Mattox estate, and the Pabst family cemetery plot remain the most nearly intact of Flanders's Upper Midwest designs. Several other projects by Flanders still show evidence of shrub borders, allées, gardenhouses, deteriorated stone work, and faint outlines of her original proposals. These existing works, along with a number of her gardens that were described in illustrated articles, demonstrate her role as a significant landscape architect of the Midwest. The Charles W. Wright estate, located in the Milwaukee suburb of River Hills, was illustrated in Annette Hoyt Flanders, "Sculptured Landscapes," *Arts and Decoration,* November 1935, 36–37, 52. Photographs of the Patton gardens were published in Annette Hoyt Flanders, "Design in Small Gardens: The Atmosphere of the Garden," *Good Housekeeping,* April 1934, 76–77, 244. The "Century of Progress" garden for the 1934 Chicago World's Fair was also illustrated in Helen Koue, "Good Housekeeping Exhibition," *Good Housekeeping,* August 1934, 54–57, 132.

10. Flanders, "Design in Small Gardens," 244.

11. "Lorgnette: Little Neo-Classic Garden Is Among the Attractions at the World's Fair," *Milwaukee Sentinel,* sec. 1, 29 May 1934, 9.

12. Topographic models of both the existing landscape and the proposed design were featured in Flanders's article "Sculptured Landscape." Today little remains of the origi-

nal estate except the entrance allée, the artificial lake, and some of the original plantings at the water's edge.

13. Flanders had been recommended by the architect Jerome Robert Cerney of Chicago. When she arrived, the Colonial Revival Lannon–stone house had already been constructed. The front entrance to the property had also been graded into a straight drive that disrupted the experience of entering the subdivision along a winding, wooded road. Flanders softened the disjuncture with groves of conifers on one side and trailing shrub roses and informal groupings of fruit trees on the other. Four large elms graced the front entrance to the house. Thorn apples, upright junipers, and lilacs at the corners of the building gave simple balance to the design.

14. In several articles Flanders discussed how border plantings could be used to "frame" a small garden and sentinel trees to frame front entrances, a secluded terrace, or natural landscapes. See Annette Hoyt Flanders, "The Value of Vistas in the Small Garden,"*Good Housekeeping,* May 1932, 19, 26; Richardson Wright and Robert S. Lemmon, eds., *House & Garden's Second Book of Gardens* (New York: Condé Nast, 1920), 20–21; and "Three Exhibition Gardens," *House Beautiful,* March 1928, 306. Borrowed vistas and scenery were also both a beautiful and an economical solution to space constraints in the small garden. See Flanders, "Design in Small Gardens," and "Coming: Design in Small Gardens," *Good Housekeeping,* February 1934, 53, 103.

15. Ronald Mattox, interview by author, 12 December 1986, Madison. Some of the features Flanders proposed for the Maddox residence were never constructed, including a lily pool, a raised paved terrace and seating area with a water fountain, and a paved, sunken area for picnics and a grill. Only a portion of the border walk was completed during the 1930s.

16. Garden Club of America, *Annual Meeting, 1947* (n.p.: privately printed, 1947), 9.

17. Flanders, the magazine's consulting garden editor from 1933 through 1934, was probably instrumental in initiating the exhibit. The garden was publicized in several issues of the magazine. The best description of the "Century of Progress" garden can be found in Helen Koues, "Good Housekeeping Exhibition," *Good Housekeeping,* August 1934, 54–57, 132. The correspondence between Flanders and the editors of *Good Housekeeping* and Flanders's sketches for the garden are at the University of Illinois at Chicago Library.

Contributors

Arnold R. Alanen is professor of landscape architecture at the University of Wisconsin at Madison.

Julia Sniderman Bachrach is preservation planning supervisor with the Chicago Park District, Chicago, Illinois.

Kurt Culbertson is president of The Design Workshop, Inc., Aspen, Colorado.

Patricia L. Filzen is an artist and landscape historian in Reedsville, Wisconsin.

Robert E. Grese is associate professor of landscape architecture in the School of Natural Resources and Environment and director of the Nichols Arboretum at the University of Michigan at Ann Arbor.

Robin Karson is executive director of the Library of American Landscape History, Inc., Amherst, Massachusetts.

Lance M. Neckar is associate dean of the College of Architecture and Landscape Architecture at the University of Minnesota at Minneapolis.

Reuben M. Rainey is professor of landscape architecture at the University of Virginia at Charlottesville.

Victoria Post Ranney, who lives in Greys Lake, Illinois, has been an associate editor with the multivolume Frederick Law Olmsted Papers project.

Miriam E. Rutz is associate professor of urban and regional planning and landscape architecture at Michigan State University at East Lansing.

William W. Tippens is an architect with the LR Development Company, Chicago, Illinois.

William H. Tishler is professor of landscape architecture at the University of Wisconsin at Madison.

Christopher Vernon is senior lecturer in landscape architecture in the School of Architecture and Fine Arts at the University of Western Australia.

Noël Dorsey Vernon is associate dean of the College of Environmental Design at California State Polytechnic University at Pomona.

Index

Page references to illustrations are in italics.

Addams, Jane, 93, 216

agriculture, 176; in greenbelt plans, 205, 208–9

Akron, Ohio, 92

Albion College (Albion, Mich.), 223

Alma, Kans., 102

Alphand, Adolphe, 6, 60, 78n.7; as influence on Jenney, 58, 65, 70

"American Garden." *See* Union Park

American Hospital (Neuilly, Fr.), 113

"An American Idea in Landscape Art" (Miller), 177

American Mercury, 203

American Park and Outdoor Art Association (APOAA), 88–89, 92, 145, 147

American Renaissance, 99, 101, 105, 107

American Society of Landscape Architects (ASLA): critics of, 4, 106–7, 114, 203–4, 233; Fellows of, 231; founders of, 2, 16, 80, 92, 218; in Great Depression, 240n.1; presidents of, 155

The American Vitruvius (Hegemann and Peets), 203

Ann Arbor, Mich., 92, 222

Anthony, Susan B., 216

APOAA. *See* American Park and Outdoor Art Association

arboretums: Cleveland as proponent of, 28, 30; in Cook County, Ill., 93, 120, 132; in Jamaica Plain, Mass., 218; in Madison, 199; Manning's design of, 145; Simonds's design of, 92

Architectural League of New York, 231

Architectural Record, 176

architecture. *See* buildings; landscape architecture

Armour, Philip, 232

Arnold Arboretum (Jamaica Plain, Mass.), 218

art: integration of, with landscapes, 117, 128–33, 137, 141n.53. *See also* monuments

Art Institute of Chicago, 31, 130, 167

Arts and Crafts movement, 3

ASLA. *See* American Society of Landscape Architects

Association of American Cemetery Superintendents, 92

Atlantic Monthly, 16

Audubon Society, 220

Ausland (German periodical), 8

Aust, Franz, 199, 214n.47

Austin Tract. *See* Columbus Park

Automobile Club, 224

Bachrach, Julia Sniderman, 67

Bailey, Liberty Hyde, 175–77, 179, 182, 191n.15

Baker, R. D., 221

Baltimore, Md. *See* Roland Park

Baum, Dwight James, 234, 239

The Beauty of the Wild (Goodman), 133

Beaux Arts principles (of landscape architecture), 159, 168–69, 223, 231–42

Bell, J. S., 151; estate of, *151*

Belle Isle Park (Detroit), 41, 50, *51,* 55n.2

Belmont Harbor (Chicago), 86

Beltsville, Md., 204–5

Belvedere (Weimar, Ger.), 100

Bennett, Edward, 167, 169, 171

Bentley, Henry ("Harry"), 208, 213n.39

Berlepsch, Baron von, 126

Bickford Park (Memphis), 108

Big Rapids, Mich., 223

Billerica (magazine), 145

Biltmore (Vanderbilt estate in North Carolina), 172n.1

"Bird Gardens in the City" (Miller), 126–27

Birkenhead Park (Liverpool, Eng.), 43, 101
Bixby, Edmund, 29
Blair, J. C., 188–89
boathouses, 86, *87, 88*
boats, 52–54
Bobbitt, Vernon, 223
Boston, Mass.: Back Bay layout in, 38n.7; landscape architects in, 2, 27; as Manning's architectural base, 142, 144; Mount Auburn Cemetery in, 10, 15, 22n.32
Boulevard and Park Association of Quincy (Illinois), 88–89
boulevards: Cleveland's interest in, 28, 32, 33, 35, *36;* Jenney's use of, 57, 61, 62, 65, 68, 78n.5; Kessler's design of, 99, 100–104, 109, *112;* legislation for Chicago, 60; Olmsted Brothers' plans for, 167; Olmsted Sr.'s advocacy of, 46, 47; Peets and Hegemann's use of, 199, 206
Bowler, Robert A., 7, 9
Boy and Frog (sculpture), 130
Brooklyn, N.Y., 27, 55n.3, 58
Bross, William, 46
Brown, Capability, 100
Bryan, Thomas Barbour, 82, 83
Buchanan, William, 9, 10, 21n.26
Buffalo (New York), 16
buildings: City Beautiful emphasis on, 164, 167, 168–71; Downing's views on, 79n.22; Jenney's treatment of, 74, *74, 75,* 76; Olmsted Sr. and Vaux's treatment of, 65; Simonds's use of, 86, 90, 91–92
Burlington & Mississippi River Railroad, 39n.21
Burnett Park (Cincinnati), 23n.47
Burnham, Daniel, 42, 50, 51, 54, 59, 162, 172n.10; and City Beautiful movement, 159, 167–71, 184
Busch, Augustus, 107
Butler University (Indianapolis), 114

Cafe Brauer (Lincoln Park), 86
Caldwell, Alfred, 79n.13
canals: in Chicago parks, 47, 51, 162, 164, 169–70; in Detroit parks, 50; filling in of, 109. *See also* lagoons (pools); rivers
Canova, Antonio, 22n.34
Catalina Island, Calif., 214n.58
cemeteries: American claims about, 177; Chinese, *15;* Cleveland's interest in designing, 27, 28; entrances to, 10, 12, 22n.27; Flanders's design of, 241nn.6, 9; Kessler's design of, 108; lakes in, 12, 13–14, 82, 83; as "museums without walls," 21n.24; roads in, 13, 23n.39, 85; rural-landscaped, 6, 10–18, 19n.3, 20n.7, 21n.23; Simonds's design of, 3, 5, 18, 80, *82,* 82–85, 96n.8, 177; Strauch's design of, 2–3, 5–24; urban, 18. *See also names of specific cemeteries*

Central Park (later, Garfield Park; Chicago): Jenney's work in, *59,* 62, *64,* 65, 66, 67–76, *69, 71, 73–75,* 78n.6; Jensen's work on, 123–24, *124,* 131
Central Park (Minneapolis). *See* Loring Park
Central Park (New York City), 38n.7; criticism of, 204; as model for other parks, 60, 62, 72, 84, 162; Olmsted Sr. and Vaux as designers of, 27, 41, 43, 55n.3, 159, 161; size of, 65
"Century of Progress" (1934 Chicago World's Fair), 238–39, 241n.9
Cerney, Jerome Robert, 242n.13
Chapman, Chandler Burwell, 196, 197
Chapman, Mary, 9
Chapultepec Heights (Mexico City), 114
Charles Eliot Traveling Fellowship (Harvard University), 200, 203, 213n.34
Chessman Memorial (Denver), 109
Chicago, Ill.: Cleveland's career in, 27–35; flatness of, 28, 30, 47, 49, 58, 66, 68, 69, 160; Great Fire in, 31–33, *32,* 49, 67, 118, 160; Jensen's work in, 118–25, 129–31; Little Fire in, 33; park development in, 27–28, 30, 46–55, 57–79, 86–87, 167–69; playgrounds in, 93, 120, 167–68, *168;* political corruption in, 97n.28, 119; Prairie School origins in, 3, 93, 95–96, 174, 178, 182; school grounds in, 131; Simonds's work in, 86–87, 92; skyscrapers in, 59; Special Park Commission of, 92–93, 120; World's Fair in, 238–39, 241n.9. *See also* Lake Michigan; *names of cemeteries, park districts, parks, and suburbs*
Chicago Academy of Sciences, 46
Chicago and Northwestern Railway, *66, 68*
Chicago Architectural Club, 122
Chicago Art Institute, 31, 130, 167
Chicago, Burlington and Quincy Railroad, 44–46
Chicago Commercial Club, 169
Chicago Evening Post, 87
Chicago Plan, 171
Chicago Playground Association, 131
Chicago River, 46
Chicago Tree Planting Society, 92
Chicago Tribune, 46
Chicago World's Fair (1934), 238–39, 241n.9
China, 14, 19n.3, 99, 112
Cincinnati, Ohio: cemeteries in, 2, 5, 9–18, 83; Eden Park in, 15, 23n.47; Greenhills near, 205; horticultural passion in, 7, 19n.3, 20n.9; Kessler's contributions to, 99, 108, 109–10; Strauch's work in, 2–3, 5, 9–18
Cincinnati, Hamilton, and Dayton railroad, 10
Cincinnati Horticultural Society, *8,* 20n.9
cities: and City Beautiful movement, 99, 102, 108, 159–73, 184; division of, into zones, 77, 110–11; flight of wealthy from, 32–33; Kessler's plans for, 114; "open," 77, 86, 92,

102–4, 204; parks' psychological benefits for residents of, 47, 57, 59, 60, 66–67, 75, 86–88, 104, 107, 126, 159; Peets on, 204; planning of, 171, 195–96, 204–11; trees in, 194. *See also* boulevards; cemeteries; grid plan (for cities); park design; parks; suburbs; *specific names of boulevards, cemeteries, parks, and suburbs*

City Beautiful movement, 99, 102, 108, 159–73, 184

City Club (Chicago), 122

City Planning for Milwaukee (Hegemann), 212n.7

civil engineering (surveying), landscape architects' training in, 26, 27, 58, 81–82, 232

Civil War, 27, 58

Clark, C. B., 238

Clarkson, W., 158n.27

The Clearing (Door County, Wis.), 2, 4, 136, *136*, 139n.33, 141n.53

Cleveland, Henry, 38nn.7, 15

Cleveland, Horace W. S., 16, *26*, 57, 62, 88, 89, 144; as Chicago landscape architect, 25–40, 49, 83, 160; Chicago office of, 28, *29*, 33; Minneapolis work of, 25, 35, 103, 147–50, 158n.16; Olmsted Sr.'s friendship with, 25, 27, 28, 30, 31, 33, 39n.21, 55n.3

Cleveland, Maryann, 31, 35

Cleveland, Ralph, 31, 35, 36, 89

Cleveland, Richard, 35

Cleveland, Ohio: cemeteries in, 16; estates in, 233; Euclid Heights in, 102; forester for, 193; Peets's practice in, 203, 204

Cleveland Cliffs Iron Company, 154

Cliff Dwellers (Chicago club), 122

Clifton, Ohio, 7, 9, 10

Codman, Henry ("Harry"), 51, 56n.3

Coffin, Marian, 218

colleges. *See* university campus design; *names of specific colleges*

Columbia, Md., 211

Columbian Exposition. *See* World's Columbian Exposition

Columbus Park (Chicago), 3, 123, 125, 126, 130, *130*, 131

Comey, Arthur, 113

community: fostering sense of, through landscape architecture, 41–56, 60, 77–78, 128–33, 137

Concord, Mass., 158n.16

conservation: and Cleveland, 27; and Gillette, 215–30; and Jensen, 117–41; lobbyists for, 132, 215, 223–25, 228–29; and Manning, 143–44; Miller on, 186; and Simonds, 80–98

conservatories, 123–24

Cook County Forest Preserves (Ill.), 93, 120, 132

Coonley, Avery, 140n.45

Copeland, Robert Morris, 27, 35, 38nn.7, 15

Cornell, Paul, 46

Cornell University (Ithaca, N.Y.), 175

Cosmos (Humboldt), 8, 14, 19n.3, 21n.15

council rings, *128*, 128–29, *129*, 131, 136, 137, 139n.33

Council Rock Spring Garden (Madison), 199

Country Beautiful movement, 184. *See also* City Beautiful movement

Country Life in America (journal), 90, 174, 176–78, 180, 182, 184, 187, 189

Country Place era designers, 241n.4

Couzens, James, 221

Cowles, Henry C., 132, 138n.20, 140n.45, 186, 191n.25

Crane, Jacob, 213n.39

cremation, 18

Crunelle, Leonard, 130

Crystal Palace (London), 7

Curtis, George, 27

Cushing family (of Boston), 9

Cutler, Herbert C., 240n.1

Cyclopedia of American Horticulture (Bailey), 175

Dallas, Tex., 219; and Kessler, 99, 100, 110–11; park near railroad station in, *110*

Daniels, Howard, 21n.26

Dawes, Charles, 92

Dealey, George, 107

Dearborn, Mich., 125–26

death, nineteenth-century views of, 10, 18, 21n.23, 83, 84. *See also* cemeteries

Dedham, Mass., 234

Delaney, Dennis, 21n.26

Deming, N.Mex., 113

democracy: Olmsted Sr.'s efforts to promote, through landscape architecture, 41–56. *See also* community

Denmark, 80, 117–18

Denver, Colo., 108–9

Design on the Land (Newton), 231

Des Moines, Iowa, 55–56n.3

Detroit, Mich.: Edsel Ford's estate in, 129; Gillette's work in, 219, 221; Olmsted Sr.'s contributions to Belle Isle Park in, 41, 50; Shipman's garden design in, 218; state parks near, 220; Strauch as consultant in, 15

Detroit Free Press, 228–29

Detroit River, 51

Der Deutsche Pionier (German American periodical), 18, 19n.3

Dickens, Charles, 43

Dixon, Ill., 92

Donahue, J., 195

Door County, Wis. *See* The Clearing

Doubleday and Page (publishers), 176

Douglas Park (Chicago), 59, *61*, 62, 65, 68, 78n.5

Downing, Andrew Jackson, 16, 102; and Central Park, 43; as Cleveland's associate, 27; death of, 43; influence of, on other landscape architects, 83; on matching buildings to landscape, 179n.22; and origins of American landscape architecture, 1, 5

Drake, Daniel, 7

drives. *See* roads

Drought, James, 207

Drury, F. E., 233

Dubuis, Oscar F., 78n.5, 120

Dugdale, George, 38n.11

Dunwoody, William H., 150, 152

Durand, J. N. L., 58

Earnshaw, Henry, 22n.28

Earnshaw, Thomas, 21n.26

Easterners: dominance of, in landscape architecture, 1–2, 4, 16, 144, 189–90n.2, 233; domination of Minneapolis by, 144

East River Parkway (Minneapolis), 148, 150

East Side Park (Minneapolis), 150, 158n.19

Eckhart, Bernard, 138n.12

Ecole Centrale des Arts et Manufactures (Paris), 58

ecology, 186

Eden Park (Cincinnati), 15, 23n.47

elevations, varying, 111–12. *See also* terraces

Eliot, Charles, 160–62, 164, 167, 172n.1. *See also* Charles Eliot Traveling Fellowship

Ellsworth, Richard, 172nn.2, 11

El Paso, Tex., 114

Emerson, Ralph Waldo, 158n.16

England: influence of, on Olmsted Sr., 42–43; influence of, on Prairie School, 184; landscape architecture in, 74–75, 83, 100–101, 177–78, 204; and Strauch, 6–7, 10, 12, 17

Ernst family (of Cincinnati), 7

Euclid Heights (Cleveland), 102

Europe: landscape architecture traditions in, 2, 4–6, 100–101, 177–78, 189–90n.2, 200. *See also names of specific countries; names of specific landscape architects*

Excelsior, Minn., 152

exotic plants: in conservatories, 76; Jenney's use of, 62, 74–75, 78n.7; Jensen's early use of, 120, 122, 126; Olmsted Sr.'s interest in, 75, 79n.20; Peets's use of, 206–8; Simonds's use of, 84

Fair Lane (Henry Ford's estate in Dearborn, Mich.), *125*, 125–26

Farm Resettlement Administration, 204

farms. *See* agriculture

Farrand, Beatrix, 218

Faust, Albert Bernhardt, 22n.34

Federal Emergency Relief Administration, 221

Federal Housing Administration, 221

Federated Garden Clubs of the State of Michigan, 224

Federated Women's Club, 224

fences, 85. *See also* hedges

Ferncroft (Bell's estate near Minneapolis), 151

Ferris, Mich., 223; park in, *219*

field houses, 168–70

Field Museum of Natural History (Chicago), 167

Fire Memorial (Central Park, Chicago), 67, 68, 70–72, 76

Fisher Boy (fountain), 130

Five of Clubs (literary group), 38n.7

Flanders, Annette Hoyt, 231–42, *232*

flatness, of Chicago and the Midwest, 28, 30, 47, 49, 58, 66, 68, 69, 160

Fletcher family (of Indiana), 38n.15

F. L. Olmsted and Company, 168. *See also* Olmsted, Frederick Law, Sr.

Folwell, William Watts, 147, 149

Ford, Clara, 126

Ford, Edsel, 127, 129

Ford, Eleanor, 127

Ford, George P., 195

Ford, Henry, 125–26

Foreman, Henry, 169, 170

Forest Park (St. Louis), 108

forests. *See* arboretums; trees; *names of specific forests*

formal styles. *See* gardens: nature-like vs. formal

Forrest Park (Memphis), 108

Forsythe House, *70*, 71

Fort Sheridan (Ill.), 85–86

Fort Wayne, Ind., 112, *112*

Foster, J. Frank, 167–68, 170

France, 6, 204. *See also* Paris

Franklin Park (Ill.), 131

French, Daniel Chester, 31, 85

French, William M. R., *30*, 31, 33

Friends of Our Native Landscape, 131, 132–33, 140n.45, *175*, 191n.25, 218, 219

Fuller, George D., 138n.20, 140n.45

Gaertner Lehr Anstalt (German school), 100

Gage, George W., 39n.27

The Galaxy (periodical), 16

Gale, Mrs. E. C., 153

Garden, Hugh M. G., 122

Garden Club of America, 127

gardenesque. *See* gardens: nature-like vs. formal

The Garden Magazine, 17, 174, 177, 178, 184, 189

gardens: characteristics of, in 1930s, 231; impermanence of, 137, 139n.31; Kessler's design of, 99; nature-like vs. formal, 3–4, 92, 100, 121–22, 125, 146–47, 159–73, 176, 180, *181*, 182, 189–90n.2, 204, 211, 223, 231–42; neo-classicism in, 193–214; thrift, 220–22. *See also* landscape architecture; *names of specific cemeteries, estates, parks, and subdivisions*

Garfield Park (Chicago). *See* Central Park
Gaspard Park (Memphis), 108
Gather, Ray, 224
Gay, Leonard, 196, 197
Geldbloom, Mara, 98n.45
General Mills (company), 150
Genevieve Gillette Nature Center (Hoffmaster
　State Park, Mich.), 225, *227, 228*
German Americans: in Cincinnati, 2, 9, 19n.3;
　as Kessler's clients, 107; in Texas, 8–9; in
　World War I, 113, 192n.45
Germany, 2, 5, 6, 8, 16, 99–100
Gilbert, Cass, 154
Gillette, Genevieve, 4, 215–30, *217*
Gilman, Arthur, 38n.7
Glasgow Necropolis (Scot.), 20n.7
Glencoe, Ill., 125, 139n.33, 180
Glenwood Children's Park (Madison), 131
God's Acre Beautiful (Robinson), 17–18
Good Housekeeping, 239
Goodman, Kenneth Sawyer, 133
Governor Lowden estate (Oregon, Ill.), 90–91,
　94
Graceland Cemetery (Chicago): Cleveland's
　expansion of, 28, *29;* Jenney's design for, 82,
　83; Simonds's work on, 3, 5, 18, 80, *82,* 82–
　85, 96n.8, 177
Graceland Cemetery Association, 84, 85
Grant, Ulysses S., 58
Grant Park (Chicago), 166–67, 171
Grayling, Mich., 220
Great Depression: landscape architecture in,
　204–8, 220–22, 240n.1
A Greater West Park System (Jensen), 124
Great Exhibition (London), 7
Greely, Samuel, 29, 31
greenbelts, 204–10
Greendale, Wis., 204–10, *205, 207–10,* 211
Greenhills (Cincinnati), 205
grid paper building plans, 58, 72
grid plan (for cities): Chicago built on, 62, 67,
　77, 169; Cleveland's view of, 32; Kessler's
　boulevards as contrasts to, 105; Peets's view
　of, 204
Griffin, Walter Burley, 184
Grosse Pointe Shores, Mich., 127, *127*
Groton, Mass., 218
Groveland (Minneapolis), 150
Grove Parkway (Chicago), 33
Gwinn, Mich., 154
Gwinn (Mather estate in Cleveland), 154

Haff, Delbert, 107
Haga Park (Stockholm), 49, 50
Hall, William Hammond, 57, 62
Halligan, Charles, 218
Hampton Court (Eng.), 204
Hannibal, Mo., 92, 102
Harbor Hills, Maine, 92

Hare and Hare (architectural firm), 114
Harrington, Charles M., 150
Harrison, Carter, 92
Hart, Phillip, 225
Hartford, Conn., 16
Hartwick, Karen, 220
Hartwick Pines State Park (Mich.), 220
Hartwig, Julius, 100
Harvard University (Cambridge, Mass.), 1–2,
　193–94, 200, 203, 204, 213n.34
Haussmann, Georges Eùgene, 6
headstones. *See* monuments
hedges, 200, 207, 233, 239. *See also* fences
Hegemann, Werner, 194–96
Henry Vilas Park (Madison), *93*
Hermann Park (Houston), *111,* 112
Hibbard estate (Winnetka, Ill.), 90, *181*
Hibbing, Minn., 154
Highcroft (Peavey estate near Minneapolis),
　146, 146–47, *147,* 150, 151
Highland Park, Ill., *34*
The Highlands (Madison), 237–38
Hinsdale, Ill., 31
Hints on Landscape Gardening (Pückler-
　Muskau), 6, 9, 12–14
Hoffmaster, Peter J., 219, 220, 223
Holabird, Samuel B., 96n.8
Holabird, William, 85, 96n.8
Home Insurance Building (Chicago), 59
The Horticulturist (periodical), 7, 43, 83
Horvath, H. U., 193
Hosack, David, 102
Hot Springs, Ark., 108
House and Garden (magazine), 176, 231
Houston, Tex., 99, *111,* 112
Houtte, Louis van, 6
"How the Middle West Can Come into Its
　Own" (Miller), 182
How to Make a Flower Garden (ed. Miller), 176
Hoyt, Frank Mason, 232
Hoyt, Hettie Jones, 232
Hubbard, Henry V., 196
Humboldt, Alexander von, 8, 14, 19n.3, 21n.15
Humboldt Park (Chicago), 59, 62, *63,* 65, 68;
　Jensen's work in, 67, 119–22, *122, 123,* 125,
　130, 178, 180, *181*
Huntsville, Ala., 92
Hyde Park (Chicago), *31,* 46, 126
Hyde Park (Kansas City, Mo.), 102
Hyde Park (London), 7
Hyde Park (New York), 102

Ickes, Harold, 140n.45
Illinois: Cleveland's exploration of, 25–26;
　legislation for Chicago parks passed in, 46,
　60; Olmsted Sr.'s view of, 41; "scenery
　types" in, 185; state park system for, 218. *See
　also names of specific cities, towns, cemeter-
　ies, and parks*

Illinois Central Railroad, 196
Illinois Out-door Improvement Association, 92
"Illinois Way," 184
Indiana Dunes, 132–33, *133*
Indianapolis, Ind., 16, 92, 99, 108
Indian Mounds Park (Quincy, Ill.), 89
Indians, 8
indigenous plants. *See* native plants
industrialism, parks as antidote to, 59–60, 76
Inness, George, 120
Interlachen Park (later, Lyndale Park; Minneapolis), 148, 150
Interlochen, Mich., 219
Iowa, 55n.3
Iron Range (of Minnesota), 142, 154–55, *156*
islands, 13–14, 18, 72, 170, 223
Italianate gardens. *See* gardens: nature-like vs. formal

Jackson Park (Chicago), 46, 47, 49, 55nn.2–3, 56n.3, 102, 160, 167; monuments in, 164, 166; as site of World's Columbian Exposition, 50–55, 162, 172n.2
Jagen, Hermann, 23n.46
Janney, T. B., 150, 152–53
Jarvis and Conklin (management firm), 102
Jenney, William Le Baron, 3, 33, 56n.3, *58*; and Chicago's West Parks, 57–79, 120; Olmsted Sr.'s influence on, 55n.3, 84; Simonds's training under, 59, 82
Jensen, Anne Marie Hansen, 118, 136
Jensen, Jens, 117–41, *118, 187*, 220; as advocate of "natural" parks and gardens, 3–4, 93, 117, 180, 182; on Greendale, Wis., 206, 207; as influence on Gillette, 218–19, 223, 225; on Miller, 188; as modifier of Jenney's West Park designs, 79nn.13, 19; and Olmsted Sr., 55n.3; and Prairie School, 3, 30, 93, 95–96, 159, 174, 178, 179, 184, 189, 193; reverence of, for prairie, 41, 80, 189–90n.2. *See also* The Clearing
John Brightmeyer and Son's Florist (Detroit), 219
John Crerar Library (Chicago), 167
Johnson, Lyndon B., 225

Kankakee, Ill., 92
Kansas City, Mo.: Hyde Park in, 102; and Kessler, 99, 102–7; parks in, 55n.2, *103–7*
Kemeys, Edward, 130
Kessler, Antoine, 99–100, 108
Kessler, Clotilde, 99–100
Kessler, Edward Carl, 99–100
Kessler, George Edward, 99–116, *100*
Kien-long (Chinese emperor), 14
Kincaid, Ill., 92
King, William S., 148, 150

Kinney, Minn., 154, *156*
Kohler, John, 195
Kohler, Walter, 195–96
Kohler, Wis., 195–96

Lafayette Club (Minnesota), 150
lagoons (pools): in Chicago parks, 47, 49, 51–55, 120–21, 160; Flanders's use of, 239; Jensen's use of, 127; in proposed Lake Forest community, 198–99; Simonds's interest in, 84. *See also* canals
Lake Cliff Park (Dallas), 111
Lake Forest, Ill., 145, 178, 236
Lake Forest (Madison), 196–99, *197, 198*
Lake Harriet (Minn.), 158n.19
Lakeland, Fla., 229n.11
Lake Michigan: and Chicago, 46, 47, 51, 87, 160; Lincoln Park's extension into, 86; and Milwaukee, 160–62, *161*; stabilization of shoreline of, 145
Lake Minnetonka (Minn.), 146, 151
Lake Park (Milwaukee), 55n.3, 160–62, *162, 163, 165*, 167
Lake Pepin (Wis.), 145
lakes: in cemeteries, 12, 13–14, *14*, 82, 83; in Jenney's park designs, 57, 67, 69, *71*, 72–73, 76, 82; on private estates, 236. *See also* islands; *names of specific lakes*
Lake St. Clair (Mich.), 127
Lakeside Reviewer (Chicago journal), 32
Lake Wingra (Wis.), *93*, 196, 198
Lancaster Park (Jackson, Tenn.), 108
land: Jensen's view of, 117, 119, 141n.53; planners for uses of, 143–44, 155, 157; shaping of, by landscape architects, 233. *See also* landscape architecture
landscape architecture, 140n.45; American style of, 174–92; Beaux Arts principles of, 159, 168–69, 223, 231–41; Cleveland's vision of, 27, 36; Eastern dominance among early American, 1–2, 4, 16, 144, 189–90n.2, 233; European traditions in, 2, 4–6, 100–101, 177–78, 189–90n.2, 200; as fine art, 83; Jensen's view of, 141n.53; maintaining designs for, 137, 139n.31; music analogies to, 241n.7; Olmsted Sr.'s vision of, 41–43, 164; sense of community fostered through, 41–56, 60, 76–77, 128–33, 137; women in, 4, 215–42. *See also* art; buildings; cemeteries; exotic plants; gardens; land; native plants; parks; "picturesque"; Prairie School ("prairie style"); "rooms"; trees; views
Landscape Architecture (journal), 2, 94, 233
Landscape Architecture as Applied to the Wants of the West (Cleveland), 33
landscape design. *See* landscape architecture
Landscape-Gardening (Simonds), 95
"The Landscape Priesthood" (Peets), 203–4
Lathrop, Bryan, 18, 83–86, 97n.28

Laurel Hill Cemetery (Philadelphia), 16, 21n.26, 82
"lawn plan," 5, 16–18
Lawton, Okla., 113
League of Women Voters, 224
Leiter Building (Chicago), 59
LeMoult's (New York City florist), 101
Lenné, Peter Josef, 100, 105
Lincoln, the Rail Splitter (sculpture), 131
Lincoln Highway (Ind.), 134, *135,* 136
Lincoln Memorial Garden (Springfield, Ill.), 127–28, *128, 129,* 139n.31
Lincoln Park (Chicago), 46, 47, *59,* 86–87, *87, 88*
Linden-Ward, Blanche, 21n.24, 23n.38
Lindsay, Vachel, 140n.45
Lisle, Ill., 92
Little Rock, Ark., 113
Liverpool, Eng., 43
Lloyd, G. W., 15
lobbyists, for conservation, 132, 215, 223–25, 228–29
"local color," 178–80, 184–85
Loeb, Albert H., 126, 127
Logan, John, 164, 166
Logan, Mrs. John, 172n.10
London, Eng., 7, 74–75
Longfellow, Henry Wadsworth, 38n.7, 149
Long Island, N.Y., 92
Longview, Wash., 114
Longworth, Nicholas, 7
Loring, Charles M., 147, 149
Loring Park (Minneapolis), *148, 149,* 158n.19
Lorrain, Claude, 21n.23
Loudon, John Claudius, 12, 16
Louisiana Purchase Exposition (1904 World's Fair), 108, 114
Lowden estate. *See* Governor Lowden estate
Lowry, Thomas, 150, 152; estate of, *152*
Lowry Hill (Minneapolis), 150, 152
Lowthorpe School of Landscape Architecture (Groton, Mass.), 218
Lyndale Park (Minneapolis). *See* Interlachen Park

Madison, Wis.: Hegemann and Peets's projects in, 195, 196–99; Henry Vilas Park in, *93;* Highlands subdivision in, 237–38; Jensen's work in, 131; Simonds's work in, 92
Magin, Francis W., 238; proposed garden house for, *239*
Manning, Ettie, 145
Manning, Jacob Warren, 144
Manning, Warren, 55–56n.3, 113, 142–58, *143*
Maria Cemetery (Cincinnati), 16
Martin, Charles J., 152; estate of, *153*
Mary, Louis Charles, 58, 69, 71
masques. *See* art; theater spaces (in parks)
Massachusetts Arms Company, 27
Massachusetts Horticultural Society, 26

Massachusetts Institute of Technology (Cambridge, Mass.), 218
Mather, Stephen, 132, 140n.45
Mather, William Gwinn, 154
Mattox, Ronald, 237–38, 241n.9
Maynard, Edward, 27
McCagg, Ezra, 46, 47
McCann, Mrs. Charles E., 240n.1
McCormick, Cyrus, 92, 145
McCormick, Harriet Hammond, 145
meadows, 126, 149, 160, 167. *See also* "lawn plan"; prairie
Memphis parks, 108
Mencken, H. L., 203
Menominee, Mich., 92
Mequon, Wis., 234–36
Merriam, Kans., 102; park in, *103*
Mexico City, Mex., 99, 114
Miami University (Miami, Ohio), 112
Michigan: Gillette's contributions to, 4, 215–30. *See also names of specific cities and towns*
Michigan Agricultural College. *See* Michigan State University
Michigan Botanical Club, 220, 223, 224
Michigan Department of Conservation, 219
Michigan Department of Natural Resources, 228
Michigan Parks Association, 224
Michigan State University (East Lansing, Mich.), 4, 92, 216, 217–18, 221, 223, 225
Michigan United Conservation Clubs, 224
Michigan Women's Hall of Fame, 225
Midway Plaisance (Chicago), 47, 49–50, 160, 164
Midwest: Cleveland's identification with, 25; Manning's view of, as a national landscape resource, 142; neglect of origins of landscape architecture in, 2, 16; Prairie School as landscape design legacy of, 174–92; unique sense of place in, 1, 3. *See also* prairie; Prairie School; *names of specific places*
Millcreek Valley (Clifton, Ohio), 9, 10
Miller, Mary Rogers, *175*
Miller, Wilhelm (later, William Miller), 90, 92, 126, 145, *175;* house of, *183;* and Prairie School, 3, 30, 174–92
Miller, William. *See* Miller, Wilhelm
Milliken, William, 225
Milwaukee, Wis.: Flanders's work in, 231–34; Hegemann's projects in, 195; parks in, 55nn.2–3, 145, 160–62; suburbs of, 199–200, 204–10, 241n.8
Milwaukee Community Development Corporation, 214n.53
Miner and Child (sculpture), 130
Minneapolis, Minn.: Cleveland's later career in, 25, 35, 103, 147–50, 158n.16; Easterners' domination of, 144; Manning's work in, 146, 147–54

Minnehaha Park (Minneapolis), 149, 150
Minnehaha Parkway (Minneapolis), 150
Minnesota: Manning's work in, 142–58. *See also names of specific cities, persons, estates, and regions*
Minnetonka Club (Minnesota), 150
Minnikahda Club (Minneapolis), 150
Mississippi River, 88–89
Moline, Ill., 113
Monett, Mo., 102
Monroe, Harriet, 140n.45
Montecito, Calif., 145
Monticello, Minn., 152
monuments: in cemeteries, 85; in parks, 67, 70–72, 76, 130, 164, 166
Morton, Joy, 92
Mount Auburn Cemetery (Boston), 10, 15, 22n.32
Mount Hope Cemetery (Chicago), 55n.3
Mount Storm (Clifton, Ohio), 7, 9
Mulligan, Charles, 130–31
Municipal Art League (Chicago), 130
Murphy, Frank, 220

Nash, John, 6
Nashville, Tenn., 16, 108
National Conference on Instruction in Landscape Architecture, 218
national lakeshores, 215, 225
national parks, 132–33, 155
"National Plan Study Brief" (Manning), 143, 144, 155
National Pomological Congress, 27
National Socialism, 21n.15
native plants: Cleveland's use of, 28, 30; Flanders's use of, 233, 237, 240; Gillette's use of, 223, 225; as invasive weeds, 84; Jenney's use of, 62; Jensen's use of, 3, 79nn.13, 19, 119, 120–21, 126–28; Manning's use of, 145; Miller on, 177–80, 184–86, 191n.25; Olmsted Sr.'s use of, 41, 52, 55, 56n.3, 75; Peets's use of, 205; Simonds's use of, 3, 80, 84, 86, 87, 89. *See also* trees
Natural Areas Council, 220, 224
natural resources management. *See* conservation
nature, 184; psychological benefits of, for urban dwellers, 47, 57, 59, 60, 66–67, 75, 84, 86–88, 104, 107, 126, 159. *See also* conservation; gardens; land; parks; wilderness (wild nature)
"Nature by Design" (Taft Museum exhibition), 21n.24
Neenah, Wis., 238
Neff, William, 9
Nelson, Swain, 29, 83, 86, 96n.5, 118
neo-classicism (in gardens), 193–214
New Jersey, 26, 27, 108, 205–6
New Jersey Horticultural Society, 26

Newman, John, 31
"The New Prairie School" (Miller), 187
Newton, Norman, 231
New York, N.Y.: Kessler's work in, 99, 108; landscape architects in, 2, 233; Woodlawn Cemetery in, 16, 23n.42. *See also* Brooklyn, N.Y.; Central Park (New York City)
Nichols Junction, Mo., 102
Nolen, John, 113, 195
non-native plants. *See* exotic plants
North Park Commission (Chicago), 60, 62
North Terrace Park (Kansas City, Mo.), *106, 107*
Norton, Charles Eliot, 27
Notman, John, 21n.26
Noyes, Laverne, 92

Oakland Housing, Inc., 221
Oakwoods Cemetery (Chicago), 16
The Oasis (Drury estate in Cleveland), 233
Oconomowoc, Wis., 232, 233, 241n.6
O. C. Simonds and Company, 86. *See also* Simonds, Ossian C.
Ogden, Utah, 102
Oklahoma City, Okla., 108
Olmsted, Frederick Law, Jr., 55n.3, 159–62, 164, 167, 171, 172n.1. *See also* Olmsted Brothers firm
Olmsted, Frederick Law, Sr., 9, *42*, 57, 99, 168; as Central Park designer, 27, 41, 55n.3, 60, 84, 159; Cleveland's friendship with, 25, 27, 28, 30, 31, 33, 39n.21, 55n.3; family of, 172n.1; influence of, on other landscape architects, 41–42, 75, 83–84, 144, 204; and Jenney, 58, 59, 62, 65–66, 75, 77; and Kessler, 101–2, 107; and Manning, 144, 145, 151; midwestern projects of, 41–56, 102, 121, 160–64; and origins of American landscape architecture, 1; on parks, 23n.47, 167; on "plaisance" treatment, 65; on prairie, 189–90n.2; on Spring Grove Cemetery, 5, 18
Olmsted, John Charles, 55n.3, 159, 169–70, 172n.1. *See also* Olmsted Brothers firm
Olmsted Brothers firm, 16, 102, 159–73, 196. *See also* Olmsted, Frederick Law, Jr.; Olmsted, John Charles
Omaha, Nebr., 108
Oregon, Ill., 90–91
The Organization Man (Whyte), 210
O'Shaughnessy, Mary, 67
Otis, F. J., 158n.27
Overton Park (Memphis), 108

Pabst, Fred, 241nn.6, 9
Pabst, Gustav, 199, 232
Pabst Farm (near Wauwatosa, Wis.), 199, *201*
pageants. *See* theater spaces (in parks)
Panic of 1873, 33, 67
Panther and Cubs (sculpture), 130

papier quadrille building plans, 58, *72*

Paris, Fr., 58, 60, 65, 74–75, 101

Park and Cemetery (magazine), 179

Park Avenue (Minneapolis), 150–51

park design: Cleveland's interest in, 27, 28, 30, 32, 33, 39n.27; Jenney's views of, 57–58; Kessler's contributions to, 102–6, 108–9; Manning's principles of, 151–53; Olmsted Brothers' views of, 159–73; Olmsted Sr. and Vaux's views of, 62, 160–61, 164, 166; Simonds's view of, 86–91; Strauch's theories of, 9

Parker, Edward J., 88

Park Forest, Ill., 210–11

Park Muskau (Silesia), 6. *See also* Pückler-Muskau, Hermann Ludwig Heinrich, Prince von

parks: cemeteries compared with, 10; commercial value of, 57, 60, 107, 149; high point, 109; Illinois legislation for, 46, 60; as industrialism antidote, 59–60, 76; Kessler's design of, 99; lack of, in early U.S., 43; multiple uses of, 62, 66, 67, 69, 71–72, 75–76, 86, 167–68; neighborhood, 167–71, *170;* Olmsted Sr.'s advocacy of, 41–56; perimeters of, 170–71; political corruption associated with Chicago, 97n.28, 119; psychological benefits of, for urban dwellers, 47, 57, 59, 60, 66–67, 75, 86–88, 104, 107, 126, 159; rural vs. city, 165–67; sense of community fostered through, 41–56, 60, 76–77, 128–33, 137; state, 4, 133, 215, 218–20, 223–25, 228; Strauch as consultant on, 2, 14–15; zones of, 71–72, 167–70. *See also* boathouses; buildings; park design; paths; playgrounds; roads; water; *names of specific parks and cities*

The Parks and Gardens of Paris (Robinson), 65

Parsons, Samuel, 22n.34, 106

Parton, James, 16

paths: Flanders's use of, 234, 236, 237–38; grass vs. paved, 85; Jensen's use of, 126; Olmsted Brothers' plan for, 171; Olmsted Sr.'s use of, 160–61; Peets's use of, 205, 210; Simonds's use of, 92. *See also* promenades

Patton, Kellogg, 234, 241n.9; estate of, *236, 237*

Paxton, Joseph, 7, 43

Peavey, Frank H., 144, 146–47, 150

Peets, Elbert, 193–214, *194*

Penhurst (Dunwoody estate in Minneapolis), 152

Pennsylvania, 16, 21n.26, 26, 82, 131

Pennsylvania Horticultural Society, 26

Père Lachaise Cemetery (Paris), 6

"Pergolas: A Suggestion" (Miller), 176

Perkins, Dwight H., 38n.15, 86, 93, 120, 138n.14

Perkins, F. B., 16

Phelps, Mason, 236

Philadelphia cemeteries, 16, 21n.26, 82

Philipp, Richard, 195, 196

Pictured Rocks national lakeshore (Mich.), 225

"picturesque," 6, 10, 12

Pillsbury, John S., 153

Pillsbury, Sarah, 153

Pillsbury (company), 150

"plaisance" treatment, 65, 75

plants. *See* exotic plants; native plants; trees

Plant Societies of Chicago and Vicinity (Cowles), 186

Platt, Charles A., 189–90n.2, 218

"players' greens," 129–30, *130. See also* theater spaces (in parks)

Playground Association of America, 172n.13

playgrounds: in Chicago, 93, 120, 167–68, *168;* Jensen's view of, 125, 131; women's efforts to establish, 216

Pleasanton, Kans., 102

Pontiac, Mich. *See* Westacres

pools. *See* lagoons (pools)

Poussin, Gaspar, 21n.23

Powderhorn Park (Minneapolis), 148, 150

Practical Tree Repair (Peets), 194

prairie: contrast of, with Jenney's landscapes, 74; flatness of, 49, 58, 180, 182, 184–85, 189–90n.2; Jensen's Columbus Park re-creation of, 3, 123, 125, 126, 130, 131; Jensen's design of scenic roads to view, 134, 136; Olmsted Sr.'s view of, 41, 47; reverence for, 41, 80, 189–90n.2. *See also* native plants; "prairie rivers"; Prairie School ("prairie style")

Prairie Club, 131–32

"prairie rivers," 120–23, 125, 130, 178, 180, *181*

Prairie School ("prairie style"): Chicago origins of, 3, 93, 95–96, 174, 178, 182; Jensen's association with, 122; as philosophy, 4, 159, 184–85; precepts of, 30, 193; Wilhelm Miller's contributions to, 174–92

The Prairie Spirit in Landscape Gardening (Miller), 145, 174, 184, 186, 188

"prairie style." *See* Prairie School ("prairie style")

Pray, Hubbard, and White (landscape architects), 194

Pray, James Sturgis, 113, 200, 202–3, 213n.34

President's Council on Recreation and Natural Beauty, 225

Preston, J. W., 34

Price, Uvedale, 43

Probasco, Henry, 9, 24n.54

Progressive era: beautification projects of, 92; ethos of, 142–44, 155; Midwest as embodiment of, 182; women's accomplishments during, 215, 216. *See also* reform movement, and park development

promenades, 45–46, 67, 72, 76, 169. *See also* paths

Les Promenades de Paris (Alphand), 65, 70

Prospect Park (Brooklyn, N.Y.), 27, 55n.3, 58
The Public Grounds of Chicago (Cleveland), 30
Public Housing Authority, 208
Pückler-Muskau, Hermann Ludwig Heinrich, Prince von, 7, 24n.54; as influence on Kessler, 101, 104–5, 109; as influence on Strauch, 9, 12–14, 19n.3; landscape design by, 6, 7, 12–14; Parsons on, 22n.34
Puerto Rico, 214n.58

Qian Long (Chinese emperor), 14
Quincy, Ill., 88–90, 89, 90

Radburn, N.J., 108, 205–6
railroads: around cities, 111–12; near parks, 66, 67, 68, 76; parks developed near, 45, 102, 110; as promoters of town development, 25, 39n.21, 59
Ramsdell, Charles, 155, 158n.27
Rattermann, Heinrich: on Earnshaw, 22n.28; on Strauch, 8, 9, 15–16, 18, 19n.3, 23nn.50–51
Rauch, John, 46, 47, 60
Red Oaks (Janney estate in Excelsior, Minn.), 152–53
reform movement, and park development, 59–60, 131
Regent Park (London), 7
"Report on the Minneapolis Parks" (Manning), 148
Repton, Sir Humphry, 6, 12, 24n.54, 43
Resor, William, 9
Reston, Va., 211
River Hills, Wis., 238, 241n.9
rivers: and Gillette, 216, 223; Jensen's use of, 67, 125–26; Olmsted Sr.'s use of, 45–46, 50; parks along, 149. *See also* "prairie rivers"
Riverside, Ill., 41, 44, 44–46, 45, 55, 60, 160
Riverside Park (Memphis), 108
Riverview Park (Quincy, Ill.), 89
roads: in cemeteries, 13, 23n.39, 82, 85; connecting parks, 102–6; on fort grounds, 85; Jensen on, 134; in parks, 62, 66, 68, 73–74, 90, 160–61, 164; near parks, 66, 68–70, 75, 171; in planned communities, 206, 208–9; on private estates, 91, 101; scenic, 134, 136, 225; in subdivisions, 102, 198. *See also* boulevards; setbacks
Robinson, Charles Mulford, 184, 195
Robinson, William: on Alphand's "mistakes," 78n.7; as influence on Jenney, 58, 65; and native plants, 184; and Olmsted Sr., 39n.21; on Strauch, 17–18, 23nn.50–51
Roche, Martin, 85, 96n.8
Rockefeller, Laurance S., 225
Rock Island, Ill., 113
rocks, 179, 184
Rodgers, Andrew Denny, 190n.10, 191n.15
Roland Park (Baltimore subdivision), 102, 106
Rome, Italy, 197

"rooms": use of vegetation to create, 73, 90, 92, 125, 126, 164, 237
Roosevelt, Franklin D., 221
Roosevelt, Theodore, 172n.13, 215
Root, John, 51, 52
Root River Parkway (Milwaukee), 209
Rosenwald, Augusta, 140n.45
Rosenwald, Julius, 126
Royal Botanic Society gardens (London), 7
Rubens estate (Glencoe, Ill.), 125, 139n.33, 180
"Rules for Stonework at Graceland Cemetery" (Simonds), 85
Rural Design Committee (of APOAA), 92

Saint-Gaudens, Augustus, 85, 172n.10
Salt Lake City, Utah, 114
San Antonio, Tex., 113
Sandburg, Carl, 140n.45
San Souci Palace (Weimar, Ger.), 100
Sargent, Charles Sprague, 218
Saturday Afternoon Walking Trips, 131, 132
Saunders, William, 82
Scammon, J. Young, estate of, 31
Scarlet Oaks estate (Clifton, Ohio), 9
"Scattered Planting versus Masses" (Miller), 176–77
Schoenberger, George, 9
Schoenbrunn Palace (Vienna), 6
school grounds, 131
Sckell, Julius, 100
sculpture. *See* art
Seal Harbor, Maine, 129
segregation, racial, 200, 210
setbacks, 208, 209
Shanghai, China, 99, 112
Shawnee National Forest (Ill.), 133
Shearer, Sybil, 140n.33
Sheboygan, Wis., 195
The Shelter (Hoyt estate in Oconomowoc, Wis.), 233
Sherman, William Tecumseh, 58
Sherman, Tex., 114
Sherman Park (Chicago), 169–71
Shipman, Ellen Biddle, 218
Shurcliff, Arthur. *See* Shurtleff, Arthur
Shurtleff, Arthur (later Shurcliff), 113
Sidway, L. B., 39n.27
Siftings (Jensen), 95, 137
Simmons, Francis T., 86, 97n.28
Simonds, Ossian C., 80–98, 81; campus designs by, 92, 164, 167; as Chicago Special Park Commission member, 120; design principles of, 80–81, 84–85, 89–90, 151; and Manning, 145; as midwesterner, 2, 16, 80; and Olmsted Sr., 55n.3, 164; and Prairie School, 3, 30, 80, 159, 174, 182, 184, 189, 193; reverence of, for prairie, 41, 80, 189–90n.2; on Strauch, 5, 18, 83; Wisconsin work of, 237
Sinissippi Farm. *See* Governor Lowden estate

skyscrapers, 59, 82

slavery, 8, 21n.15

Sleeping Bear Dunes national lakeshore
    (Mich.), 225, *226, 227*

Sleepy Hollow Cemetery (Concord, Mass.),
    158n.16

Sloane, David, 21n.24

Smith, Leonard, 213n.20

Smith-Lever Act, 184

"Some Design Aspects of City Street Trees"
    (Peets), 194

Song of Hiawatha (Longfellow), 149

South Bend, Ind., 112

Southopen Ground (Washington Park, Chi-
    cago), 47

South Park (Allegheny County, Pa.), 131

South Park (Chicago), 46, 47, *48,* 55n.2, *59,* 62,
    65, 102, 160, *168. See also* South Park Com-
    mission

South Park (Quincy, Ill.), *90*

South Park Commission (Chicago), 30, 33, 35,
    39n.27, 46–47, 49, 60, 162, 167–69

Special Park Commission (Chicago), 92–93,
    120

Spencer, Robert, 138n.14

Spoon River (Ill.), *135*

Springfield, Ill., 92, 127–28

Springfield, Mo., 102

Spring Garden nursery (Cincinnati), 7

Spring Grove Cemetery (Cincinnati), 2, 5, 9–
    18, *11, 13, 14, 17,* 83

Spring Grove Cemetery (Strauch), 14, 16, 19n.3

Star Commonwealth Schools, 223

Starved Rock State Park (Ill.), 133, *134, 175, 179*

state parks: Gillette's work to establish, 215,
    218, 219–20, 223–25, 228; Jensen's work to
    establish, 133

St. Bonifacius, Minn., 153

Steele, Fletcher, 241n.4

Stein, Clarence, 108

Stevens, Thomas Wood, 132

stewardship. *See* conservation

St. Joseph, Mo., 112

St. Louis, Mo., 99, 108

Stockholm, Swed., 49, 50

Stout, James H., 144

St. Paul, Minn., 144

Strang, John, 10

Strauch, Adolph, 2–24, *6,* 83

Strauch, Mary Chapman, 9

Strauch Island (Spring Grove Cemetery, Cin-
    cinnati), 13–14, 18

"Street Trees in Built-up Districts of Large
    Cities" (Peets), 194

suburbs: Cleveland's design of, *34;* Flanders's
    design of, 237–38, 241n.8; Olmsted Sr.'s
    plans for, 44–46; Peets's contribution to,
    193, 194, 196–200, 204–11; restrictive cov-

enants in, 200; rise of, 32–33, 176. *See also
names of specific suburbs and subdivisions*

Sullivan, Louis, 3, 59, 159, 192n.42

Summit Cemetery (Oconomowoc, Wis.),
    241n.6

Sunnyside Gardens (N.Y.), 108

surveying. *See* civil engineering (surveying),
    landscape architects' training in

Sutermeister, Eda, 108, *109,* 114

Syracuse, N.Y., 108

Taft, Lorado, 85, 130

A Talk about Dahlias (Miller), 175

Tawas Point State Park (Mich.), 220

Taylor, A. D., 113

Taylor, Myron C., 233

Taylor, Rose, 217

tea houses, 236, *238*

terraces, 234, 237, *237,* 239, *240. See also* eleva-
    tions, varying

Terre Haute, Ind., 92, 112

Texas, 8–9, 99, 100, 110–14, 219

Thayer, Mo., 102

theater spaces (in parks), 129–30, *130,* 132–33,
    133, 137, 139n.33

Thomas, Walter, 206, 213n.39

Thompson's Harbor State Park (Mich.), 229

Thorwaldsen, Bertel, 22n.34

thrift gardens, 220–22

Tippens, William, 67

trees: as buffers, 75; Cleveland's plans for
    planting, 33, 35, 39n.21; Flanders's use of,
    233–35, 239; as flat terrain enhancement, 47,
    48, 50; fruit, 222; Jenney's use of, 72, 73;
    Jensen's use of, 126, 128; Manning's map-
    ping of, 143; Miller on, 176–78; Olmsted
    Brothers' use of, 171; Olmsted Sr.'s use of,
    51; Peets's use of, 194, 199–200, 206–7;
    Simonds's use of, 84. *See also* arboretums;
    Cook County Forest Preserves (Ill.)

Tri-State Fairgrounds (Memphis), 108

Trollope, Anthony, 43

Turtle Creek Parkway (Dallas), 111

Tyler, Moses Coit, 174

Union Park (Chicago), 3, 56n.3, 119

United States: centennial of, 101; Indian wars
    of, 8; lack of landscape architecture train-
    ing in early, 5; Strauch's obscurity in, 16

university campus design: Cleveland's, 31;
    Gillette's, 223; Kessler's, 112, 114; Manning's,
    153–54, *154, 155;* Simonds's, 92, 164, 167

University of Chicago, 31, 164, 167

University of Illinois, 182, 184, 187–89, 232

University of Maryland, 92

University of Michigan, 81, 92, 174, 220, 223

University of Minnesota, 153–54, *154, 155*

University of Nanking (China), 112, *113*

University of Wisconsin, 2, 199

Upland Farm (Gale estate in St. Bonifacius, Minn.), 153
urban planning. *See* cities: planning of
urn burial, 18
U.S. Department of Agriculture, 204
U.S. Sanitary Commission, 46

Valentine, Patrick, 232
Van Alyea, Thomas, 234–35, 238
Van Bergen, John S., 134
Vanderbilt, George W., 172n.1
Vanderbilt University (Nashville, Tenn.), 108
Vaux, Calvert, 57; as Central Park designer, 27, 55n.3, 60, 84, 159, 162; collaboration of, with Olmsted Sr., 30, 43–45, 47–51, 58, 60, 160; on "plaisance" treatment, 65
Vernon, Nol Dorsey, 2–3
Versailles Palace (Fr.), 6, 204
views: broad, 87, 90, 185, 186, *186;* long, 87, 90, 125, 185, 186, *187, 188;* Pückler-Muskau's emphasis on, 101; Simonds on, 91
Virginia, Minn., 154
Vitale, Brinckerhoff and Geiffert (landscape architects), 232

Wade Mine (Kinney, Minn.), *156*
Wahl, Christian, 172n.5
Walden (McCormick estate in Lake Forest, Ill.), 145
Walker, C. I., 15
walks. *See* paths; promenades
Wallace, Henry, 206
Ward, Montgomery, 232
Warder, John Aston, 7, 9
Warren Woods. *See* Columbus Park
Washburn Crosby (milling company), 150–52
Washington, D.C., 197, 203
Washington Highlands (Wauwatosa, Wis.), 199–200, *201, 202*
Washington Park (Chicago), *35,* 47, 49–50, 55n.3, 102, 160
Washington Park (Milwaukee), 55n.3, *165*
Washington University (St. Louis), 55n.2
water: as flat terrain enhancement, 65. *See also* canals; lagoons (pools); lakes; rivers; *names of specific bodies of water*
Wauwatosa, Wis., 199–200, *201*

Wayzata, Minn., 151
Weidenmann, Jacob, 16, 23n.49, 55n.3, 57
West, J. Roy, 98n.34
Westacres (Pontiac, Mich., housing project), 221–23, *222*
The Western Horticultural Review, 7
West Park (Milwaukee). *See* Washington Park
West Park District (Chicago), 46, 55n.3; "chain of verdure" parks in, 62, 68; Jenney's contributions to, 57–79, 120; Jensen's work with, 3, 57–79, 118–24, 129; remains of, 67
What England Can Teach Us about Gardening (Miller), 178, 179
"What Is the Matter with Our Water Gardens?" (Miller), 180
White, Stanley, 214n.47
Whiteley, Harry, 225
White Rock Parkway (Dallas), 111–12
Whitney, William Channing, 146, 150, 152
Whyte, William, 210
Wichita, Kans., 92
Wichita Falls, Tex., 114
wilderness (wild nature), 4, 161, 215
wildlife, 117, 126–27, 205
Williamsburg, Va., 206
Winnetka, Ill., 90, 91–92
women: in landscape architecture, 4, 215–42; suffrage for, 215–16
Woodlawn Cemetery (New York City), 16, 23n.42
Woodmere (Detroit), 15
World's Columbian Exposition (1893), *52–54;* City Beautiful vision of, 102; Manning's work at, 144, 145, 151; Olmsted Sr.'s contributions to, 41, 49, 50–55, 121, 160, 162, 164
World's Fair (1904), 108, 114
World War I: and landscape architects, 113–14, 155, 189, 192n.45, 199
Wright, Charles W., 236, 241n.9
Wright, Frank Lloyd, 159, 187, 189n.1, 192n.42, 206
Wright, Henry, 108
Wright, Peter B., 192n.40
Wright, Richardson, 231

Young, Mrs. Mitchell, 234–36

University of Illinois Press
1325 South Oak Street
Champaign, IL 61820-6903
www.press.uillinois.edu